Movie Magick

ALSO BY DAVID HUCKVALE
AND FROM McFARLAND

*A Green and Pagan Land: Myth, Magic and Landscape
in British Film and Television* (2018)

Music for the Superman: Nietzsche and the Great Composers (2017)

*A Dark and Stormy Oeuvre: Crime, Magic and Power
in the Novels of Edward Bulwer-Lytton* (2016)

Hammer Films' Psychological Thrillers, 1950–1972 (2014)

Poe Evermore: The Legacy in Film, Music and Television (2014)

*The Occult Arts of Music: An Esoteric Survey
from Pythagoras to Pop Culture* (2013)

*Ancient Egypt in the Popular Imagination: Building a Fantasy
in Film, Literature, Music and Art* (2012)

*James Bernard, Composer to Count Dracula:
A Critical Biography* (2006; paperback 2012)

*Visconti and the German Dream: Romanticism, Wagner
and the Nazi Catastrophe in Film* (2012)

*Touchstones of Gothic Horror: A Film Genealogy
of Eleven Motifs and Images* (2010)

Hammer Film Scores and the Musical Avant-Garde (2008)

Movie Magick
The Occult in Film

DAVID HUCKVALE

McFarland & Company, Inc., Publishers
Jefferson, North Carolina

LIBRARY OF CONGRESS CATALOGUING-IN-PUBLICATION DATA

Names: Huckvale, David, author.
Title: Movie magick : the occult in film / David Huckvale.
Other titles: Movie magic
Description: Jefferson, North Carolina : McFarland & Company, Inc., Publishers, 2018. | Includes bibliographical references and index.
Identifiers: LCCN 2018043236 | ISBN 9781476674377 (softcover : acid free paper) ∞
Subjects: LCSH: Occultism in motion pictures.
Classification: LCC PN1995.9.O28 H83 2018 | DDC 791.43/615—dc23
LC record available at https://lccn.loc.gov/2018043236

BRITISH LIBRARY CATALOGUING DATA ARE AVAILABLE

ISBN (print) 978-1-4766-7437-7
ISBN (ebook) 978-1-4766-3375-6

© 2018 David Huckvale. All rights reserved

No part of this book may be reproduced or transmitted in any form or by any means, electronic or mechanical, including photocopying or recording, or by any information storage and retrieval system, without permission in writing from the publisher.

Front cover: Scene from the 1922 Swedish-Danish film *Häxan (Witchcraft Through the Ages)*

Printed in the United States of America

McFarland & Company, Inc., Publishers
 Box 611, Jefferson, North Carolina 28640
  www.mcfarlandpub.com

Table of Contents

Introduction ... 1

One. Decadence ... 11
Two. Symbolist Horrors ... 28
Three. Occult Fantasy Before the Movies ... 40
Four. Silent Magick ... 50
Five. Ritual ... 64
Six. Willpower ... 82
Seven. Return of the Magi ... 102
Eight. Theological Horror ... 115
Nine. Theosophy ... 129
Ten. Psychedelia ... 143
Eleven. Conspiracy ... 158
Twelve. Faust ... 170
Thirteen. Animagick ... 179

Chapter Notes ... 189
Bibliography ... 196
Index ... 199

Introduction

Sigmund Freud identified the origins of magical thinking in what he considered to be his best book, *Totem and Taboo,* first published in 1913. Under the section "Animism, Magic, Omnipotence of Thoughts," he wrote:

> Thus the first picture which man formed of the world—animism—was a psychological one. It needed no scientific basis as yet, since science only begins after it has been realized that the world is unknown and that means must therefore be sought for getting to know it. Animism came to primitive man naturally and as a matter of course. He knew what things were like in the world, namely just as he felt himself to be. We are thus prepared to find that primitive man transposed the structural conditions of his own mind into the external world.[1]

By 1915, Sir James Frazer had devoted 12 volumes to the subject in *The Golden Bough,* usefully highlighting in this passage the differences between religion and magic:

> Thus in so far as religion assumes the world to be directed by conscious agents who may be turned from their purpose by persuasion, it stands in fundamental antagonism to magic as well as to science, both of which take for granted that the course of nature is determined, not by the passions or caprice of personal beings, but by the operation of immutable laws acting mechanically. In magic, indeed, the assumption is only implicitly, but in science it is explicit. It is true that magic often deals with spirits, which are personal agents of the kind assumed by religion; but whenever it does so in its proper form, it treats them exactly in the same fashion as it treats inanimate agents, that is, constrains or coerces instead of conciliating or propitiating them as religion would do.[2]

The difference between religion and magic is a crucial one, for the former is necessarily a moral structure, and consequently legislative in a social sense. The latter is not really concerned with morality, and works independently of established social structures. It claims to be a science and to work without the need for divine intervention, its aim being to make the practitioner a god. "The Microcosm is an exact image of the Macrocosm," Aleister Crowley explains in *Magick in Theory and Practice*; "the Great Work is the raising of the whole man in perfect balance to the power of Infinity."[3] Monotheistic religions, particularly Judaism and Christianity, have always attempted to normalize the irrational basis of their thinking, censuring "superstition," while simultaneously promoting divinity, parthenogenesis, resurrection, immortality, and transubstantiation. Indeed, Crowley sensibly isolates the Eucharist as the "most complete of magick ceremonies": "Take a substance symbolic of the whole course of Nature, make it God and consume it."[4] Having done so, the Magician "becomes filled with God, fed upon God, intoxicated with God. Little by little his body will become purified by the internal lustration of God; day by day his mortal frame, shedding its earthly elements, will become in very truth the Temple of the Holy Ghost. Day by day matter is replaced by Spirit, the human by the divine; ultimately the change will be complete: God manifest in flesh will be his name."[5] But this is a distinctly occult interpretation of the Eucharist. *Becoming* God is not the presumptuous aim of the church.

I have adopted Crowley's particular spelling of magick, following his definition of it in *Magick in Theory and Practice,* as "the Science and Art of causing Change to occur in conformity with Will."[6] This is very different from "mere" conjuring or the metaphorical use of the word we find in fairy tale situations, recently made immensely popular in the Harry Potter novels and films. Harry Potter—like magic is in fact very mechanistic, being entirely reliant on learning the right gestures, but it has very little in common with the invocational and will-based approach of magick. In fact, its very attainability via acquired technique complements the Internet age of instant gratification in which the original audiences of the stories grew up: Potter's wand technique differs very little from the skill of a ten-year-old adept of the computer keyboard to call up any information or image. In contrast, Chic and Sandra Cicero have summed up the aims of classical magic as follows:

THE BEAST: **Aleister Crowley in robes for the Rites of Eleusis in 1910.**

Magic is primarily a technique for sharpening the magician's latent psychic senses. Quite simply, it is a method for learning how to increase and focus one's faculties of willpower, imagination, memory and intuition. The more one is able to train these faculties, the greater the chance of being in alignment with the divine forces that govern the universe. It has often been said that the principle of magic is based on four fundamental truths: (1) that the physical universe is only a part, and by no means the most important part, of total reality; (2) that human *willpower* is a real force, capable of changing its environment and producing physical effects; (3) that this *willpower* must be directed by the *imagination*; (4) that the universe is not a mixture of chance factors and events, but an ordered system of *correspondences*...; and that the understanding of the pattern of these correspondences enables the magician to use them to effect change.[7]

The adoption of magickal processes rather than religion by Nazi Germany is one of the reasons for the continuing fascination of the Third Reich, especially as such a catastrophe emerged from a well-established Christian and more recently industrialized society. Later, I will be exploring the occult aspects of Leni Riefenstahl's *Triumph des Willens* (1935), which is a kind of cinematic hagiography of Hitler's magickal persona. Hitler's considerable powers of persuasion, regardless of his fundamental mediocrity, were claimed by his adherents as evidence of his supernatural ability to make the impossible possible—a true triumph of the will, in Crowley's sense of the term. Of course, Hitler's success required more than his "magickal" aura; economic and social conditions were a prerequisite. As the most recent historian of Nazi occultism, Eric Kurlander, explains, quoting C.G. Jung,

> After the First World War, objective reality had for many Germans "collapsed into a psychic disorder of apocalyptic proportions," which rendered millions of people susceptible to "some higher power or charismatic messiah-guru," an idea, a movement or an individual that "elicited the conversion experience and the sense of liberation that comes with it." For those who were "starving for the unattainable," who have been "unsuccessful in the battle of life," National Socialism was the "great worker of magic." By translating the "religious mysteries of Nazism" for the German people, Hitler became "the master-enchanter and the high priest," the nation's supreme magician.[8]

The cultural and economic vacuum caused by the First World War and its aftermath was not the only cause of the occult anomaly of the Third Reich. Even before Madame Blavatsky arrived on the scene with her theories of Root Races, Atlantis, magical powers and a Tibetan occult conspiracy lying behind the development of the world's religions, Christianity had been under attack from science. In England, Shelley, the ultimate Romantic poet, had made his assault on conventional faith while still a student, finding himself expelled from university after publishing a pamphlet in 1811, entitled *The Necessity of Atheism*. In Germany, Arthur Schopenhauer had dispensed with God by 1819 with the first publication of his atheistic, but nonetheless still mystical treatise, *The World as Will and Representation*. The pessimistic outlook of Schopenhauer's philosophy was only compounded by Darwin's demonstration that humanity was not an immutable, God-created species. By the time Friedrich Nietzsche arrived on the scene towards the end of the nineteenth century, Christianity was so moribund that he famously pronounced God to be Dead. "We have killed him," he added. "What were we doing when we unchained this earth from its sun? Where is it moving now? Where are we moving to? Away from all suns? Are we not continually falling? And backwards, sidewards, forwards, in all directions? Is there an up and a down left? Aren't we straying as through an infinite nothing? Isn't empty space breathing at us?"[9]

Nietzsche regarded the death of God not only as a supremely liberating event but also a profoundly troubling one, for how was society to survive without its divinely ordained moral structures? A world without the proscriptions of God and the meaning religion had imposed upon it would now be revealed to be a meaningless chaos. Nietzsche's philosophy, unlike Schopenhauer's, aimed to find a way to embrace the new conditions in a creative and optimistic manner; but for many others at the end of the nineteenth-century, the vacuum left by conventional Christian faith sucked out all their confidence and joy of living. Out of this (for some) profoundly distressing state of affairs, alternative systems of belief emerged, and occultism began to enjoy a revival unprecedented since the Middle Ages. Blavatsky's Theosophical Society attempted a synthesis of pseudo-scientific procedures with occult doctrines derived from Eastern religions, promising a new Grail to assuage the apparently unquenchable human thirst for meaning. This existential crisis took many forms alongside theosophy: the *fin de siècle* occultism of organizations such as the Order of the Golden Dawn, the Anthroposophy of Rudolf Steiner, Wagnerism, symbolism, the writings of Aleister Crowley, Nazi supernaturalism in the 1930s and '40s, the Hippy culture of psychedelia in the 1960s, and what we now call "New Age" philosophy.

The movies were quick to exploit this explosion of magickal thinking. In the survey of the films that follows, my aim is to discover how they reflect the wider occult scene that gave rise to them. Film is the ideal medium for the representation and dramatization of occultism, with its unprecedented ability to replicate unconscious imagery and convincingly realize non-causal phenomena. (This is why so many examples of fairy tale magic have been adapted for the screen.) That the birth of film coincided with the development of Freudian psychoanalysis seems to provide evidence for what the later Freudian apostate Jung termed the "collective unconscious." Certainly, no artistic technique had previously offered such a fluid and fecund means of representing the apparently impossible and meaningful irrationality of dreams. Our ideas of religion and the supernatural derive largely from the reservoir of our dream imagery, as Freud observed in 1900 when describing "clear-headed men, without any extravagant ideas, who seek to support their religious faith in the existence and activity of superhuman spiritual forces precisely by the inexplicable nature of the phenomena of dreaming."[10]

Most films (not unlike religions) impose rational structures on their occult content, such as, for example, Hammer Films' adaptation of Dennis Wheatley's *The Devil Rides Out* (dir. Terence Fisher, 1968), in which occult imagery is superimposed upon a traditional abduction thriller. The non-linear, "dream-like" approach of Luis Buñuel's *Un chien Andalou* (1929), even though it is not concerned with occult imagery, is far more unsettling and closer to the psychological processes that give rise to magickal thinking than Fisher's film. Similarly, the "Desire" segment of Hans Richter's surrealist film *Dreams That Money Can Buy* (1947) specifically references two plates from Max Ernst's 1934 novel in collage, *Une semaine de bonté*. Ernst's re-arranged reality in that work (cut-and-pasted from nineteenth-century illustrated magazines) turns women in bustles into winged gryphons, and gives smartly dressed young men the heads of birds and lions; women float over staircases; lion-headed gentlemen indulge in atrocities, and men in African masks attack women in railway carriages. Despite the specific connection between *Une semaine de bonté* and "Desire," which was written and directed by Ernst, Georges Franju's 1951 *L'hôtel des Invalides* and *Judex* (1963) perhaps summon

THE IMPORTANCE OF BEING ERNST: **Channing Pollock in the title role of *Judex* (dir. Georges Franju, 1963).**

the general mood and imagery of Ernst's unnerving vision rather more powerfully. The former, commissioned by the French government as a straightforward documentary film, was transformed by Franju into a surreal anti-war montage, creating a dream-like world from the shadows of tourists, disabled old soldiers, suits of armor and statues, many of which echo the bird- and lion-headed men in Ernst's "novel." The effect is both social commentary and occult nightmare. *Judex,* concerning the activities of the eponymous vigilante, features a masked ball where many of the guests, including the mysterious Judex, wear bird-head masks with their formal evening dress, very much in the style of Ernst's collage visions. Though intended as no more than a visual conceit, such imagery strongly suggests, via *Une semaine de bonté,* the mystical associations of the gods and goddesses of ancient Egypt.

Two of Ingmar Bergman's films also achieve this combination of occult and dream imagery. *Wild Strawberries* (1957) begins with a sequence in which an elderly man walks down a deserted street. A mood of apprehension, created by Bergman's oblique lighting, crisp shadows and slow tracking shots, is comparable to the unnerving urban desolation found in the surreal paintings of Giorgio de Chirico. The man passes a clock without hands, suggesting that time has run out for him. He encounters a Magritte-like figure, which reveals a lumpen face of clay. The figure then collapses into a heap of clothes as a hearse appears. A hand emerges from the coffin inside the hearse, and drags the man inside: The dream is obviously a premonition of the man's death. In Bergman's *The Magician* (1958), a series of occult hoaxes are played on a pathologist. These include an eyeball staring up from an inkwell (reminiscent of the floating eyeballs of Odilon Redon's engravings), a disembodied hand and ghostly reflections in a mirror. Though explained as hoaxes, perpetrated from motives of revenge, their uncanny effect marvelously conveys the mood of a dream and the supposed possibilities of occult phenomena. Jung was particularly interested in this connection:

> Those who are not convinced should beware of naïvely assuming that the whole question of spirits and ghosts has been settled and that all manifestations of this kind are meaningless swindles. This is not so at all. These phenomena exist in their own right, regardless of the way they are interpreted, and it is beyond all doubt that they are genuine manifestations of the unconscious. The communications of "spirits" are *statements about the unconscious psyche,* provided that they are really spontaneous and are not cooked up by the conscious mind. They have this in common with dreams; for dreams, too, are statements about the unconscious, which is why the psychotherapist uses them as a first-class source of information.[11]

Each of this book's 13 chapters will help to illuminate a different facet of occultism's dark jewel. I begin with the decadent movement of the 1890s, a period in which occultism was first taken up by the literary world, and subsequently influenced horror films of a particular kind. Among these are Edgar G. Ulmer's *The Black Cat* (1934), Stuart Walker's *WereWolf of London* (1935), Lew Landers' *The Raven* (1935), Albert Lewin's *The Picture of Dorian Gray* (1945), Roger Corman's *Pit and the Pendulum* (1961), Hammer vampire, mummy and Frankenstein films and the extraordinarily decadent esthetic of Terence Fisher's *The Two Faces of Dr. Jekyll* (1960).

Chapter Three explores the literary background to later occult films, contrasting Marlowe's play with Goethe's *Faust*, before discussing the demonic elements in Wagner's *Parsifal*, Baudelaire's Satanic imagery, Huysmans' *Là-bas*, and Strindberg's *Inferno* and *Occult Diary*.

The possibilities of film to realize occult fantasy had been eagerly exploited by filmmakers from the very beginning of the medium's history with the fantasies of Georges Méliès. Chapter Four consequently explores the occult background to Stellan Rye's *The Student of Prague* (1915), Henrick Galeen's *The Golem* (1920), F.W. Murnau's *Nosferatu* (1922) and *Faust* (1926), Benjamin Christensen's *Häxen* (1922), Fritz Lang's *Dr. Mabuse—Der Spieler* (1922), *Faust* (1926), *Metropolis* (1927) and *The Testament of Dr. Mabuse* (1933), Arthur Robison's *Warning Shadows* (1923), Carl Dreyer's *Vampyr* (1932) and, in particular, Rex Ingram's 1926 adaptation of Somerset Maugham's 1908 novel *The Magician*, its connections with Aleister Crowley and its influence on later occult films.

Chapter Five is devoted to the significance and expression of ritual, magickal processes being largely articulated by it. Ritual plays a particularly significant role in Hammer's vampire films, which became increasingly structured around an occult framework, derived from operatic examples. Ritual is really what transforms Dennis Wheatley's *The Devil Rides Out* from an abduction thriller to an occult one, a fact of which Hammer was well aware in its two adaptations of Wheatley novels. This approach was echoed in Paul Campion's 2011 film *The Devil's Rock*, in which Wheatley-esque black magic ritual joins forces with the Third Reich.

Magick being a "science" of the will, Chapter Six explores ways in which willpower has been articulated in film, including perhaps the most disturbing manifestation of it in Leni Riefenstahl's *Triumph des Willens* (1935). Riefenstahl's film is, however, the end product of a tradition in German Romanticism as a whole, derived in part from Wagner's *Parsifal*, Robert Wiene's *The Cabinet of Dr. Caligari* (1919) and several other classics of the Weimar period. Other famous historical exponents of willpower who also inspired the movies include Rasputin (interpreted by two of the great masters of horror films, Conrad Veidt and Christopher Lee, along with one of the most popular of

Dr. Whos, Tom Baker). A modern-dress Australian version of the Rasputin legend appeared in Simon Wincer's *Harlequin* (1980) starring Robert Powell as the mysterious hypnotist Gregory Woolf. Parallel themes feature in Archie Mayo's *Svengali* (1931), with John Barrymore in the title role.

That Svengali was a Jew brings us back to the triumph of the will that was Adolf Hitler, whose career was unnervingly foreshadowed in Otto Rippert's German film serial *Homunculus* (1916). Willpower lies at the heart of Wolf Rilla's *Village of the Damned* (1960), which is also an expression of the fear of parenthood that we find in films such as Roman Polanski's *Rosemary's Baby* (1968), Peter Sasdy's *I Don't Want to Be Born* (1975), Donald Cammell's *Demon Seed* (1977), David Lynch's *Eraserhead* (1977) and Ridley Scott's *Alien* (1979). *The Omen* (dir. Richard Donner, 1977) combines these two aspects in a particularly powerful manner.

The Magus figure is the subject of Chapter Seven, bringing us into the contrasting worlds of George Lucas' *Star Wars* (1977), Erle C. Kenton's *Island of Lost Souls* (1932), Sherlock Holmes and most significantly John Fowles' 1964 novel *The Magus*, which was adapted for the screen by Guy Green in 1968. In the character of Conchis, Anthony Quinn creates the archetypal Magus figure in a perhaps unjustly criticized film.

Chapter Eight focuses on the realistic approach taken by William Friedkin's *The Exorcist* (1974) and *The Omen*, while Chapter Nine explores theosophical aspects of the Indiana Jones films, *The Frozen Dead* (dir. Herbert J. Leder, 1967), *Village of the Damned*, *Quatermass and the Pit* (dir. Roy Ward Baker, 1967), *The Lost Continent* (dir. Michael Carreras, 1968), *Warlords of Atlantis* (dir. Kevin Connor, 1978), *The City Under the Sea* (dir. Jacques Tourneur, 1965) and the cosmic horror of Lovecraft in *The Dunwich Horror* (dir. Daniel Haller, 1970).

Because of the close connection between the occult revival and hippy culture in the "long" 1960s (a mood that carried on until the arrival of punk rock in 1976 and was finished off by the seismic appearance of *Star Wars* in 1977), Chapter Ten is devoted to ways in which psychedelic imagery and altered states of mind (due mainly to hallucinogenic drugs) informed the occult elements in the Beatles' films, Alejandro Jodorowsky's *The Holy Mountain* (1973) and "the ultimate trip" in Stanley Kubrick's *2001: A Space Odyssey*, a sequence that was updated in Scott Derrickson's *Doctor Strange* (2016). *Doctor Strange* brings us back to the connection between occultism and the Third Reich, all of which has its origins in Blavatsky's ideas.

Chapter Eleven addresses how occult films have so often exploited conspiracy as its motivational principle. One might say that all religion is a form of conspiracy, attempting to explain reality by means of hidden agendas.

Blavatsky's theosophy is no exception. Nazi occultism has also been a lucrative aspect of this approach, exemplified by Franklin J. Schaffner's *The Boys from Brazil* (1978) in which Hitler is cloned, and more recently, in *The Da Vinci Code* (dir. Ron Howard, 2006), all manner of occult conspiracies have coalesced.

The Faust legend, explored in Chapter Twelve, has formed the basis of films specifically about the character made famous by Marlowe and Goethe, and also those in which pacts are made with the forces of darkness. Murnau's *Faust* (1926) is a conflation of various strands of German Romantic imagery. Jan Svankmajer's 1994 version of the story updates it, simultaneously using puppetry and animation to create a world of magical realism. Horror films often improvise on the general theme. *From Beyond the Grave* (dir. Kevin Connor, 1974), for example, features a demonic antiques dealer (Peter Cushing) who ensnares his shop's customers. Fraser Clarke Heston's film adaptation of Stephen King's *Needful Things* (1993) continues the same idea.

Finally, after considering the field of animation, we close the covers of this cinematic grimoire in the hope that what might once have been hidden will to some extent have been revealed.

CHAPTER ONE

Decadence

The occult revival at the end of the nineteenth century was but one aspect of the wider decadent movement. Before I turn my attention to the occult in more detail, I feel it would be helpful to explore the esthetic of decadence that nurtured it. This, in turn, influenced the more traditional kind of horror films from which the specifically occult variety emerged.

In his study of the dancer Maud Allen, Wilde's play *Salomé* and the backlash against the perceived decadence of British society in the years prior to the First World War, Philip Hoare usefully identified two of the reasons for the nineteenth-century occult revival. "In the *fin de siècle*," he argues, "such pagan mysticism proliferated as a reaction to encroaching and irrevocable change, of the recent past (the effects of the industrial society) and the near future (its acceleration into the modern era)."[1] But decadence originated in Paris, and only reached London after Wilde had imported it. After completing *À Rebours* (1884), which came to be regarded as the bible of *La décadence*, J.-K. Huysmans wrote *Là-bas* (1891), with its specifically occult themes, the crimes of Gilles de Rais and the literary underworld of *fin de siècle* Paris. Huysmans' aim was to apply the naturalistic technique of Zola to decadent subject matter, and by so doing resolve the impasse he perceived in contemporary literature:

> In France right now the purely corporeal recipe has brought upon itself such discredit that two clans have arisen: the liberal, which prunes naturalism of all its boldness of subject matter and diction in order to fit it for the drawing-room, and the decadent, which gets completely off the ground and raves incoherent in a telegraphic patois intended to represent the language of the soul—intended rather to divert the readers' attention from the author's utter lack of ideas.[2]

The climax of *Là-bas* takes us to a Black Mass. It is presided over by the notorious Satanist Canon Docre, whom Huysmans based on a Belgian abbot called Van Haeke:

> He evokes the Devil, and he feeds white mice on the hosts which he consecrates. His frenzy for sacrilege is such that he had the image of Christ tattooed on his heels so that he could always step on the Saviour![3]

Modern occultism and decadence grew from the same root, and have become firmly associated in the popular imagination ever since, as we see in Richard Gilman's amusing word-association exercise at the beginning of his *Decadence—The Strange Life of an Epithet,* where he lists

> elegant opium dens with suave, slinky hostesses; bedrooms with mirrored ceilings and black satin sheets on the emperor-sized beds; women in high heels, black stockings and garter belts; Marlene Dietrich in *The Blue Angel* with Emil Jannings crowing like a rooster; bathrooms with purple or zebra-striped tiling; Tangiers; Pompeii; a Black Mass; Turkish pashas in their playrooms; *Les Fleurs du mal;* a drag-queen costume ball; a voyeur with expensive binoculars trained on the windows of a girls' boarding-school dormitory; Oscar Wilde and the green carnation...[4]

Robert W. Gutman also identifies the occult aspects of Wagner's final, distinctly decadent music drama *Parsifal,* first performed in 1882:

> In *Parsifal,* with the help of church bells, snippets of the Mass, and the vocabulary and paraphernalia of the Passion, he set forth a religion of racism under the cover of Christian legend. *Parsifal* is an enactment of the Aryan's plight, struggle and hope for redemption, a drama characterized not only by the composer's naively obscure and elliptical literary style, but also by the indigenous circumlocutions of allegory, the calculated unrealities of symbolism, and, especially, the sultry corruptions of decadence. The temple scenes are, in a sense, Black Masses, perverting the symbols of the Eucharist and dedicating them to a sinister god. And the Black Mass, so fascinating to the *fin de siècle* decadents, was but one of their obsessions weaving its spell around the aging Wagner and his *Parsifal*.[5]

Charles Baudelaire, high priest of *La décadence,* accused the nineteenth-century bourgeois of being "an enemy of roses and scents, a fanatic of utility; he is an enemy of Watteau, of Raphael, an arch enemy of luxury, of the fine arts and literature."[6] Significantly, Madame Blavatsky made a similar attack in the opening pages of her first major work, *Isis Unveiled* (1877), complaining of

> an unspiritual, dogmatic, too often debauched clergy; a host of sects, and three warring great religions; discord instead of union, dogmas without proofs, sensation-loving preachers, and wealth and pleasure seeking parishioners' hypocrisy and bigotry, begotten by the tyrannical exigencies of respectability, the rule of the day, sincerity and real piety exceptional.[7]

Not that Blavatsky regarded her "solution" to the soulless state of affairs at the time as decadent: theosophy would rise above it; but, nonetheless, the connection remains, and the period's fascination with the occult would never have arisen in the way it did without the decline of established religion and its social consequences. The attraction of occultism was in many ways the same as decadence, for both are transgressive.

So what exactly is decadence? Friedrich Nietzsche defined the typical *décadent* as a type that "always chooses the means harmful to him."[8] For Nietzsche, decadence weakens the instincts: "What one ought to shun is found attractive.

One puts to one's lips what drives one yet faster into the abyss."⁹ Decadence has developed considerably since then, but the legacy of its *fin de siècle* style continued to resonate in twentieth-century popular culture. In the 1960 and '70s, Hammer Films and its many competitors were much indebted to decadent and symbolist literature, which had explored many of those films' themes, and also inspired their often elaborate *décor*. The symbolist movement, out of which *fin de siècle* decadence emerged, was primarily concerned with using art to express ideas. For symbolist artists, reality was just a raw material; for some, reality itself was merely a product of the mind. In his symbolist manifesto of 1886, poet Jean Moréas proposed that "symbolist poetry endeavors to clothe the Idea in a form perceptible to the senses that nevertheless does not constitute an ultimate goal in itself, but, while helping to convey the Idea, remains subordinate."

> The Idea, in turn, must not allow itself to be deprived of the sumptuous trappings of external analogies; for the essential character of symbolic art is never to reach the Idea itself.¹⁰

The use of the word "sumptuous" here links symbolism to the obsession with *décor* and eroticism that typifies the writings of Oscar Wilde in England and Huysmans and Jean Lorrain in France.

DECADENT DR. GLENDON: **Henry Hull as Dr. Glendon and Warner Oland as Dr. Yogami, contemplating exotic orchids in** *WereWolf of London* **(dir. Stuart Walker, 1935).**

Via pulp fiction, there were, of course, echoes of *fin de siècle* decadence in the American horror films of the 1930s, long before the arrival of the Hammer esthetic. Think of the frog-eating orchid in *WereWolf of London*. "Fancy!" exclaims a guest who is present at its dinnertime, "Bringing a beastly thing like that into Christian England!" That line might well have been applied by many people to Oscar Wilde himself at the time of his trials. But Warner Oland's Dr. Yogami speaks up for eccentricity: "Nature is very tolerant," he smiles. "She has no creeds." And to Henry Hull's Dr. Glendon, he adds: "May I congratulate you, sir, on the amazing collection of plants you have assembled here. Evolution was in a strange mood when that creation came along. It makes one wonder just where the plant world leaves off and the animal world begins."

Such ambivalence was central to *fin de siècle* decadence as a whole—not least the sexual ambivalence of Wilde himself. Wilde's fictional spokesman Dorian Gray comments on the "metaphors as monstrous as orchids,"[11] which he reads in what is clearly intended, though never actually specified, as Huysmans' *À Rebours*. Arthur Symons, a less sensational though no less persistent advocate of decadence in England, admitted in his 1895 poem "Lilian I: Proem," "The orchid mostly is the flower I love." Violets do not move him, but violets that grow in a hothouse, and take on the orchid's coloring, become "the artificial flower of my ideal."[12] This aloof imagery of hybrid, unnatural and cultivated abnormality soon trickled down to a more popular level, as we see in Fred M. White's story "The Purple Terror," first published in *Strand Magazine* in 1899. This features a man-eating orchid: "Most orchids have a kind of face of their own; the purple blooms had a positive expression of ferocity and cunning. They exhumed, too, a queer, sickly fragrance. Scarlett had smelt something like it before, after the Battle of Manila. The perfume was the perfume of a corpse."[13] Such stories were the conduit through which the elitist imagery of decadent poets was transferred to the democratic movie screen.

Dracula, another poisonous flower of decadence, bloomed in the Gothic gloom of Universal Studios at the beginning of the 1930s. Bela Lugosi's florid pallor and serpentine body language have something of the orchid and the tendril about them too. Dracula's habit of spending the daylight hours in his coffin was also practiced by the great actress of *La décadence*, Sarah Bernhardt. She claimed it helped her to study her parts, but she was no doubt also fully aware of its publicity value.

> I found it quite natural to sleep every night in this little bed of white satin which was to be my last couch. One day my manicurist came into the room to do my hands, and my sister asked her to enter quietly, because I was still asleep. The woman turned her

head, believing that I was asleep in the armchair, but seeing me in my coffin she rushed away shrieking wildly. From that moment all Paris knew that I slept in my coffin, and gossip with its thistle-down wings took flight in all directions.[14]

All this seems to have foreshadowed Martin Landau's recreation of Lugosi in *Ed Wood*, Tim Burton's 1994 homage to Hollywood at its endearing worst. We first encounter Lugosi in a funeral parlor trying out coffins for size. "Too constrictive!" he complains. "I can't even fold my arms! This is the most uncomfortable coffin I've ever been in!" In fact, we don't see Lugosi in his coffin at all in director Tod Browning's 1931 film, merely his hand emerging from it and the sound of the coffin lid falling aside as he steps out of it, off camera. An insect and a rodent, with their own miniature coffins, stand in for him as the camera cuts away. Browning does allow us to see one of Dracula's vampire brides sitting up in her coffin, as Sarah Bernhardt no doubt sat up in hers.

Lugosi's Poe fanatic, Dr. Vollin, in *The Raven* is another child of Parisian *décadence*. He is a kind of deranged Baudelaire, for Baudelaire had been equally smitten by the Bard of Baltimore. Baudelaire, however, confined himself to translating Poe's works into French rather than constructing a torture chamber of pendulums and contracting walls, which are Dr. Vollin's psychopathic pastimes. In *The Black Cat*, *décadence* was transformed from *fin de siècle* to modernist Bauhaus style for a story of Satanism that in fact had little to do with Poe. A story of vengeance, necrophilia, Satanism and, most important of all, architecture, it stars Lugosi and Boris Karloff. Karloff plays a namesake of the architect Hans Poelzig, who had designed *The Golem* for Paul Wegener in 1920. Lugosi plays a medical man with the marvelously alliterative name Vitus Verdegarst. Together, Karloff and Lugosi offer twice the macabre allure, but the modernist Bauhaus interiors of Poelzig's fortress residence are the real stars of the film. With their tubular steel chairs, chrome-trimmed sliding doors, art-deco intercom speakers, goldfish-bowl wash basins, digital clocks and a streamlined staircase, these sets are redolent of the decadent Weimar Republic, while the concrete-clad cellars with their riveted steel doors and industrial bulkhead lighting bring to mind the bunkers Hitler was building around the same time the film was being shot, and in which he would eventually commit suicide. As David Manners' hero Peter Alison says, Poelzig is just the man to design a "nice cozy lunatic asylum."

Germany, for all its technology and cutting-edge design, was already dabbling with the Devil, like Poelzig and his fellow Satanists. Hitler had been invoked by the German people (which was why Ulmer found himself in Hollywood, as a refugee), and *The Black Cat*, like so many Hollywood horror films of the time, responded subliminally to the threat from the Old World. Ostensibly, *The Black Cat* was about unfinished business from the First World

ART-DECO DECADENCE: **Boris Karloff as Hjalmar Poelzig in** *The Black Cat* **(dir. Edgar G. Ulmer, 1934).**

War (Poelzig's betrayal of Verdegast), but the general feeling of the film aired anxieties about the possibility of a Second: When we watch Verdegast flay Poelzig alive at the end, it is hard not to associate this horror with Nazi atrocities.

Ulmer's film also regards Modernism as worryingly "other" and more disorientating than traditional Gothic. Its sweeping lines and pared-down geometry implied a cold rationality far more troubling than any crumbling castle. The alienation of this architectural nightmare frightens the newlyweds far more than Karloff's angular haircut and Lugosi's elongated vowels. Even the Black Mass at the film's climax is modernized, with its slanting, inverted double cross, metallic obelisks and Expressionist dagger-shaped *décor*; but tradition is maintained by the ironic use of the poignant Adagio from Bach's

Toccata, Adagio and Fugue in C Major, which, in this context, is a musical equivalent of the inverted cross. That Poelzig's character was also loosely inspired by Aleister Crowley adds to the disturbing modernity of the proceedings, while simultaneously enhancing its decadence.

The Black Cat also retained the motif of the *femme fatale* so dear to the symbolists and decadents alike, who obsessed about Salome dancing before the severed head of John the Baptist: In *The Black Cat,* Poelzig preserves the mummified corpse of his wife in his underground bunker. This perhaps more appropriately echoes Poe's "Ligeia," in which the spirit of the dead beloved actually returns in another woman's body. Poe's work, via Baudelaire's translations, was a major influence on the French *décadents.* The neurasthenic Roderick Usher in Poe's "The Fall of the House of Usher," whose soul is like the string of a suspended lute, vibrating at the slightest touch, is the literary ancestor of Des Esseintes, the hero of *À Rebours.* Both isolate themselves and devote their lives to estetic experiences, and Wilde's Dorian is their direct descendent.

Albert Lewin's glossy MGM adaptation of *The Picture of Dorian Gray* exploited the marvelous settings of Cedric Gibbons, Hans Peters and Edwin B. Willis to suggest the diabolic undertones of Dorian's estheticism. They are modeled on the opulent Regency style of Joseph Gandy (1771–1843) with their classical statues, oversized urns and furnishings supported by the wings of mythological beasts. We are shown black-tiled floors with white diamond inserts, reversing, like a film negative, the black diamond inserts with white titles more commonly found in such checkerboard schemes. Ebonized doors and door frames complement black picture frames, a black stair carpet fillets the white marble of the steps on either side, and the use of heavy shadows helps to emphasize the richly textured monochrome contrasts, eschewing chiaroscuro.

The demonic connotations of this kind of *décor* are in fact the most important aspect of the film, signaling what is never made explicit in the action. Dorian's "crimes" are only ever alluded to and never explained, but the *décor* reveals all. The neoclassical trimmings, such as the Greek key motif around the fireplace, signal Wilde's "paganism," the demonic element of which (selling one's soul in exchange for eternal youth) is really only a disguise for the story's homosexual agenda. But in making this a morality tale in which Dorian's gayness corrupts him, Wilde subverts his own subversion and colludes with the late-Victorian public opinion that ultimately sent him to prison.

Though *Dorian Gray* only suggests its hero's debaucheries, Huysmans' *Là-bas,* Octave Mirbeau's *Torture Garden* (1899) and Jean Lorrain's *Monsieur de Phocas* (1901) are all much more explicit in their descriptions of violence and even sadism, and it is appropriate to see these writers, even more than Poe, as the progenitors of a film such as Corman's *Pit and the Pendulum* (1961). Like Lorrain's Phocas, Vincent Price's Nicholas Medina in *Pit and the Pendulum* is both attracted to and repelled by the idea of torture and murder. Disturbed by the crimes of his Inquisitorial father, he is finally driven insane when he discovers that his wife (Barbara Steele), whom he believed dead, is in fact still alive. He also learns that she has been deliberately terrorizing him with the aim of inheriting his estate, which she intends to enjoy with her lover. The sensitive Nicholas now channels the spirit of his Inquisitorial father. (Nicholas, as a boy, had watched as his mother was murdered by his father.) As Nicholas taunts his wife, he calls her by the name of his mother, Isabella:

> I'm going to torture you, Isabella. I'm going to make you suffer for your faithlessness to me. Before this day is out, you will be begging me to kill you, to relieve you of the agony of Hell into which your husband is about to plunge you. Harlot! You will die in agony! Die!

The *décadent* obsessions of Lorrain's Phocas are similar: "My cruelty has also returned: the cruelty which frightens me. It lies dormant for months, for years, and then all at once awakens, bursts forth and—once the crisis is over—leaves me in mortal terror of myself."[15] The impulse to strangle "made my hands feverish and caused my fingers to clench involuntarily."[16] At the end of the novel, Phocas does indeed commit murder, and his victim's death throes are described with a salacious attention to detail of which Medina himself would have approved: "a heavy sweat beaded his face, and his breast rose and fell like bellows. His two vitreous eyeballs rolled up, like two billiard-balls, towards the suddenly creased temples—then they capsized beneath the eyelids which no longer contained anything but whiteness, and his whole body lost its rigidity, becoming black."[17]

Jimmy Sangster, screenwriter for most of the early Hammer horrors, also recognized the tradition in which he was working, referring to the moment in *The Curse of Frankenstein* (dir. Terence Fisher, 1957) when Peter Cushing's Baron Frankenstein asks his cousin to "pass the marmalade" after a particularly gruesome murder in the previous scene.[18] Black comedy has always been part of decadence, and *À Rebours* is in fact a very amusing book, which it is unwise to read with too straight a face: Huysmans was fully aware of the absurdity of his hero's ultra-esthetic obsessions, while being simultaneously fascinated by them. Oscar Wilde also took a playful and ironic approach to decadence, which Lorrain perhaps did not.

Hammer's original 1958 adaptation of *Dracula* (dir. Terence Fisher) is even more of a study in decadent estheticism than the old-fashioned Gothic style of the Universal approach. The obsessive attention to detail in Bernard

Robinson's lushly upholstered, *bric-à-brac*–filled sets are also derived from decadent fiction. The castle sets are dust-free and in excellent repair, their barley-twist Solomonic columns and artfully arranged interiors being closer to Bram Stoker's description of "a well-lit room in which a table was spread for supper, and on whose mighty hearth a great fire of logs flamed and flared,"[19] than anything we find in Charles D. Hall's spectacular Gothic fantasies for the Tod Browning adaptation. Robinson's set also corresponds in some ways to the description of the castle in Villiers de L'Isle Adam's famous 1890 symbolist drama *Axël*:

> [At right a stone stairway is built into the wall; at the top of the stairs an arched doorway leads to one of the towers.]
> [It is already deep twilight.]

ORNATE COFFIN: **At right Noel Willman as Dr. Ravna looms over the evenings proceedings in *The Kiss of the Vampire* (1963). Director, Don Sharp (center) gives instructions.**

> [The depth of the hall gives the impression of a colossal pile dating from the early years of the Middle Ages.—At right in the vast fireplace an immense fire lights the stage. …
>
> [In the foreground doors at right and left; hangings and tapestries of high warp hand over the doors.]
> [In the middle of the hall a table is laid for a banquet.][20]

I will be returning to Villiers—and Axël—later. Meanwhile, the Victoriana, the carefully arranged paintings and the *eau-de-Nil* paneling in the study of Peter Cushing's Van Helsing in Fisher's *Dracula* also suggest the estheticism of Wilde. Noel Willman's Dr. Ravna in *The Kiss of the Vampire* (dir. Don Sharp, 1963) is a kind of undead Des Esseintes, who shuts the world out of his hermetically sealed esthetic retreat. Ravna refers to his exquisitely furnished castle, where music and artifice help entrap his victims, as an "ornate coffin." In *The Brides of Dracula* (dir. Terence Fisher, 1960), David Peel's oedipal vampire, Baron Meinster, is an undead Dorian Gray, a golden-haired dandy who attacks his own mother before converting virgins to vampirism as an esthete might collect blue and white china. Indeed, Wilde's description of Dorian is remarkably similar to the admittedly brown-eyed David Peel, being "wonderfully handsome, with his finely curved scarlet lips, his frank blue eyes, his crisp gold hair."[21] That the virgins whom Meinster vampirizes are female is merely a concession to popular taste, as the evidence suggests that the baron is in fact attracted in quite the opposite direction, and would no doubt have been very much at home in the Café Royal with Oscar and his acolytes.

It is, indeed, at the Café Royal that Ralph Bates' demonic aristocratic Lord Courtley in Peter Sasdy's *Taste the Blood of Dracula* (1970) discusses his plans to resurrect the arch vampire. In this, he is aided by a dissolute trio of Victorian hypocrites who are all eventually destroyed by their taste for dangerous novelty, just as Wilde was destroyed by his. What makes Hammer's first foray into ancient Egypt, *The Mummy* (dir. Terence Fisher, 1959) interesting is not so much the Mummy (excellent though Christopher Lee is as the bandaged nemesis), but rather the eloquent excellence of the luxurious settings. *The Mummy* doesn't have much of a story, but it looks extraordinarily impressive. Its *décor* is really its entire justification: The living room of Peter Cushing's John Banning is a model of estheticism with its fluted columns, scalloped niches, screen, tastefully arranged paintings, tooled volumes, globe-shaded gasoliers and gas brackets, fringed lampshades and sculptures on columns flanking the French windows. ("I love beautiful things that one can touch and handle," writes Wilde in *Dorian Gray*, "Old brocades, green bronzes, lacquer-work, carved ivories, exquisite surroundings, luxury, pomp, there is much to be had from all these."[22]) *Eau-de-Nil* again forms part of the decorative scheme, which nicely complements Yvonne Furneaux's mauve negligée. (The 1890s were known both as the "yellow" '90s and "the mauve decade." "The laburnum will be as yellow next June as it is now," we read in *Dorian Gray*, "In a month there will be purple stars on the clematis."[23]) Like an Egyptian Dorian, George Pastell's Mehemet keeps a private shrine to the god Karnak in his living room. (Lewin interestingly has Hurd Hadfield's Dorian read from Wilde's poem "The Sphinx"), and Mehemet's curious domestic arrangements also have certain things in common with the first appearance of Hadaly, the female android that features in another work by Villiers de L'Isle Adam, his 1886 symbolist-decadent science fiction novel, *The Future Eve*:

> As the professor called out this mysterious name, a section of the wall at the extreme south of the laboratory turned on its hinges, silently bringing to view a narrow retreat fashioned between the slabs of stone. All the light from the electrical globes was suddenly focused on this spot.
>
> The concave and semi-circular walls were covered with rich draperies of black velvet, which fell luxuriously from an arch of jade to the white marble floor. The heavy folds were hooked back and fastened by retainers of gold, caught here and there through the rich material.
>
> On a dais in the centre of this niche was standing a being whose aspect bore the impression of the Unknown.[24]

In *The Man Who Could Cheat Death* (dir. Terence Fisher, 1959), Charles Bonnard (Anton Diffring) is a part-time sculptor who hosts elegant parties in his atelier. Again like Dorian, he is older than he looks, but although he sculpts pretty women, he doesn't have a portrait to age for him, instead relying on an elixir. To keep up supplies, he must murder his sitters for their pituitary glands. Everything is photographed in golden light, echoing that phrase once used to describe the bible of the esthetic movement, Walter Pater's *The Renaissance*, as "the golden book of English prose."

Perhaps the most decadent (if dramatically less interesting) Hammer presentation, Terence Fisher's *The Two Faces of Dr. Jekyll* depicts the good doctor as an unattractive, bearded bore and Mr. Hyde as an engaging, angel-faced monster. This gleeful youth, played by Paul Massie without the aging makeup he needs for Jekyll, is yet another Dorian. This time, Fisher and his photographer Jack Asher bathe everything in mauve and pink light: There is mauve and pink satin, mauve and pink upholstery, and lilac lampshades. Jekyll's unfaithful wife, Kitty (Dawn Addams), wears the mauve negligée previously modeled by Yvonne Furneaux in *The Mummy*, and thus attired she similarly compliments the esthetic *eau-de-Nil* paintwork of Dr. Jekyll's staircase. (All this is not unlike the boudoir decorated with "mauve satin" and "pink candles"[25] in which a son stabs his own mother after she attempts to seduce him, in Jean Moréas' decadent tale "La Faënza" (1886). M.P. Shiel's decadent detective from 1894, Prince Zaleski, is similarly fond of "dim violet, scarlet and pale-rose lights."[26])

A nightclub scene featuring a snake dancer is similarly decked out in a riot of pink and mauve but this time with turgid green light flooding the dance floor. The film's composer, Monty Norman, once told me he was asked to visit the Raymond Revue Bar in London's Soho to interview the woman who performed this role in the film: "She showed me all the things that you can do with a snake," he explained, and we too are shown a fairly comprehensive set of moves in the film. The whole thing is reminiscent of the most famous painting by the decadent Munich painter, Franz von Stuck, whose 1893 canvas *Die Sünde* (*Sin*) scandalized Europe with its snake-draped but otherwise naked *femme fatale*. There are also echoes here of Salome dancing in the overheated interiors of Gustave Moreau's paintings, which were lauded by Huysmans and Lorrain as quintessential expressions of *La décadence*. Musicians wearing fezzes accompany the snake dance in *The Two Faces of Dr. Jekyll*, which even includes an acknowledgment of Loïe Fuller's famously billowing fabrics, before the snake lady suggests fellatio by placing the snake's head in her mouth and sucking hard. Lines from Lorrain's *Monsieur de Phocas* demonstrate the *fin de siècle* origin of this sort of thing. Two Javanese dancers are entertaining a group of opium eaters in elegantly decadent surroundings:

> Now, as they stood on tiptoe, very slender in their exaggerated nakedness, it was as if two long black serpents shot forth from the cones of the two diadems had begin a delicious and lugubrious dance within the bluish vapors.[27]

Alternatively, we might glance at the "Andante of Snakes" by that other British advocate of decadence, Arthur Symons:

> Ancestral angers brood in these dull eyes
> Where the long-lineages venom of the snake
> Meditates evil; woven intricacies
> Or Oriental arabesques awake.[28]

But the snake is only the beginning of Hyde's journey into perversion. Like Dorian—like Monsieur de Phocas—he wants much more than opium dreams and high living. He seeks out lowly drinking dens, gaudy whores and rough boxing matches before he is thrown down in the mud of the streets and robbed. This degradation is also experienced by Lorrain's Phocas, who is corrupted by an English esthete called Ethal, a character possibly modeled on Oscar Wilde:

> Ethal has given me a taste for the slums; he has awakened in me a dangerous curiosity regarding streetwalkers and guttersnipes. The bulging eyes of cut-throats, the soliciting

eyes of suburban strumpets, all the acute and brutal depravity of beings reduced by wretchedness to the elementary gestures of instinct, attracts and fascinates me.

I arrive in the outer lying boulevards in the evening, to prowl about interestedly, surveying the scene, on the look-out for whores. Low prostitution excites and entices me with its reek of musk, alcohol and white grease-paint.[29]

Despite the fashion for contemporary settings in vampire films of the singularly occult 1970s, the decadent heritage of the undead remained. This is particularly the case in the two Count Yorga films, which went on to inspire Hammer's self-consciously modish but less daring approach to updating vampire narratives. Robert Quarry, an enthusiastic horror-film fan himself, played the eponymous role in both films very much in the style of a Sadean decadent from the 1890s. In *Count Yorga—Vampire* (dir. Bob Kelljan, 1970), Yorga has left his native Bulgaria to refresh himself in contemporary Los Angeles, shots of which open the film. The action begins with a séance, over which Yorga presides, firmly embedding this vampire tale in the occult milieu of the time, which was still absorbing the New Age hippiedom of the 1960s. Later, Yorga, the ultimate outsider, will fascinate a young woman and attack her. Eventually he meets his end, though not before he has infected another victim.

Combining camp, cool and brief but shocking moments of bloody horror, Quarry's performance is unnervingly effective. Formally, sometimes even theatrically dressed, with an understandable penchant for scarlet and black, he cuts a suave, ironic but also genuinely frightening figure, assisted by his grotesque, disfigured and presumably resurrected servant Brudah (Edward Walsh). Amid the somewhat chilly modern furnishings of Yorga's home are more traditionally Gothic details such as crimson candles, and even a kind of throne in the basement, which Quarry's commanding presence manages to make weird rather than absurd. The contemporary setting of the film is, in fact, rather more suited to Baudelaire's observation that modern metropolitan life "is rich in poetic and marvelous subjects. We are enveloped and steeped as though in an atmosphere of the marvelous; but we do not notice it."[30]

> He alone will be a painter, the true painter, who proves himself capable of distilling the epic qualities of contemporary life, and of showing us and making us understand, by his colouring and draughtsmanship, how great we are, how poetic we are, in our cravats and our polished boots.[31]

Stoker's *Dracula*, after all, takes place in what was, for its first readers, the contemporary setting in late–Victorian London. What more appropriate environment for a decadent vampire than a modern city?

To aid this sense of modernity, Kelljan employed up-to-date techniques such as the use of a hand-held camera, which immediately lends the narrative a quality of *cinéma verité*, predating the impact hand-held camera work had on the television police series *Hill Street Blues* by a decade. Kelljan also effectively uses montage with voice-over dialogue for a conversation between the two male leads early in the film; the action shows them walking through various Los Angeles locations.

Crucially, this general approach also required a different approach to the soundtrack. Traditional "horror music" is kept to a minimum. Instead, eerie wind effects help heighten the mood without the aid of music. Silence, in particular, is also an extremely effective tool, especially when the count stares at his opponents in the particularly unsettling way that Quarry perfected for this role. And during surprise attacks by Yorga, his hands outstretched and fangs bared, the Yorga films' composer William Marx (adopted son of harp-playing Harpo Marx) relies simply on a kind of electric bell effect, the unexpected nature of which very successfully heightens the intended shock in a particularly contemporary manner. Yorga staggers back, impaled and bloody, but complete silence reigns for a good ten seconds before his exaggerated screams and final death agony.

Wind effects return to even greater effect in *The Return of Count Yorga*, directed by Kelljan the following year. The main attack scene features a group of female vampires who burst into a contemporary living room and slaughter nearly everyone in it. This is played out entirely with naturalistic sound effects—screams, footsteps, furniture being moved, etc.—but without a note of music. It has a similar impact to the brutal murder scene in Hitchcock's *Torn Curtain* (1966), for which Bernard Herrmann scored a cue in his habitually intense symphonic style; Hitchcock rejected it. However, the effect of Herrmann's score has subsequently been demonstrated, and while heightening the dramatic effect, it might also be said to weaken its brutality by reassuring the audience that this is "only" a film, with the kind of film music we have grown to expect at such a moment. By removing the music, the action becomes much more disturbing and "real." *The Return of Count Yorga* also experimented with electronic manipulation of musical sounds, such as phasing, which was still a relatively unfamiliar and hence unnerving sound on film soundtracks in 1971.

Marx confines his orchestrations to chamber music proportions, creating a more intimate, even claustrophobic style, appropriate to the decadent sterility of Yorga's environment and the arid modernity of the contemporary settings. Spare string writing often features solo timbres, playing atonal material. In the opening shots narrated by George Macready, and during the séance that follows, the string writing is suitably reminiscent of the second movement Adagio of Schoenberg's Third String Quartet. Occasionally, these string textures are expanded with the addition of harp or percussion (as in the final killing scenes set in Yorga's cellar). Flutes also join in during the séance, as they do during the initial drive to Yorga's creepy mansion; but Marx saves fuller string resonance for the love scene between Erica (Judith Lang) and her boyfriend. Later, there are touches of more traditional horror timbres, such as the use of an organ and low register flute when Yorga paces through his domain at night. String glissandi also accompany Yorga raising a storm, but Marx restrains his use of these more hackneyed effects. Sometimes all he needs is a snare-drum rhythm, as in the scene during which the menfolk drive over to Erica's apartment only to find her assuaging her newfound thirst for blood by feasting on a kitten.

Before Yorga attacks Erica in the camper van in which she and her lover are stranded, Marx and Kelljan again remove music from the soundtrack and rely on sound effects to raise the dramatic tension. Cicadas and barking dogs provide the crescendo and musical punctuation that a traditional vampire film score would have used at this moment. The result is not only more naturalistic, but in 1970 it would also have been much more unnerving, in the way that the replacement of music with naturalistic sound effects in Tod Browning's 1931 *Dracula,* would have been to audiences who had been accustomed to wall-to-wall musical accompaniment in so-called "silent" films.

At one moment, Yorga even plays the piano himself, ironically strumming the film's "love" theme, and perhaps referencing the way in which so many silent films in the past were once accompanied. The self-conscious irony here also enriches the decadence of Yorga's persona. Yorga is nothing if not a poseur, a kind of undead *flâneur* as described by the arch-priest of decadence, Baudelaire, one of whose poems is indeed entitled "Le Vampire:"

> The crowd is his element, as the air is that of birds and water of fishes. His passion and his profession are to become one flesh with the crowd. For the perfect *flaneur,* for the passionate spectator, it is an immense joy to set up house in the heart of the multitude, amid the ebb and flow of movement, in the midst of the fugitive and the infinite. To be away from home and yet to feel oneself everywhere at home; to see the world, to be at the centre of the world, and yet to remain hidden from the world—impartial natures which the tongue can but clumsily define. The spectator is a prince who everywhere rejoices in his incognito. The lover of life makes the whole world his family, just like the lover of the fair sex who builds up his family from all the beautiful women that he has ever found, or that are or are not—to be found; or the lover of pictures who lives in a magical society of dreams painted on canvas. Thus the lover of universal life enters into the crowd as though it were an immense reservoir of electrical energy. Or we might liken him to a mirror as vast as the crowd itself; or to a kaleidoscope gifted with consciousness, responding to each one of its movements and reproducing the multiplicity of life and the flickering grace of all the elements of life.[32]

The similarity with Yorga here is an almost perfect match. Yorga is indeed the passionate spectator, away from home and yet everywhere at home, hidden from the world, and building a family from beautiful women, filled with "electrical" energy. He is obviously "different," but is quite able to integrate into the world around him. History is one long period of contemporaneity to him.

A different kind of undead populate Don Sharp's *Psychomania* (1973), in which motorcycle-riding Hell's Angels learn that one can become immortal by committing suicide. Visually, the film updates the imposing sterility of Dorian Gray's Gandy-inspired interiors to an equally chilly '70s esthetic for this story about a homely occultist (Beryl Reid) who makes a pact with the Devil (George Sanders as a formally attired butler). Black candles, a black metronome and black leather chairs are contrasted with orange (the defining color of the decade). Instead of black, the door frames, fireplace and skirting boards are salmon pink (or possibly even metallic copper), while neoclassical opulence is replaced by abstract shapes decorating the otherwise empty walls. One might also consider the *tout ensemble* as a '70s version of the kind of decadent opulence described by Prince Youssoupoff, the immensely wealthy, transvestite and self-indulgent assassin of Rasputin. His residence overlooking London's Hyde Park featured scandalously black carpets:

> To the right of the hall was a white dining-room decorated with blue Delft pottery; the carpet was black, the curtains of orange silk, the chairs were covered with *toile de Jouy* in the same shade as the pottery. The room was lit by a blue glass bowl hanging from the ceiling, and by silver candlesticks on the table with orange shades.[33]

Yousouppoff had experimented with black carpets before, when occupying a Curzon Street flat. Its connotations caused much alarm to two elderly spinsters whom he employed to decorate it:

> All went well until I ordered a black carpet. They must have thought me the devil in person, for, from that day, whenever I entered their shop, they disappeared behind a screen, and nothing could be seen of them but two quivering little lace caps. My carpet set a fashion in London—it even became the cause of a divorce. An Englishwoman ordered one against her husband's wishes. He considered it funereal: "Either me or the carpet," he said, which was rash, for she chose the carpet.[34]

Francis Ford Coppola also acknowledged the connection between Gothic horror, decadence and symbolism in his flawed and partly stylized attempt to bring *Bram Stoker's Dracula* to the screen in 1992. Bram Stoker's *Dracula* it was not (nowhere in the book does the count wear scarlet, Kabuki-style robes), but the production design takes as many opportunities to refer to late-Victorian and Symbolist art as possible. Dracula's castle is based on František Kupka's 1903 painting *The Black Idol*, which echoes an ancient

Egyptian statue; the headboard of Lucy Holmwood's bed features concentric circles framing her head in the manner of Alphonse Mucha, while Gary Oldman's Dracula at one stage models a robe inspired by the example of Gustav Klimt.

The symbiosis of decadence and the occult may well be due to the fact that both decadents and occultists ritualize existence, removing it from the mundane to inhabit a richer imaginative arena. Both are also dependent upon language: "In the beginning was the word," "enchantment," "invocation," "summoning"—all magickal processes depend upon the allusive power of language; both are, indeed, constructed *out* of language. As Richard Gilman points out:

> Not exactly "world-weary" or "self-indulgent" or "ultrarefined" or "overcivilized"; not "debauchery," "effeteness," "depravity," "hedonism" or luxuriousness"; certainly not simply "decay" or "degeneration" or "retrogression," "decadence" seems to gather in all these meanings and implications and to exist precariously and most cabalistically beyond them.[35]

Gilman's final adjective here sets the seal on our first.

CHAPTER TWO

Symbolist Horrors

All the films mentioned so far inhabit far more the *décadent* milieu of Jean Lorrain, Wilde and Huysmans than that of traditional Gothic. Such decadent writing grew out of the symbolist movement, with which it shares many similarities. Villiers de l'Isle Adam, whose writing has much in common with later horror films, is an excellent example of a writer who was both a symbolist and a proto-decadent. A decadent, according to the novelist Paul Bourget, loves "languid music, rare antiques for his furniture, and singular paintings." His thoughts are "morbid" or "petulant," and he prefers authors like Poe, who stretch their nervous mechanism "to the point of hallucination, rhetoricians of a troubled life whose 'language' is 'laced with the green of decay.'"[1] Similarly, a symbolist hero "would rather drop out of the common life than have to struggle to make themselves a place in it—they forgot their mistresses, preferring dreams."[2]

Despite his impressive name and lineage, Jean-Marie-Mathias-Philippe-Auguste, Comte de Villiers de l'Isle Adam (1838–1889) spent most of his life in abject poverty. His ancestors included a Grand Master of the Order of the Knights of Malta, a naval officer and a Marshal of France, but his own father, Joseph, found himself in much reduced circumstances and became obsessed by the pursuit of buried treasure. He purchased vast tracts of land, convinced that somewhere beneath the surface lay the fabulous wealth of aristocrats exiled during the French Revolution. This particular obsession was echoed by Sir Arthur Conan Doyle, whose 1890 Sherlock Holmes story "The Sign of Four" features a similar kind of treasure hunt, undertaken by the curious Sholto brothers. Thaddeus Sholto explains how excited he and his brother were by the idea of the treasure spoken of by their recently deceased father, who, we later learn, had acquired it when out in India in the company of three others who formed a pact of loyalty, identified by the "Sign of Four."

"For weeks and for months we dug and delved in every part of the garden without discovering its whereabouts. It was maddening to think that the hiding-place was on his very lips at the moment that he died."[3] Thaddeus himself lives in exotic Hindu splendor like one of Villiers' characters, giving Doyle an opportunity to describe the kind of decadent *décor* that would eventually be replicated by Hammer's Bernard Robinson in *The Reptile* (dir. John Gilling, 1966):

> The richest and glossiest of curtains and tapestries draped the wall's looped back here and there to expose some richly mounted painting or oriental vase. The carpet was of amber and black, so soft and so thick that the foot sank pleasantly into it, as into a bed of moss. Two great tiger-skins thrown athwart it increased the suggestion of Eastern luxury, as did a huge hookah which stood upon a mat in the corner.[4]

The 1987 Granada Television adaptation of "The Sign of Four," starring Jeremy Brett as Holmes, emphasized this oriental extravagance alongside the Gothic grotesquerie of the tale by showing immense mounds of earth around the forbidding Pondicherry Lodge, where Thaddeus' brother had been digging before his unexpected and gruesome death.

MASTER OF SYMBOLISM: Jean-Marie-Mathias-Philippe-Auguste, Comte de Villiers de l'Isle-Adam.

Villiers' father had been just as unsuccessful in finding treasure as the Sholto brothers. Finding nothing, he sold the land for much less than he paid for it, and finished off the family's financial security for good, ending up bankrupt. His son similarly followed a blind obsession to unearth literary treasures from his imagination. Though he inherited his father's bad luck and failed to convert his literary achievements into cash, he did gain the priceless accolade of being admired by Baudelaire, enjoying friendly relations with Richard Wagner, and being regarded as a genius by that unequivocal genius of French symbolist poetry, Stéphane Mallarmé. Villiers' output contained many horror tales with decadent–Gothic settings. He was also regarded by critic Edmund Wilson as the spiritual father of literary modernism, the title of his immense symbolist drama, *Axël,* informing the title of Wilson's famous book on the subject, *Axël's Castle.*

Villiers' writing glitters with opulence and theatricality, strangeness, satire and Gothic gloom. He also flirts with science fiction and adopts at all times an aloofly aristocratic manner that found its cinematic equivalent in the patrician performance styles of Peter Cushing and Christopher Lee, who had themselves suffered hard times before finding fame. Anticipating the way in which Hammer films in particular overcame the limitations of low budgets, Villiers' style also belies the squalor in which his works were written. He would scribble on wine-stained scraps of paper, for he usually wrote in cafés and restaurants, being to all intents and purposes a homeless itinerant. As his biographer A.W. Raitt puts it, describing the short stories in Villiers' 1883 collection *Cruel Tales*, "[T]he sumptuousness of their style, the richness of their settings, the apparent remoteness from any confessional element, even the resoundingly aristocratic name of their author, could easily give the impression that they were the pastime of some elegant and moneyed amateur—and that is no doubt how Villiers would have liked them to be read."[5]

Villiers' most famous work, *Axël,* was the last thing he wrote, and this vast symbolist drama is really a paean to the powers of the imagination, its hero having more than a dash of Poe's neurasthenic aesthete Roderick Usher about him. Whereas Usher lives in a crumbling mansion, symbolizing his unstable state of mind, Axël lives in a vast castle in the Black Forest, symbolizing his towering, death-devoted and jewel-studded imagination. Edmund Wilson describes it as "half–Wagnerian, half–romantic-Gothic,"[6] and Villiers' description of the crypt of Axël's castle is indeed almost a blueprint for the castle sets of Hammer and its competitors:

> [At right and left along the complete length of the hall are mausolea of white marble.—Statues of knight and chatelaines, the former standing or kneeling upon their tombs, the latter, wearing the costumes of their particular century, their hands joined in prayer, are stretched out the length of the sepulchre blocks;—sculptured marble greyhounds at their feet.]
>
> [A funerary lamp suspended from the central vault dimly lights the mortuary.—Near a porphyry holy-water fount is a large prie-dieu in ebony with worn cushions of violet Utrecht velvet and tarnished gold tassels.] [At left at some distance in the passageway, in the angle of the wall, there is a high terrace window with panes bearing an iron rose-window tracery on the outside; black drapery half conceals it. Near left centre there is a low door hollowed into the thickness of the wall.]
>
> [At right at the back of the gallery and opposite the door above three steps lead to a massive ogival iron door with two leaves which open onto a steep spiral stone staircase.]
>
> [In the centre a bronze perfume-pan on a tripod burns low among the tombs.][7]

In this symbolic environment, Villiers also commemorated his own father's obsession with buried treasure: When Napoleon's armies had rampaged over Germany, the entire wealth of the Frankfurt National Bank, where the population had deposited their treasure for safekeeping, was buried underground somewhere on Axël's fictional estate; but as in Conan Doyle's "The Sign of

Four," the location of the treasure has been kept a jealously guarded secret. Axël's mother is the only person her husband informed of its whereabouts, but she died without revealing the secret. Villiers treats the image of the treasure as a symbol of the unrealizable treasures of the imagination. He was fascinated by the imbalance between the immense wealth of the mind and the frustrating limitations of reality. Indeed, he doubted that reality was as real as the imagination, and subscribed to the philosophical speculation that reality is in fact the product of the mind, rather than vice versa.

All this is an important part of the driving force behind a belief in the occult—that desire to transcend the mundane and to inhabit a magical environment, where what previously could only be *imagined* is actually made manifest. In artistic and social terms, symbolist art was unashamedly elitist; and despite Crowley's insistence to the contrary, much of the appeal of magick and the occult is that it is also so often a secret affair for initiates only. The high priest of symbolism in *fin de siècle* Paris, Joséphin Péladan, who liked to be referred to as Sâr Péladan, was also interested in occultism, as were so many of his followers, and his pursuit of the ideal in art differs very little from the pursuit of the "impossible" by magickal means:

> What determines the worth of a feeling also determines the strength of a doctrine. It so happens that tradition is steadfast, and its teachings can be summarized thus: *the work of art is the feeling of an idea sublimated to its highest level of harmony, or of intensity, or of subtlety.* As for hierarchy, I do not even dare utter its name; it is strangely seditious at this point in our history; I shall nevertheless say that if France is glorious, it is through the heroism of its knights and not the probity of its recorders of deeds. The artist must be an ever-struggling medieval knight in symbolic pursuit of the Holy Grail, a furious crusader against the bourgeoisie![8]

It is to be expected, then, that after trying various justifications for living (honor, pleasure and politics), Axël turns, like Faust, to magick:

> Shall I be able to transmute metals like Hermes? displace magnets like Paracelsus? resuscitate the dead like Appollonius of Tyana? Shall I too find pentacles to compel or dispel love? the Elixir of long life? the Powder of projection like Raymond Lulle? the Philosopher's Stone—like the Cosmopolite? Will I be like the magi of the great tradition?[9]

But in the end, even the occult world is seen as no more than a metaphor of the imagination:

> Quick forces which assemble the laws of substance, occult Beings which give birth to generations of elements, accidents, phenomena,—oh! if you were just not impersonal! Suppose the abstract terms, the hollow symbols wherewith we veil your presence were only vain human syllables! ... Ah! what difference does it make to me! it is too gloomy! I want life! *Not more knowledge!*[10]

The fullest life is the one that is lived most imaginatively, and Axël now realizes that imagination is all that matters to him, just as it would do for little Hanno in Thomas Mann's 1901 novel *Buddenbrooks*. In Hanno's case, it is the magic of Richard Wagner's music dramas that seduces him away from the workaday world, which, for him, is the opposite of the kind of life he wants to lead. Promised a performance of *Lohengrin*, he grows so excited that he cannot be bothered to do his homework: "What was Monday to him? Was it likely it would ever dawn? Who believes in Monday, when he is to hear *Lohengrin* on Sunday evening? He would get up early on Monday and get the wretched stuff done—and that was all there was to it."[11] In that sentence alone, Mann, another member of the decadent movement initiated by Villiers, encapsulates the whole argument of *Axël*. Mann was equally aware of death's enchantment, for it raised the possibility, even if only symbolically, of release from the mundane. His Hanno catches typhoid—a metaphor for the ultimate artistic imaginative freedom, just as, in the very different world of Lisa Alther's 1976 novel *Kinflicks*, death is the "ultimate orgasm."

Axël commits suicide with the woman who has discovered the whereabouts of the fabulous wealth buried in the castle grounds. "Live?" he asks in his final moments, "our servants will do that for us … oh, the external world! Let us not be made dupes by the old slave, chained to our feet in broad daylight, who promises us the keys to a palace of enchantments when it clutches only a handful of ashes in its clenched black fist!"[12] Reality can only disappoint. Far better the imagination; but total freedom can only be imagined in death—the kind of *Liebestod* envisioned by Wagner's Isolde, indeed; and that is exactly what Axël and Sara do at the end of Villiers' play, drinking poison surrounded by jewels and fabulous wealth.

These vicarious concerns were echoed in Michael Reeves' 1967 film, *The Sorcerers*. Boris Karloff plays Prof. Montserrat, a discredited hypnotist who has invented a machine that permits him to experience another man's perceptions and emotions without having to leave the comfort of his own home. The machine indeed provides a kind of psychological virtual reality some decades in advance of current computer technology. Ian Ogilvy plays the bored youth who submits to the experiment, while Catherine Lacey plays Montserrat's originally kindly wife, who is corrupted by her husband's invention. She rapidly becomes addicted to the vicarious pleasure of experiencing Ogilvy's acts of violence, which she is actually able to *will* him to perpetrate. The process backfires when Ogilvy dies in a car crash and the two pensioners suffer the same fate, spontaneously combusting at a not-so-safe distance, so to speak. Reality has its revenge, and the film ends with a shot of Lacey and Karloff lying charred and very dead in their humble sitting room.

Villiers had always been preoccupied by this theme of imagination vs. reality. His story "Véra," from *Cruel Tales*, was inspired by his understanding of that aspect of G.W.F. Hegel's philosophy, as expounded in *Philosophy of Mind* (1807), which, in one part of its complex vastness, proposes that reality is actually our own creation. As Peter Singer expresses this idea: "Hegel claims to be able to demonstrate the necessity of absolute idealism: that the only thing that is ultimately real is the absolute idea, which is Mind, knowing itself as reality."[13] It was not an idea unique to Hegel, who shared it to some extent with Immanuel Kant's contention that as we cannot know the real world, whatever that is, by any means other than our five senses; all we can know about reality is indeed largely our own creation. In "Véra," a widower is reunited with his dead wife by imagining her back to life. Villiers' narrator explains, "Ideas are living creatures; and since the count had hollowed out in the air the shape of his love, that space had to be filled by the only creature which was homogeneous with it, or else the Universe would have collapsed."[14] Raitt explains: "[T]he reappearance of the dead Véra is only the creation of D'Athol's imagination—since only our thoughts are real to us, we are free to create our own reality if we believe in it with sufficient urgency."[15] To cement the connection with Hegel, Villiers commemorated the Hegelian scholar Augusto Véra, from whom he gained most of his knowledge of Hegel's metaphysics, as both the name of Count D'Athol's wife and that of the story itself. Again, we can trace a connection with Reeves' *The Sorcerers* here.

In the flamboyant recklessness of horror film characters such as Vincent Price's Prince Prospero in Roger Corman's *The Masque of the Red Death* (1964), of Lon Chaney, Claude Rains and Herbert Lom's respective Phantoms of the Opera, along with the irresponsibly obsessive, well-dressed Frankensteins of Peter Cushing, we find cinematic descendants of Villiers' symbolist heroes, who frequently throw discretion to the winds, as did Villiers, in their pursuit of beauty, ego and the ideal. In Terence Fisher's *The Revenge of Frankenstein* (1958), Cushing carefully adjusts his buttonhole after a catalogue of horrors—an idiosyncrasy he repeats in *Frankenstein Must Be Destroyed* (Fisher, 1969). Indeed, his attitude toward the three elderly men with whom he shares the boarding house of Veronica Carlson's Anna Sprengel, results in some delightful bourgeois-baiting, fully the equal of Villiers' contempt for this class, which he missed no opportunity to attack. Overhearing his fellow boarders' medical prejudices, Frankenstein asks if they are doctors. When they insist they are not, Cushing, dressed in a red velvet smoking jacket with pink satin lapels, apologizes: "I beg your pardon. I thought you knew what you were talking about."

You're damn rude, sir.

I'm afraid that stupidity always brings out the worst in me. ... It is fools like you who have blocked progress throughout the ages. ... Had man not been given to invention and experiment, then tonight, sir, you would have eaten your dinner in a cave. You would have strewn the bones about the floor and then wiped your fingers on a coat of animal skin. In fact, your lapels do look somewhat greasy. Good night.

We might usefully compare such acid wit with this passage from Villiers' tale "Two Augurs," in which a writer gets a job on a newspaper by professing to be a second-rate hack, realizing that this is the only kind of author the Parisian press can sell to an unenlightened public:

"What's that?" cries the editor, trembling with joy. "You actually claim that you have no literary talent, you presumptuous young man?"

"I can prove to you, here and now, my incompetence in that respect."

"Impossible, I'm afraid! ... You're boasting!" stammers the editor, obviously stirred to the depths of his oldest and most secret hopes.

"I am," the stranger continues with a gentle smile, "what is known as a dull, mediocre scribbler, endowed with wonderfully stupid ideas and a marvelously trivial style ... a commonplace writer *par excellence*."

"You are? Get along with you! Oh, if only it were true!"[16]

BONE OF CONTENTION: **Laird Cregar as the homicidal pianist George Harvey Bone in** *Hangover Square* **(dir. John Brahm, 1945).**

British horror films' list of esthetic monsters continued after Hammer's heyday with Vincent Price's crazed Dr. Phibes, who wears a false face to hide his hideous disfigurement while surrounding himself with art deco extravagance. Tom Baker played a painter who uses voodoo to slay his critics in Roy Ward Baker's *Vault of Horror* for Amicus in 1973, and one might also include, alongside the Phantom of the Opera, all those psychotic musicians of the movies such as Laird Cregar's murderous concert pianist in *Hangover Square* (dir. John Brahm, 1945) and the piano-playing Barry Warren in *The Kiss of the Vampire*. All are symptomatic of the esthetic artist at odds with his society and taking refuge in an alternative world of their own creation—a world that frequently involves the destruction of those who intrude upon it.

Other episodes from *Cruel Tales* have their cinematic parallels. "The Very Image," for example, is a satire on the bourgeois bankers Villiers despised. In this story, they have killed their own souls to make money, and Villiers compares their bank to a morgue filled with the corpses of people who have murdered their bodies (*"the second glimpse* [i.e., the bank] *is more sinister than the first!* [the morgue]"[17]). The atmosphere created in the morgue section foreshadows the crepuscular anxiety conjured by Roy Ward Baker in the "Midnight Mess" episode from *Vault of Horror,* in which Daniel Massey stumbles across a town of vampires (including one played by Massey's real-life sister Anna). These gourmet bloodsuckers assemble in the evenings at a restaurant to enjoy such culinary delights as blood-clot soup. The restaurant is eerie but inviting. In Villiers' tale, the equally eerie morgue is also described as having a "certain cordial air of hospitality about it which reassured me."

> "The people who live here," I said to myself, "must surely be sedentary folk. This threshold has an inviting look: isn't the door open?"[18]

In "The Desire to Be a Man," also from *Cruel Tales,* an actor bemoans the fact that he has been "playing other men's passions without ever feeling them—for at bottom I have never felt anything."[19] Consequently he sets about committing a sensational crime in order to feel a genuine emotion of remorse. He burns down a theater, rather in the manner of Vincent Price's Edward Lionheart at the end of *Theatre of Blood* (dir. Douglas Hickox, 1973). And in his egoistic desire to cause eccentric mayhem, Villiers' actor sounds like Dr. Phibes as well. "What a triumph!" he exclaims on reading about the disaster. "What a wonderful scoundrel I am! How I'm going to be haunted! How many ghosts I'm going to see!" But, as the narrator explains later, "Contrary to all his hopes and expectations, his conscience failed to torment him. Not a single ghost appeared. He felt nothing, *absolutely nothing!*"

> "Ghosts! ... For the love of God! ... Let me see one ghost at least! ... *I've earned it!"* But the God he was invoking did not grant him that favour—and the old actor died, still expressing, in his vain rhetoric, his ardent longing to see some ghosts ... *without realizing that he himself was what he was looking for.*[20]

The downbeat ending could be applied to most of the esthetic horror film villains, for they, too, are often defeated by reality in one way or another.

In the Cruel Tale "The Duke of Portland," Villiers created another antihero along the lines of the Phantom of the Opera. Villiers' Duke of Portland lives in the splendor of a "massive crenellated mansion, built in ancient times in the midst of gloomy gardens and wooded lawns, on Portland Bill"[21]; but the Duke of Portland is a hideously disfigured recluse due to being "the last leper in the world."[22] In 1989, Herbert Lom found himself in a similar role to his earlier interpretation of the Phantom for Terence Fisher in 1962, when playing Ludwig in Harry Alan Towers' remake of *The Masque of the Red Death* (dir. Alan Birkinshaw, 1989). In this unfaithful but nonetheless interesting adaptation, Lom's Ludwig (the equivalent of Poe's Prince Prospero) appropriately lives in King Ludwig II of Bavaria's Neuschwanstein castle (a location opportunity that is hopelessly lost, despite some exterior shots being filmed there). Like the Duke of Portland, Lom's Ludwig holds grand parties but never appears at them. The point of Villiers' story is really an excuse to indulge in yet more descriptions of exotic décor, the interiors of the Duke of Portland residence being "covered with huge Venetian mirrors."

> The floor was now laid with marble flagstones and brilliant mosaics. High-warp curtains, hanging from twisted cords, were the only partitions between a string of wonderful rooms where, beneath sparkling golden chandeliers ablaze with light, Oriental furniture embroidered with precious arabesques was set out among tropical plants, scented fountains playing in porphyry tropical basins, and beautiful statues.[23]

As we have seen with regard to *The Mummy,* Hammer's opulent environments, like Villiers', invest often quite scanty subject matter with considerably more significance than it would have in other surroundings. One of Hammer's Frankenstein films, however, shares rather more with the general theme of Villiers' 1886 novel *L'Eve future* (*The Future Eve*) than merely its settings. The home of the Frankenstein-like professor in Villiers' novel is, as one would expect, a riot of extravagance:

> The concave and semicircular walls were covered with rich draperies of black velvet, which fell luxuriously from an arch of jade to white marble floor. The heavy folds were hooked back and fastened by retainers of gold, caught here and there through the rich material.[24]

The professor later reveals his inner sanctum, revealing an excess of *objets, bric-à-brac* and what we would now call interior design, which form a decadent-esthetic equivalent of Charles D. Hall's magnificently theatrical laboratory scenes in James Whale's 1935 *Bride of Frankenstein*:

> "Come," he said jocularly, "in going into the realm of the ideal, we must first pass through the kingdom of the commonplace. We will now leave the earth's surface."
> ... Lord Ewald saw before him a spacious subterranean hall such as might have intrigued the fancy of the caliphs under the city of Bagdad.
> "You may go in," said the professor. "You have been introduced."
> Lord Ewald went forward, walking on the skins of wild animals which covered the floor. A clear blue light lit up the vast hall with the brilliance of a radiant summer day. Tremendous pillars, placed at intervals, supported the interior circuit of a dome of

basalt, and formed a gallery to the right and left of the entrance, running back to the half circle of the hall.

This abode was gorgeously decorated in Syrian fashion. Large sheaves and garlands of silver were entwined on a bluish background. In the centre of the vault, suspended from a long golden chain, was a cluster of powerful electric lights shaded with blue globes.

... Picturesque waterfalls flowed and cascades bubbled, and under the caress of an imaginary breeze wonderful flowers of the Orient grew in profusion. Birds from southern climates warbled gaily in this garden of artificial flora.[25]

Like the imagery of immense treasure in *Axël*, Villiers uses opulent décor as a metaphor for the riches of the imagination. He reiterates this point in *L'Eve future* when he suggests that we should "say farewell to the pretended reality, the everlasting deceiver, and accept the artificial and its novel incitements."[26]

Hammer's *Frankenstein Created Woman*, directed by Terence Fisher in 1967, has a great deal in common with *L'Eve future*, but the settings are surprisingly less extravagant than Fisher's earlier Frankenstein films. Even the laboratory scenes are understated and out of proportion with the story's grandly metaphysical, distinctly magickal theme. The soul of an executed man is placed in the body of a woman who spends half the film crippled and disfigured before being transformed by Peter Cushing's Baron Frankenstein into a *femme fatale*. (The title is a tongue-in-cheek reference to Roger Vadim's 1956 *And God Created Woman*.) By the time of Cushing's appearance in *Frankenstein Must Be Destroyed* (dir. Terence Fisher, 1969), the baron had nothing but contempt for the female of the species, blackmailing Veronica Carlson's unfortunate Anna and using her as a coffee-making slave, before raping and eventually stabbing her to death in a fit of exasperated fury. In *Frankenstein Created Woman*, he is less ruthless—indeed, rather charming—but he has no conception of the sufferings of his creation or of the incongruity and danger of transplanting a male brain into a female body. Poor Christina, at first the female victim and then the seductive avenger of Fisher's film, doesn't really know who she is.

In *L'Eve future*, the fleshy android called Hadaly, created by the professor for the decadent Lord Ewald, is wholly the product of male desire, imbued not only with the will of the professor and Lord Ewald, but also the personality of the professor's mysterious assistant Sowana. Lord Ewald has almost committed suicide because his human lover, while being beautiful, was, to put it bluntly, stupid. He therefore inspires the professor to manufacture a being for him who combines beauty with intelligence, artistry with submissiveness. Like all fashionable accessories, she even has her own carrying case: a coffin made of ebony and upholstered in black silk. Both *Frankenstein Created*

Woman and *L'Eve future* end in disaster: Frankenstein's creation commits suicide, while Lord Ewald and his perfect artificial woman are drowned when the ship that is to take them to America sinks. Again, reality intrudes and destroys the imagination, so perhaps reality is not merely our own invention after all.

Villiers' also relishes the opulent approach to gore favored by Hammer Films. He describes "a human arm and hand lying on a violet silk cushion. The blood appeared to be congealed around the humeral section. Some crimson splashes on a piece of white linen, which had been thrown down beside it, attested to a recent operation."[27] Villiers even uncannily envisions Peter Cushing's features in his description of the professor:

> Although the inventor's hair was greying on the temples, his face was boyish, his smile was frank and winning. Around his mouth were little lines which told of the struggles and hardships which he had encountered in the early days of his career. It has been bitter uphill work—but he now stood on the pinnacle of fame.[28]

Villiers' complicated 1866 story *Claire Lenoir* was first translated into English by England's answer to Baudelaire himself, poet-critic Arthur Symons; it has subsequently been adapted in English translation by Brian Stableford and retitled *The Vampire Soul,* which is somewhat confusing as it has nothing really to do with vampires in the literal sense of the term. It is, however, concerned with a variety of equally abstruse issues, including Hegelian philosophy, the occult and the satire of bourgeois pomposity; but its plot revolves around a subject that was to feature in Gene Martin's 1972 film *Horror Express,* which starred Hammer's famous double act of Cushing and Lee as British travelers on the Trans-Siberian Express. The subject in question is the optogram, which Villiers describes as follows:

> The Academy of Sciences in Paris has determined the authenticity of a most surprising fact. It is henceforth established that animals destined for our nourishment, such as sheep, cattle, lambs, horses and cats, retain in their eyes, after the fatal stroke of the butcher's sledge-hammer, the imprint of the objects of their last gaze. It is a veritable photograph of paving-stones, stalls, gutters and vague figures, among whom can nearly always be distinguished that of the man who strokes them down. The phenomenon lasts until decomposition sets in.[29]

He concludes his story with the last truly weird vision of his heroine:

> On examining the eyes of the dead woman the first thing I saw, distinctly outlined, as if it were a frame, was the strip of violet paper which ran around the top of the wall. And within this frame, like some kind of echo, I saw a picture which is beyond the expression of any language under the Sun and the Moon, alive or dead—and I say that without a single moment's hesitation.
> Oh, how to describe it? ...

> Yes! The sky! Distant waves, a huge rock, the fall of a starry night! And upright on the rock, larger than life, stood a man like an inhabitant of the archipelagoes of the Dangerous Sea![30]

What the dead woman actually saw was a vision of her husband's vengeful soul, reincarnated as a savage cannibal, decapitating her guilty lover on a remote desert island. *Horror Express,* however, concerns a prehistoric embodiment of evil causing havoc on the Trans-Siberian Railway, during which Cushing and Lee examine one of the monster's eyeballs and discover there a retinal image of its last victim. Also connected with Villiers' style are the elaborately presented, somewhat decadent interiors of the train carriages in this film.

Villiers' infatuation with the imagination, his relentless interiorization of experience is very close to the psychology of occultism. We have seen how Villiers' *Axël* uses the occult as a symbol for the power of the imagination. In his Cruel Tale "Occult Memories," he links highly decadent descriptions such as those of "monstrous flowers ... streaked with blue, tinged with fire, veined with vermilion like the radiant remains of a triad vanished peacocks," with the loaded word "occult" in the title: Both the decadent esthete and the practitioner of occult power avoid, with the narrator of this story, "the harmful company of human beings."

> Yes, I avoid them when I walk like this, alone with my dreams. For then I feel that I carry in my soul the light of the barren riches of countless forgotten kings.[31]

Those riches are really the isolating treasures of unfettered imagination—the ultimate dream of the Romantic artist. And it is in this tradition that occult films have their roots.

CHAPTER THREE

Occult Fantasy Before the Movies

Occult fantasy as we recognize it today began in 1592 with Christopher Marlowe's play *Doctor Faustus*. Like Hammer Films at their best, it was designed both to moralize and vicariously to thrill its audiences with the promise of forbidden things. Marlowe's language was naturally rather more elevated than that of Jimmy Sangster or even Richard Matheson (who made such a splendid job of adapting Wheatley's *The Devil Rides Out* for the screen), but there are revealing parallels. Magic, and the material benefits that it is supposed to make possible, are the play's main attractions. As Faustus himself puts it:

> These metaphysics of magicians
> And necromantic books are heavenly;
> Lines, circles, schemes, letters and characters:
> Ay, these are those that Faustus most desires.[1]

Faustus conjures up the Devil with Latin, which is, of course, so much more impressive than mere English, a lesson learned well by later screenwriters: "*Orientis princeps, Belzebub inferno ardentis monarcha, et Demogorgon, propitiamus vos, ut appareat, et surgat, Mephostophilis.*"[2] Faustus wishes to be the emperor of the world, and if he had as many souls as there be stars, he'd give them all for Mephistopheles. Marlowe's moral aim, which is to demonstrate the folly of such a pact, is really overshadowed by the excitement of observing the magical processes that lead to it. As Mephisto says, when devils appear and dance around Faustus, it all means nothing "but to delight thy mind,/And let thee see what magic can perform."[3] Angels appear to persuade Faustus to repent, but to no avail. Thunder and lightning are called for, and the final dread of damnation as the midnight hour approaches, provides the template for cinematic horrors yet to come:

> Now hast thou but one bare hour to live,
> And then thou must be damn'd perpetually.
> Stand still, you ever-moving spheres of heaven,
> That time may cease and midnight never come.[4]

Faustus is indeed damned. His fate inspired the ending of Matthew Lewis' celebrated Gothic novel *The Monk* (1796), in which the eponymous Ambrosio, having formed a pact with the infernal one, must face the music at the end:

> Our contract? have I not performed my part? What more did I promise than to save you from your prison? Have I not done so? Are you not safe from the Inquisition—safe from all but for me? Fool that you were to confide yourself to a devil! Why did you not stipulate for life, and power, and pleasure? Then all would have been granted: now, your reflections come too late. Miscreant, prepare for death: you have not many hours to live![5]

This supernatural fate was frowned upon by the mistress of the Gothic novel, Ann Radcliffe, who was firmly of the opinion that no matter how supernatural her mysteries appeared to be, everything should be rationally explained in the end. Sir Walter Scott, though not always averse to the supernatural in his novels, nonetheless ended his series of *Letters on Witchcraft and Demonology* (1830) with skepticism. Having described his own visit to the apparently haunted castle of Dunvegan, wherein he experienced nothing more than a Romantic view and a comfortable bed, he concluded:

> From this I am taught to infer that tales of ghosts and demonology are out of date at forty years and upwards; that it is only in the morning of life that this feeling of superstition "comes o'er us like a summer cloud," affecting us with fear which is solemn and awful rather than painful; and I am tempted to think that if I were to write on the subject at all, it should have been during a period of life when I could have treated it with more interesting vivacity, and might have been at least amusing if I could not have been instructive. Even the present fashion of the world seems to be ill suited for studies of this fantastic nature; and the most ordinary mechanic has learning sufficient to laugh at the figments which in former times were believed by persons far advanced in the deepest knowledge of the age.[6]

Scott's fascination with the occult and his simultaneous rational approach to the subject was matched by Goethe, who had deeply inspired Scott as a young writer. Goethe's 1808 version of *Faust* is a much more philosophical and allegorical version of the legend than Marlowe's. At the end of Goethe's play, the spirit of Gretchen, the girl Faust seduces and then abandons, redeems Faust's soul. (This anticipates the final sentiment of the much longer and more philosophically complex second part, summed up in the famous line, "Das ewige Weibliche zieht uns hinan"—"the Eternal Feminine Leads us on.") Goethe enjoyed the magical elements in the story, but these seem incidental in the very different context of his play. Mephisto's conjuration in Goethe's *Faust* is in fact bathetic: After an impressive build-up, he announces himself with the line, "What's all this fuss? How can I serve you, sir?"[7] Ironic humor characterizes Goethe's Mephisto, in a way that it does not in Marlowe's vision, and humor also infuses the magical scenes: Faust is made young again in the Witches' Kitchen. "Why do we need this hag?" he asks. "The Devil's busy, sir!" Mephisto replies. "Why, I could build/A thousand bridges by the time that stuff's distilled!"[8] Later, an homunculus is created, which is again treated ironically. Indeed, "ironico" was the marking Liszt used for the third movement of his *Faust* Symphony, being a musical portrait of the spirit of denial, which distorts the noble motifs associated with Faust's character.

Somewhat ironically too, Goethe's profounder version formed the basis for Gounod's delightful though more superficial opera, which concentrated on the romantic elements of the play at the expense of Goethe's more philosophical intention. In 1924, Marlowe's more sensational approach informed the much more serious opera by Ferruccio Busoni. Richard Wagner had considered writing a *Faust* Symphony of his own, reconciling himself instead to an Overture on the subject in 1840; but it was Klingsor, the wicked magician in his final music drama *Parsifal* (1882), who provided the first modern role model for later fictional and cinematic Satanists. Éliphas Lévi had provided the iconography of classical magic in his *Dogma et Rituel de la Haute Magie* (1856), to which Wagner added the psychological elements.

Klingsor already has many of the characteristics of Huysmans' Canon Docre in *Là-bas*, Maugham's Oliver Haddo in *The Magician* and Wheatley's Mocata in *The Devil Rides Out*. To begin with, there is something suspect about Klingsor's sexuality, a trait he shares with all the fictional Satanists who followed him: Haddo's "heavy, sensual lips" inspire both ecstasy and loathing in the heroine he seduces, "physical attraction mingled with physical abhorrence"[9]; Docre is a "scoundrel, but he is learned and perverse, and then he is so charming,"[10] while Mocata is variously described as a "fleshy, moonfaced man"[11] with "pudgy fingers," a "slightly lisping voice"[12] and a penchant for chocolates, all of which are Wheatley euphemisms for a homosexual.

In fact, Klingsor is even more effeminate than this, having drastically castrated himself: "Ohnmächtig, in sich selbst die Sünde zu ertöten,/an sich legt er die Frevlerhand, die nun dem Grale zugewandt, verachtungsvoll des Hüter von sich stiess"[13] ("Unable to kill the sinful, raging lust within him, his hand upon himself he turned/to gain the Grail for which he yearned,/and by its guardian he with scorn was spurned"), as Gurnemanz, the old sage of the opera explains, before we meet Klingsor in person. "Bist du keusch?"[14] ("Are you chaste?") laughs his schizophrenic slave, Kundry, a woman who once laughed at Christ and has been cursed with immortality like the Wandering Jew. Having been compelled to enter Klingsor's magic garden, her role is now to seduce the knights of the Grail with the aim of furthering her master's ultimate ambition: to gain the Grail for himself. This is indeed a similar state of affairs to that in Charles Williams' 1930 novel *War in Heaven,* in which an unscrupulous Satanist attempts to use the Holy Grail for unholy ends. In fact, one of the (Jewish) conspirators in the novel is all for destroying the Grail when they eventually possess it:

WIZARD OF BAYREUTH: Theodor Schild as Klingsor in Wagner's *Parsifal* at Bayreuth, 1914.

Don't you understand that yet? They build and we destroy. That's what levels us; that's what stops them. One day we shall destroy the world. What can you do with [the Grail] that is so good as that? Are we babies to look to see whether a man has a gluttonous heart? To destroy this is to ruin another of their houses, and another step towards the hour when we shall breathe against the heavens and they shall fall. The only use in anything for us is that it may be destroyed.[15]

Wagner was quite clear about Klingsor's magical nature, providing his castle keep with the appropriate tools of the trade, calling for "Magical and necromantic apparatus." We first see Klingsor "on the offset of the tower to one side, sitting before a metal mirror."[16] Before this scrying glass, he summons Kundry from her somnambulant trance. Though lacking genitalia, Klingsor seems nonetheless to be psychologically homosexual at least: "Er ist schön, das Knabe,"[17] ("He is pretty, this lad,") Klingsor observes as the young, pure fool, Parsifal, ventures into his enchanted domain.

Most magical of all is Klingsor's domination of others by means of that powerful will. If, as Crowley suggests, the object of magic is to effect change by means of the will, Klingsor is the first modern antihero to demonstrate this technique. He draws Kundry to him, enslaving her by the strength of his personality. His invocation is the blueprint for so many later cinematic equivalents:

Herauf! Herauf! Zu mir!	Arise! Arise! To me!
Dein Meister ruft dich Namenlose,	Your master calls you nameless woman,
Urteufelin! Höllenrose!	first she-devil! Rose of Hades![18]

Though Kundry tries to resist, just as Marie Eaton attempts to resist Mocata on the sofa of her sitting room in *The Devil Rides Out,* Klingsor insists: "Wohl willst du, denn du musst." ("You'll do it, for you must.")

KUNDRY: Du ... kannst mich ... nicht ... halten.	You ... cannot ... compel me!
KLINGSOR: Aber dich fassen.	But I can force you.
KUNDRY: Du?	You?
KLINGSOR: Dein Meister.	Your master.
KUNDRY: Aus welcher Macht?	And by what power?
KLINGSOR: Ha!—Weil einzig an mir deine Macht nichts vermag.[19]	Ha!—Because I'm immune from your power—I alone."

This short scene is one of Wagner's most fascinating musical dialogues. Eero Tarasti[20] has identified the pulsing chromatic energy of the music as a classic example of the kind of "demonic" that would later be imitated by film composers. Klingsor's stillness has been much imitated. Wheatley emphasizes the "quiet, altered voice" and "steady gaze"[21] of his Satanist, Mocata, qualities so well realized by Charles Gray in Fisher's film. (The same can be said of Paul Wegener's Oliver Haddo in Rex Ingram's adaptation of Maugham's *The Magician*.) In Hans-Jürgen Syberberg's 1982 film version of *Parsifal,* Aage Haugland plays Klingsor as a kind of Nazi, evoking the mesmeric power of Hitler, who entranced an entire nation and whose National Socialist movement was indeed informed, if only in part, by occult ideology.

Wagner became a cult in the nineteenth century. Baudelaire, the spiritual founder of the decadent movement, had been an early admirer of Wagner's art, having been overwhelmed by *Tannhäuser* when it was first performed in Paris in 1861. He wrote a fan letter to the composer, which he followed up with an entire pamphlet expressing the full nature of his enthusiasm: "I felt myself released from the *bonds of gravity,* and found again in memory the extraordinary *thrill of pleasure* which lives and moves *in high places.*"[22] Huysmans later went further towards decadence in his Moreau-esque response to the same work: "The darkness retreats, light floods the scene, wreaths of mist and cloud take on the contorted forms of writhing hips and heaving, throbbing breasts. Avalanches of blue sky are gradually filled with naked shapes. From the orchestra the music rises in shrill cries of unbridled desire, piercing screams of lewd sensuality...."[23]

Baudelaire's interest in Satanic imagery, is reflected in his most famous collection *Les Fleurs du Mal* (1957), in which we find such lines as "Satan, I worship thee!,"[24] "The Devil in my upper room,/ Arrived to visit me today,"[25] "The Devil stirs beside me,"[26] "From Satan or from God, seraph or fiend,/ What matter, if ... /You make the world less grim, time faster fly?"[27] "Great Lucifer" appears in "L'Irréparable,"[28] while an entire poem is devoted to "Les Litanies de Satan." Interspersed with the repeated invocation, "Satan, have mercy on my long distress!," the text literally plays Devil's advocate, praising the spirit of denial "whose great hand conceals the precipice/From the somnambulist whom roofs entice," "Thou who in Death, your mistress old and strong,/Breeds Hope—delightful aberration!," "Thou who, consoling frail mankind in pain,/Taught us to make our guns and gun-cotton."[29]

Baudelaire recognized the Satanic (because erotic) nature of Wagner's music and poetry, which was later identified by Nietzsche as an art of decadence,[30] with Wagner himself cast as Klingsor, "this old magician,"[31] who seductively combines beauty with sickness. Wagner thus became a crucial cornerstone of European decadence at the turn of the century. A journal was dedicated to his ideas and esthetics: the *Revue Wagneriènne,* edited by Édouard Dujardin, whose stream-of-consciousness technique, derived from the example of Wagnerian monologues, later influenced James Joyce and Virginia Woolf. Wagner was invariably present in much decadent writing. Huysmans' refers to him in *À Rebours,* where he argues,

> [T]here was not a scene, not a phrase in any opera of the mighty Wagner that could be detached from its context without ruining it.
>
> The scraps thus cut from the whole and served up at a concert lost all meaning, all sense, for, like the chapters in a book that mutually complete each other and all concur to bring about the same conclusion, the same final effect, his melodies were used by Wagner to define the character of his personages, to incarnate their thoughts, to express their motives, visible or secret, and their ingenious and persistent repetitions were only intelligible for an audience which followed the subjects from its first opening and watched the characters grow little by little more clearly defined, observed them develop in surroundings from which they could not be separated without seeing them perish like branches severed from a tree.[32]

Huysmans became involved with Satanists, suffering a psychic attack after having exposed them in his next book, *Là-bas.* Canon Docre's perverse invocation in the closing pages of this, has much in common with Baudelaire's "Litanies":

> Master of Slanders, Dispenser of the benefits of crime, Administrator of sumptuous sins and great vices, Satan, thee we adore, reasonable God, just God!
>
> Superadmirable legate of false trances, thou receivest our beseeching tears; thou savest the honour of families by aborting wombs impregnated in the forgetfulness of the good orgasm ...

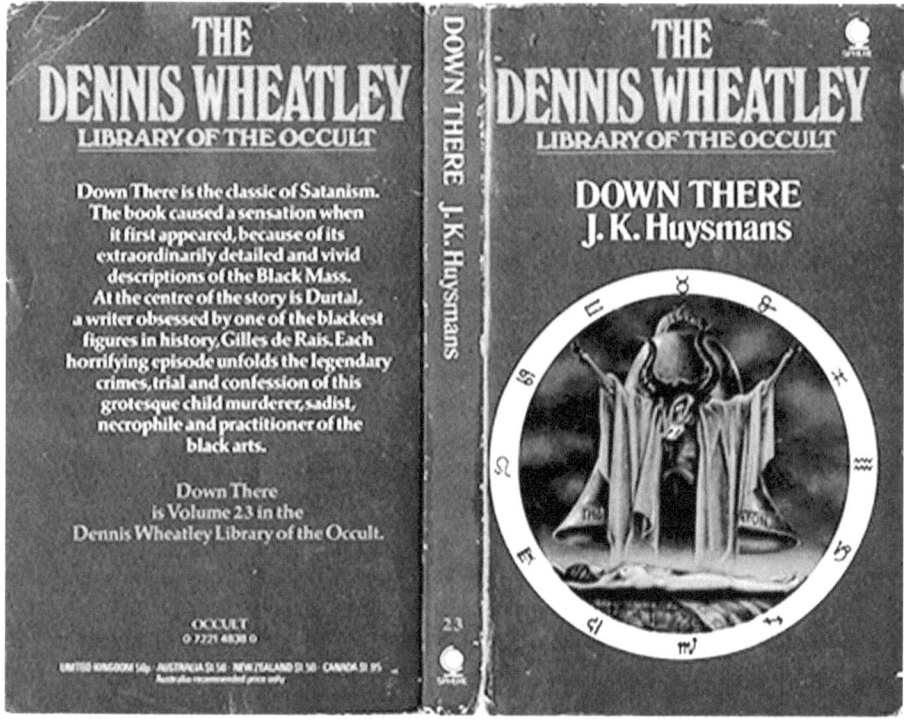

PAPERBACK SATANISM: **J.K. Huysmans gets the Dennis Wheatley treatment.**

> Mainstay of the despairing Poor, Cordial of the Vanquished, it is thou who endowed them with hypocrisy, ingratitude and stiff-neckedness...
>
> Treasurer of old Hatreds, thou alone dost fertilize the brain of man whom injustice has crushed; thou breathest into him the idea of meditated vengeance, sure misdeeds; thou incitest him to murder...[33]

Earlier in the novel, Huysmans' hero, Durtal, researches the life of Gilles de Rais and describes a magical invocation, complete with a magic circle. This no doubt influenced Dennis Wheatley, who included the book in his "Library of the Occult" in the 1970s:

> On the ground he traces a great circle and commands his two companions to step inside it. Sillé refuses. Gripped by a terror which he cannot explain, he begins to tremble all over. He goes to the window, opens it, and stands ready for flight, murmuring exorcism under his breath. Gilles, bolder, stands in the middle of the circle, but at the first conjurations he too trembles and tries to make the sign of the cross.[34]

The manner in which a magic circle should be prepared had been described at length in Francis Barrett's influential treatise *The Magus* (1801), the first important manifestation of the modern occult revival, which is really a conflation of various sources, mostly Cornelius Agrippa's famous *Three Books of Occult Philosophy* (1510). Barrett's prescription for the most effective magic circle is rather more complex than we see in popular manifestations of this ancient practice, and is in fact a close description of the Great Magic Circle in *Les Oevres Magiques de Henri Corneille Agrippa*, first published in Rome in 1744. As we shall be encountering numerous magic circles later, Barrett is worth quoting in full, but first here is Agrippa's original text, as translated by Robert Turner in 1655:

> These things being considered, let there be a Circle framed in the place elected, aswel for the defence of the Invocant, as for the confirmation of the Spirit. And in the Circle it self there are to be written the divine general names, and those things which do yeild defence unto us; and with them, those divine names which do rule this Planet, and the Offices of the Spirit himself; there shall also be written therein, the names of the good Spirits which bear rule, and are able to binde and constrain that Spirit which we intend to call. And if we will any more fortifie and strengthen our Circle, we may adde Characters and Pentacles agreeing to the work; then also if we will, we may either within or without the Circle, frame an angular figure, with the inscription of such convenient numbers, as are congruent amongst themselves to our work.[35]

And here is Barrett's gloss on this along with a description of the illustration:

> The forms of circles are not always one and the same, but are changed according to the order of spirits that are to be called, their places, times, days and hours...: therefore, to begin, let there be made three circles of the latitude of nine feet, distant one from another about a hand's breadth. First, write in the middle circle the *name of the hour* wherein you do the work; in the second place, write *the name of the angel of the hour*; in the third place, the seal of the angel of the house; fourthly, the name of the angel that rules the day in which you work, and the names of his ministers; in the fifth place, the name of the present time, and their *presidents*; seventhly, the name of the head of the sign ruling in the time; eighthly, the name of the earth according to the time of working; ninthly, and for the completing of the middle circle, write the name of the sun and moon, according to the said rule of time: for as the times are changed so are the names: and in the outer circle let there be drawn, in the four angles, the names of the great presidential spirits of the air that day wherein you would do this work, *viz.* the name of the kind and his three ministers. Without the circle, in four angles, let *pentagons* be made. In the inner circle write four divine names, with four crosses interposed: in the middle of the circle, *viz.* towards the east let be written Alpha; towards the west, Omega; and let a cross divide the middle of the circle.[36]

In his essay "Religion and Art" (1880), Wagner argued that when the symbols of religion are no longer believed in a literal sense, "it is reserved for Art to save the spirit of religion by recognizing the figurative value of the mythic symbols which the former would have us believe in their literal sense."[37] Huysmans also regarded the *fin de siècle* interest in the occult as the consequence of a similar spiritual vacuum: "[T]he unsatisfied need of the supernatural was driving people, in default of something loftier, to spiritism and the occult."[38] Occultism manifested itself in various ways. Huysmans' half-ironic, half-serious approach to the subject was taken a step further in the *Inferno* and *Occult Diary* of August Strindberg, which are based on diaries he kept between 1896 and 1908. These works cover a variety of subjects and provide a commentary on Strindberg's distinctly disturbed state of mind after two divorces, poverty, professional failure and rejection in his native Sweden; but the fashion for decadent occultism provided him with a platform, not to mention a therapeutic occupation. In these works, Strindberg discusses Blavatsky and theosophy, seems convinced that his chemical experiments have revealed the secrets of the alchemical quest, mentions many a seemingly "significant" coincidence, interprets chance occurrences as symbolic manifestations of personal relationships or states of mind, and devotes an entire section to his reading of Emanuel Swedenborg, whose description of Hell fitted in remarkably well with Strindberg's life at the time.

> Hell? But I had been brought up to regard Hell with the deepest contempt as an imaginary conception, thrown on the scrap-heap along with other out-of-date prejudices. All the same, I could not deny a matter of fact, the only thing I could do was explain eternal damnation in this new way: we are already in Hell. It is the earth itself that is Hell, the prison constructed for us by an intelligence superior to our own. ...
>
> Hell-fire is our desire to make a name for ourselves in the world. The Powers awaken this desire in us and permit the damned to achieve their objectives. But when the goal is reached and our wish fulfilled, everything is found to be worthless and our victory meaningless.[39]

Strindberg also records many dreamlike incidents, apparently genuine experiences. For example, on September 19, he found five sticks in an enormous chest, "but they were arranged on the bottom of the chest to form a pentagram. Who has played this trick on me and what does it mean?"[40] A later passage looks forward to what happens in *The Exorcist*:

> I was told of a man possessed by a devil who had changed the unfortunate creature's character and forced him to go about uttering blasphemies against his will. After looking for an exorcist for a long time, at last they found a young Franciscan monk, a virgin and well known for his purity of heart. He prepared himself for his task by fasts and penances and, when the great day arrived, the possessed man was led to the church, where he confessed before the whole congregation. *Coram populo.* Then the young monk went to work with prayers and invocations from morning till late at night, when he at last succeeded in ousting the Devil. The latter fled in a manner so horrifying that the spectators never dared to tell of it.[41]

The whole point of *The Exorcist* is that it *does* dare to tell and *show* what happens, with all the blasphemies, spider-walking and head-rotating antics of Linda Blair's Regan, which would no doubt have fascinated Strindberg had he lived to see them. He also tantalizingly warned his readers against practicing magic themselves, just as Wheatley does at the beginning of *The Devil Rides Out* with his "Author's Note" strongly urging readers "to refrain from being drawn into the practice of the Secret Art in any way." Strindberg's earlier version of this ruse is curiously similar:

> By playing with those mysterious powers out of pure folly I had given the reins to my evil desires, but they, guided by the hand of the Unseen, had struck at my own heart.
> I am not trying to excuse myself. I am only asking the reader to bear these facts in mind, should he ever be tempted to practice magic, particularly the kind known as bewitchment, or witchcraft in the true sense of the word.[42]

CHAPTER FOUR

Silent Magick

The Devil was present virtually from the very beginning of cinematic history. He made a spectacular entrance in Georges Méliès' three-minute *The Devil in a Convent* (1896), which was based on a Francis Oscar Mann short story. Méliès' Devil leaps out of a convent font, impersonates a man of the cloth, terrifies the nuns, materializes imps and demons out of an impressive hell mouth, before riding a giant frog and being overcome by the archangel Michael and vanishing in a puff of sulfur. A distant ancestor of Ken Russell's *The Devils* (1971), *The Devil in a Convent* pursues a similar theme of demonic infiltration, which Mann's original story makes even more explicit. Releasing their repressions, "the eyes of all the nuns danced after his dancing legs, and their ears hung on the clear sweet notes he struck out of his cithern as he walked."

> He took his place with his back against the great hall door, in such an attitude as men use when they play the cithern. A little trembling ran through the nuns, and some rose from their seats and knelt on the benches, leaning over the table, the better to see and hear him. Their eyes sparkled like dew on meadowsweet on a fair morning.[1]

Méliès brought the Devil back in 1906 with the six-minute *The Merry Frolics of Satan*. Here Satan enjoys a celestial coach ride, and the hell mouth returns, flanked by decorous maidens holding fans in the underworld.

The ability of film to realize the impossible by means of trick photography made supernatural subjects the obvious choice, but it was in Germany rather than France that their potential was most persuasively exploited, thanks largely to the heritage of nineteenth-century German Romanticism and twentieth-century occultism on which early German films so voraciously fed.

Berlin, where the famous Babelsburg studios were situated, enjoyed an active occult subculture of its own. Though it is well-known that Albin Grau (1884–1971), the man behind F.W. Murnau's 1922 vampire classic *Nosferatu—Eine Symphonie des Grauens*, was the occultist, very little is known about Grau himself. He remains almost as shadowy a figure as Max Schreck, the

Four. Silent Magick

TWENTY SHADES OF GRAU: Max Schreck as Count Orlok in *Nosferatu* (dir. F.W. Murnau, 1922). The document he holds was prepared by the film's occult art director Albin Grau.

actor who played the lead role of Graf Orlok, the renamed Count Dracula of *Nosferatu*. A member of the esoteric German group Fraternitas Saturni, Grau also had dealings with Aleister Crowley. (There is a rumor that he actually filmed Crowley in Berlin, though no one has ever found this potentially fascinating visual record.) He also founded the company Prana Films, referring to the Hindu concept of divine energy, and which Grau complemented with a corporate Yin-Yang symbol. His intention was to produce a series of occult features. Alas, his infamous copyright infringement of Bram Stoker's novel put an end to this ambition after his first film. But *Nosferatu* as directed by Murnau is a masterpiece, which is surely legacy enough. In his capacity as production designer, Grau also managed to infuse a much more overtly occult mood into Stoker's more straightforwardly orthodox Christian context. It thus foreshadowed Hammer's later occultization of the Dracula myth, beginning with *Taste the Blood of Dracula* (dir. Peter Sasdy, 1970) and reaching its peak with *The Satanic Rites of Dracula* (dir. Alan Gibson, 1973). Grau conceived the grotesque appearance of Orlok and designed the film's overall style, furnishing the production with the documents Orlok exchanges with the real estate agent Crook. The symbols in these documents are rumored to include elements of the mystical Enochian alphabet, which had apparently been revealed to the Elizabethan magician John Dee and his assistant Edward Kelly, who considered it to be the language of angels. The *Nosferatu* documents include a variety of other magical symbols: a swastika, magic squares, a snake, a skull and crossbones, astrological sigils and sequences of numbers. The sigil of the Fraternitas Saturni (the astrological symbol of Saturn within a triangle enclosed by a circle), which one might expect to find here, disappointingly does not appear, and no one has yet deciphered what the other mysterious symbols actually mean, if they mean anything; Grau claimed they were based on magical rituals, but their esthetic function is clearly to create an appropriately occult "mood." Similarly, the film's renaming of Van Helsing as Dr. Bulwer references the English occult novelist Edward Bulwer-Lytton (1803–1873).

Grau was also the production designer for Robinson's *Warning Shadows* (*Schatten—Eine nächtliche Halluzination*), an allegorical tale. The shadows of a group of Biedermeir aristocrats are detached from their bodies while they dine, and henceforth act out the tragedy that would have occurred had they not been forewarned in this magical way. All rivals for the love of a baron's wife, they learn that the baron would eventually have killed them all. Shadows have long been regarded as symbols of the soul, a convention Gustav Meyrink succinctly summed up in his 1921 novel *The White Dominican*, "Our shadows: the bond that ties us to the earth, the black ghost that emanates from us, revealing the death within us, when light strikes our bodies."[2] More importantly, the shadows in *Schatten* are manifestations of the hidden intentions of the characters—of their *wills*.

Film itself is an art of shadows *par excellence*. They appear in Carl Dreyer's early sound film *Vampyr* (1932), representing dead souls dancing, in a sequence that is curiously similar to lines from Oscar Wilde's poem "The Harlot's House," though Wilde's shadows are cast by the living rather than the dead:

> Like strange mechanical grotesques,
> Making fantastic arabesques,
> The shadows raced across the blind.
>
> We watched the ghostly dancers spin
> To sound of horn and violin,
> Like black leaves wheeling in the wind.[3]

In 1922, Benjamin Christensen directed the curious docudrama *Häxen* (usually known as *Witchcraft Through the Ages*). Inspired by the *Malleus Maleficarum*, the infamous medieval manual for the persecution of witches, Christensen's sequence of tableaux depicting the activities of witches, the

Devil and his attendant demons are in fact far more disturbing than anything to be found in Hammer's *The Devil Rides Out* or even *The Exorcist*. One of the reasons for this is the overtly sexual imagery employed, quite extraordinary for the time, and Christensen's use of atmospheric lighting and shock tactics: a demon leaps up from behind a lectern where a monk is reading holy scripture, flickering his tongue like a snake; and in one astonishing sequence, we observe witches lining up to kiss the backside of the Devil. Christensen's demons are truly grotesque, their rapid movements, as they cavort, torment and play infernal musical instruments, having a comparable effect to Murnau's use of accelerated time-lapse photography in *Nosferatu*. The Black Mass at which the Devil's backside is venerated also involves the disturbing sacrifice of babies; witches transform themselves into cats as two demons in animal form keep watch at the church door; skeletal fingers caress the naked back of another witch, and a demon incites a nun to sacrilege and murder, peering from behind the door of her study in one of the film's most unnerving images.

These visceral and grotesque demons capture something of the sexual hysteria that lay behind the *Malleus Maleficarum* in the first place, and seem to bypass the more literary demons of later Satantic fantasies. It even pales the impressive Mephistopheles of Emil Jannings in Murnau's *Faust* (1926), which loosely follows Goethe's incarnation of the tale, with Faust redeemed at the end. Murnau's Faust throws himself on the pyre at which Gretchen is being burned at the stake, and his soul ascends with hers into paradise. An angel destroys the contract between Faust and Mephistopheles, Mephisto is denied his prize, and the word "Liebe" appears in the final frames, surrounded by rays of shimmering light. But even more impressive are the much earlier shots showing Faust raising Mephistopheles. A plague having been spread by this demon, whose cloak releases a black cloud over the town, Faust is unable to save anyone and in despair throws all his books on the fire. He even consigns his Bible to the flames, but rescues an occult grimoire at the last moment, using this for his invocation. He traces a circle with the book as he stands at a deserted crossroads by moonlight, and then holds the grimoire over his head. The circle begins to burn, spawning flaming rings which rise over him like the electronic halos that bring the famous robot of Fritz Lang's *Metropolis* to life. (That an inverted pentagram is suspended behind that robot is not merely a decorative device but evidence of the combination of science and magic that features throughout *Metropolis*. Hanging upside down, this pentagram is definitely of the sinister sort. Éliphas Lévi insisted, "The Pentagram signified the domination of the mind over the elements. ... The direction of the points of the star is in no sense arbitrary, and may change the entire character of an operation."[4])

According to Crowley, once the magic circle "is made and consecrated, the Magician must not leave it, or even lean outside, lest he be destroyed by the hostile forces that are without."[5] Stoker includes a magic circle in *Dracula*: Towards the end of the story, Van Helsing and Mina are confronted by Dracula's vampire brides. "I drew a ring so big for her comfort, round where Madam Mina sat; and over the ring I passed some of the wafer, and I broke it fine so that all was well guarded."[6] Gerald Savory's 1977 BBC television adaptation *Count Dracula* and Francis Ford Coppola's *Bram Stoker's Dracula* (1993) notably dramatize this scene; but this persistent imagery in occult fantasy on film largely derives from the haunted screen of German "silent" films.

Nineteen twenty-six was also the year that Adolphe Menjou's Satan appeared as a well-dressed Italian aristocrat in a top hat and an astrakhan collar in D.W. Griffith's adaptation of Marie Corelli's late-Victorian novel *The Sorrows of Satan*. Thus disguised (as Prince Lucio de Rimanez), he first appears as a shadow, immediately after the writer Geoffrey Tempest (Ricardo Cortez) curses God and swears that he would sell his soul to the Devil for money. Corelli describes the Devil's first entrance in the novel thus:

> The door opened,—and from the dense obscurity enshrouding me I could just perceive a tall shadowy figure standing on the threshold. I remember well the curious impression the mere outline of this scarcely discerned Form made upon me even then,—suggesting at the first glance such a stately majesty of height and bearing as at one riveted my attention.[7]

Accordingly, Griffith responds to Corelli's vocabulary ("shadowy," "obscurity" and "outline") by ingeniously merging both the prince's silhouette, which advances and grows bigger, and his shadow, which grows smaller until both meet as Rimanez steps over the threshold. Shadows play an important role in Griffith's realization of the Devil in this film: later, when Rimanez appears before Tempest in his true form, we see only the shadow that his immense wings and clutching talons casts over Tempest and the wall behind him.

The presentation of the Devil as a wealthy man of the world certainly makes sense, given what money and the world are capable of. Similar imagery had been used by Fritz Lang in *Dr. Mabuse—Der Spieler* (1922), wherein the criminal mastermind Mabuse (Rudolf Klein-Rogge) wears a comparably plutocratic outfit of fur-lined collars and fur hats. Like a magician, he is a skilled hypnotist and can make others do his will. The way in which Lang superimposes Mabuse's face over the deserted stock market trading hall, having caused slumps and booms, powerfully suggests the demonic power of that will, which foreshadowed the equally demonic authority of Hitler. Mabuse's will manipulates the actions of all who are subjected to its power, and his eyes stare with the intensity of the Führer's later ecstasies. Lang's film is an astonishing pre-

Four. Silent Magick 55

FINGERS AND THUMBS: A séance in *Dr. Mabuse—der Spieler* (dir. Fritz Lang, 1922).

diction of what would soon befall Germany. Lang called it "a documentary about the current world."[8] As Kracauer observes, however, the expressionist artificiality of its style is hardly the stuff of a documentary film, "but it is a document of its time."[9] The film's fascination with séance and occult imagery also eerily predicts the Nazi exploitation of superstition, occultism and the irrational. Mabuse is more Klingsor than criminal. In Kracauer's words, "Mabuse's face gleams out of the jet-black screen ... upon the audience,"[10] which was exactly how Hitler was sold to voters in the famous Nazi election poster of 1932. With hindsight, the image suggests an entranced medium rather than a politician, which is part of what the quasi-mystical term "Führer" implies.

In the sequel, Lang artfully exploited the new advantages of sound. *The Testament of Dr. Mabuse* (1933) expresses a truly demonic interpretation of crime more along the lines of Milton's Satan than American film noir. In his study, lined with tribal masks and human skulls, the psychiatrist in charge of the insane Mabuse reads the eponymous testament, with its description of "The Empire of Crime." "Humanity's soul must be shaken to its very depths," Mabuse insists, "frightened by unfathomable and seemingly senseless crimes. Crimes that benefit no one, whose only objective is to inspire fear and terror. Because the ultimate purpose of crime is to establish the endless empire of crime. A state of complete insecurity and anarchy, founded on the destruction of the ideals of a world doomed to annihilation." The monstrous-eyed ghost of Mabuse appears before the psychiatrist and appears to enter his body, symbolizing the corrupting power of these ideas. The doctor now *becomes* Mabuse, just as Germany "became" Hitler under the persuasive power of his poisonous will.

We can experience this process in science fiction films, which have no overt connection with Nazi Germany, but nonetheless allegorize the psychological-magical continuum. In Nigel Kneale's screenplay for *Quatermass and the Pit,* an ancient instinct (which we would now call ethnic cleansing) has been implanted in humanity by Martians millennia ago. When a spaceship is discovered during the excavation of a London underground station, these regressive instincts are stimulated, inspiring the population in the Hobbs Lane area to become murderous lunatics, attacking and slaughtering anyone who appears to be "different." The political implications of all this are just as apparent here as the magical aspects of the will that lies behind them: the power of persuasion, and the political "art" of unleashing the primitive instincts of the Id.

German film in the 1920s and early 1930s, as Siegfried Kracauer observes in his famous book on the subject, fully explored the fractured psychology of a country that was soon to be engulfed by a criminal state, unleashing irrational and monstrous urges. Monsters had also been a staple of the golden age of German film. *Nosferatu* began the cinematic career of Count Dracula, while Frankenstein and Mummy films had been anticipated by Paul Wegener's Golem in three films about the clay automaton, the first of which (now mostly lost) appearing as early as 1915. The only film of this trilogy to have survived in its entirety dates from 1920. *The Golem—How He Came into the World* is often credited as an adaptation of Gustav Meyrinck's best-selling novel *The Golem,* which Wegener certainly knew, but which in fact has very little in common with the film's much more straightforward story. Although Meyrinck based his novel on the legend of the clay Golem, created by Rabbi Lowe in Prague to defend the ghetto against pograms, he also used the Golem as a psychological symbol rather than stomping nemesis. For Meyrinck, the Golem was a representation of the self, which he used in a way that Jung found highly satisfactory.[11] Predating *Nosferatu* by several years, Wegener's production designer Robert A. Dietrich decorated the pages of the ancient book that describes how one goes about creating a Golem with astrological sigils (Scorpio, Libra and Pisces are clearly visible). In fact, the rabbi's finger points to the sigil for Libra, which tarries with the following inter-title: "Venus is entering the Libran constellation, and time now favors the invocation." It continues: "I must now wrest the crucial life-giving word from the dreaded spirit of Astaroth that will bring the Golem to life." Like a Semitic Faust, the rabbi sets about his necromantic work, first modeling the figure from clay. Wegener then superimposes the six-pointed Seal of Solomon over the face of the Golem in anticipation of the life-giving ritual soon to follow. The rabbi announces this with, "The hour has come!," which curiously echoes Klingsor's first line in *Parsifal* ("Die Zeit is da!"—"The time has come!"). The rabbi dons an extraordinary piece of headgear, vaguely resembling a chef's hat and decorated with magical symbols. He raises his wand to begin the invocation, watched with wide-eyed wonderment by his assistant, who joins him in the magic circle. This, like Faust's circle in Murnau's film, then begins to glow and smoke. Astral flames dance around them as, brandishing his Seal of Solomon, the rabbi commands Astaroth to appear. (Astaroth would be summoned again many years later in Hammer's distinctly unfaithful adaptation of Dennis Wheatley's *To the Devil a Daughter* [dir. Peter Sykes, 1976], a distant descendent of this 1920 classic.) Astaroth materializes, with bulging eyes staring out of what is actually a carved wooden mask. Vapor emerges from the demon's lips, forming the magic word of life: "AEMHET." Just as Mephisto would later appear with lightning flashes in Murnau's film, so here Astaroth departs with similar electrical fury. The rabbi writes the words onto a scrap of parchment, securing it within the pentagram on the Golem's breast, whereupon it stomps off to do his work.

Along with the Pygmalion myth and Mary Shelley's famous creature, the Golem also shares certain characteristics with the scarecrow in Nathaniel Hawthorne's 1852 story "Feathertop," which Frank Tuttle filmed as *Puritan Passions* in 1923. In Hawthorne's tale of New England necromancy, the witch, Mother Rigby, imbues a scarecrow with life by thrusting her pipe between its pumpkin jaws and making it blow. The smoke brings him to life. Like the Golem, the scarecrow also wears a star on its breast to cover a hole in his jacket which reveals the broomstick spine that lies within.

The Devil had appeared in Wegener's earlier 1913 film, based on a conflation of *Faust*, Poe's doppelgänger story "William Wilson" and a poem by Alfred de Musset, which were whipped up into a script by Germany's popular purveyor of the bizarre, Hanns Heinz Ewers, for *The Student of Prague*. It was directed by Stellan Rye at a time when the whole of Europe, plunged into war, seemed also to have made a pact with Satan. But the Devil in this film takes the super/annuated human form of Scapinelli, who offers the student Balduin untold wealth in return for his reflection, which promptly walks out of the mirror and becomes Balduin's crime-bent doppelgänger. Remade twice, with Conrad Veidt and then Anton Walbrook as Balduin, these demonic alternatives to *Dr. Jekyll and Mr. Hyde* gave their respective directors many opportunities to explore the imagery of German Romanticism in general and to reference the paintings of Caspar David Friedrich in particular: The diagonal slant of the tree in Friedrich's "Two Men Contemplating the Moon" (1825–1830) is directly echoed in Galeen's 1926 version, during which Werner Krauss' Scapinelli observes and magically influences the outcome of a hunt. Krauss' entire body echoes the shape of the tree, his umbrella held out in parallel with the trunk, while his bent arm, shielding his eyes from the light, echoes the angle of the contorted branch. Such imagery presents the Devil very much as a bourgeois Romantic figure in the tradition of E.T.A. Hoffmann's demonic characters. Later, Scapinelli's immense shadow is cast on the wall above which Balduin and his lover are embracing. Whereas the shadow cast by the Devil in *The Sorrows of Satan* suggests his medieval winged form, here Scapinelli retains his bourgeois appearance and umbrella, but the shadow itself is somehow able to interact with the action as his arm reaches up and throws to the ground a letter resting on the edge of the balcony. The shadow therefore becomes the manifestation of Scapinelli's will—the power on which all magical processes are dependent.

The immense, largely negative publicity surrounding Aleister Crowley made his persona the inevitable inspiration for several cinematic occultists, the first being based on the character of Oliver Haddo in Maugham's *The Magician*. The two men had met by chance in Paris some years before. Maugham had instinctively disliked Crowley (he instinctively disliked many people), but he also found him intriguing. "He was a liar and unbecomingly boastful," he recalled, "but the odd thing was that he had actually done some of the things he boasted of."[12] Their meeting took place in 1897, the year in which Stoker's *Dracula* was first published, and though Oscar Wilde was by then already disgraced and in prison, there was still a sense of the decadent "Yellow" Nineties in the air, particularly in Paris. Maugham acknowledged that there was "something of a vogue in Paris" for Satanism, in which Crowley was, as he put it, "dabbling." This he urbanely put down to the interest in Huysmans' *Là-bas*, and in many ways, Maugham's *The Magician* is its English equivalent. "The style is lush and turgid," he wrote in his retrospective introduction to later editions of the novel, "not at all the sort of style I approve of now, but perhaps not unsuited to the subject."[13] Maugham isn't usually associated with the occult, but he certainly did his research on the subject for this early novel and took a perhaps more than merely commercial and exploitative interest in the subject implied by his retrospective comment, "I wondered how on earth I could have come by all the material concerning the black arts which I wrote of. I must have spent days and days reading in the library of the British Museum."[14]

Crowley offers a different explanation for Maugham's esoteric learning: Not only did he claim that the protagonist's "witty remarks were, many of them, my own," but also that Maugham's friend, artist Gerald Kelly, whom Crowley had introduced to the Order of the Golden Dawn, provided the author with the details of Crowley's private life along with a list of volumes "which I had told Gerald to buy. I had never supposed that plagiarism could have been so varied, extensive and shameless. *The Memoirs of a Physician, The Island of Doctor Moreau, The Blossom and the Fruit* and numerous other more or less occult works of fiction had supplied the plot, and many of them the incidents. *The Kabbalah Unveiled, The Life of Paracelsus, The Ritual and Dogma of Transcendental Magic* and others had been transcribed, whole pages at a time, with such slight changes as 'failed' for 'resulted in failure,' and occasional additions and omissions. ...*The Magician* was, in fact, an appreciation of my genius such as I had never dreamed of inspiring."[15] Maugham's partner Gerald Haxton also apparently told Maugham's cousin Robin that the novelist had sold his soul to the Devil to attain his immense success as a popular novelist.[16]

Oliver Haddo is a grotesque amplification of the, some would say, already grotesque Crowley. "I made my character more ruthless than Crowley ever was," Maugham explained. "I gave him magical powers that Crowley, though he claimed them, certainly never possessed."[17] The result was so compelling that it inspired one of the most famous silent films, directed by Rex Ingram in 1926, and also directly inspired Dennis Wheatley's much more famous occult classic *The Devil Rides Out* (1934), filmed by Hammer in 1968 with Charles Gray playing the Crowley/Haddo-inspired Mocata. That film paved the way for the occult blockbusters *The Exorcist* and *The Omen*. Crowley returned to the screen in the shape of Simon Callow in Julian Doyle's uneven but still intriguing *Chemical Wedding* (2008).

The plot of *The Magician* is quite similar to *The Devil Rides Out*: An unscrupulous practitioner of the black arts seduces an innocent virgin whom he sacrifices for occult ends. In Haddo's case, he requires her blood to nourish the homunculi he is growing. Wheatley was no doubt inspired by this aspect of Maugham's novel when writing his subsequent occult thriller *To the Devil a Daughter*, in which Canon Copley-Style (this time modeled on writer Montague Summers) does much the same thing. The results are suitably revolting: "a living lump" that resembles a tumor, an embryo child "shaped vaguely like an infant, but the legs were joined together so that it looked like a mummy rolled up in its coverings," something with four arms and four legs and other "ghastly counterfeits of humanity."[18] And Maugham's reference to that infamous grimoire *The Clavicule of Solomon* was not lost on Wheatley, who has the Duc de Richleau discover a copy of it, suitably bound in human skin, in Simon Aron's occult observatory in *The Devil Rides Out*.

Even more than all this, Haddo is a Nietzschean antihero in his quest for *power*. "And what else is it that men seek in life but power?" he asks. "If they want money, it is but for the power that attends it, and it is power again that they strive for in all the knowledge they acquire."[19] Perhaps Maugham also knew of Crowley's belief in himself as a reincarnation of the French magus Éliphas Lévi, as he also mentions him in *The Magician*. But even more significant is how Maugham describes Haddo as a kind of decadent superman, combining du Maurier's Svengali with Huysmans' Des Esseintes, and foreshadowing Sax Rohmer's Fu Manchu in the process. Like Fu, Haddo is "cruel" and "merciless," seems to have been everywhere including a monastery in India, is highly educated and frequents opium dens in the East End of London. Like Svengali, Haddo dominates Margaret, who becomes "an automaton" under his overpowering will; and like Des Esseintes and Lorrain's equally decadent Monsieur de Phocas, he is well-versed in the strange allures of French symbolist imagery. One of his seductions is an oriental fantasy suggestive of the kind of thing Tristan Klingsor described in the poem Maurice Ravel set to music as *Shéhérazade*:

> He told her of strange Eastern places where no infidel had been, and her sensitive fancy was aflame with the honeyed fervour of his phrase. He spoke of the dawn upon sleeping desolate cities, and the moonlit might of the desert, of the sunsets with their splendour, and of the crowded street at noon. The beauty of the East rose before her. He told her of many-coloured webs of silken carpets, the glittering steel of armour damascened, and of barbaric, priceless gems.[20]

Haddo is also an admirer of Gustave Moreau's Salome paintings, with their "clustered colours, emerald and ruby, the deep blue of sapphires, the atmosphere scented chambers," "the strange sense of sin"[21] and so forth. He even quotes from Wilde's play on the subject ("I am amorous of thy body, Iokannan!") and begins his esthetic assault on his hapless victim by reciting Walter Pater's famously decadent description of the Mona Lisa: "She is older than the rocks among which she sits; like the vampire, she has been dead many times, and learned the secrets of the grave; and has been a diver in deep seas, and keeps their fallen day about her; and trafficked for strange evils with Eastern merchants."[22] Having prepared the way with art, Haddo continues with a piano improvisation to deliver the *coup de grâce*: "His fingers caressed the notes with a peculiar suavity, and drew out of the piano effects which she had scarcely thought possible." The exotic music is "strange and terrifying"[23] and does the trick. Poor Margaret, due to be married to a nice doctor, is unable to resist Haddo's will and ends up marrying him instead.

Haddo's musical seduction lingered in later films. In *House of Dracula* (dir. Erle C. Kenton, 1945), John Carradine's Count Dracula inspires Martha O'Driscoll's Miliza to transform "Moonlight Sonata" into something much more troubling than Beethoven intended. "You like it?" she asks. Carradine stares back: "It breathes the spirit of the night." Composer Edgar Fairchild then cleverly injects the influence of Debussy into the piece. Miliza has obviously never played Debussy before: "I've not heard this music before, yet I'm playing it." "You're creating it. For me," explains the count. Scriabin takes over from Debussy, and despite hailing from Transylvania, the count insists, "It is the music of the world from which I come."

In Albert Lewin's adaptation of *The Picture of Dorian Gray*, released the same year, Hurt Hatfield's Dorian uses a Chopin prelude to impress Angela Lansbury's Sybil Vane. "Does it have a name?" she asks. "A kind of name," Dorian replies. "It is called 'Prelude.'" Haddo's sinister serenade also looked forward to James Bernard's "Vampire Rhapsody" in *The Kiss of the Vampire* with which Barry Warren's vampire, Carl Ravna, hypnotizes Jennifer Daniel's Marianne Harcourt. "Something of your own, perhaps, Carl?" suggests his father. Carl willingly obliges.

Maugham initiated all this in his early novel, but in one detail at least, he may also have been thinking about Edward Bulwer-Lytton's 1850 occult thriller *A Strange Story*, in which the evil magician Margrave charms a squirrel from the trees, only cruelly to kill it when it bites him. Haddo does much the same thing to a dog when it bites him.

Ingram's film is remarkably faithful to Maugham's novel until it alters the ending, which is significant. Maugham has his heroine murdered by Haddo, who is himself killed in a kind of psychic wrestling match with the good doctor to whom Margaret was originally betrothed. In the film, the combat is physical and *mano a mano*, Haddo being thrown into a suitably symbolic fiery furnace; and Margaret is rescued, allowing a happy ending. Wegener's moon-faced Haddo captures something of the fleshy monstrosity Maugham describes in the novel and thus the florid features of Crowley himself. Ingram also incorporates a sinister tower as the setting for Haddo's laboratory, which Maugham places merely in the attic of Haddo's mansion, Skene. (The name Skene echoes Crowley's Scottish retreat, Boleskin House, on the shores of Loch Ness, again suggesting that Maugham knew rather more about Crowley than he later wished to admit.) Ingram's tower had far-reaching consequences, as it inspired the gloriously Gothic watchtower lab of James Whale's *Frankenstein* (1931). Dwight Frye's hunchback assistant in that film also echoes the deformed dwarf sidekick employed by Haddo in Ingram's film.

Ingram naturally invested as much movement and visual interest as he could in his adaptation, but despite his embellishments, compressions and the happy ending, he remained faithful to the spirit of Maugham's book. Careful viewing reveals how he adapts a single set by a lick of paint and a change of furniture (the operating theater, in white, becomes the library of the Arsenal, in mahogany), which reminds one of how Hammer turned Dracula's castle in *Dracula—Prince of Darkness* (dir. Terence Fisher, 1966) into Rasputin's grace-and-favor palace in *Rasputin the Mad Monk* (dir. Don Sharp, 1966). Ingram also injects some humor into the scene (again derived from the novel) in which we visit a snake charmer's circus booth. A bowler hat floats aloft on a balloon and a child blows a party whistle in a lady's ear; but the scene's dramatic function is to demonstrate Haddo's magical powers: He takes the snake and allows it to bite him. No harm having been done, the snake then bites the unfortunate Indian girl who has been playing a drum, and she promptly expires. (Less drastically, Maugham has the snake kill a rabbit instead.)

When Haddo calls on Margaret in her studio, his hypnosis of her on the sofa seems to have been the inspiration for the virtual reprise of the situation in *The Devil Rides Out,* when Mocata imposes his will on Marie Eaton. Mocata is, however, not as musically talented as Haddo, who, as we have seen, backs up his mind control with a piano recital and then, obedient to Maugham again, performs a ritual with a bowl of water, which begins to burn. Ingram has no time to explain the full implications of this effect, but in the novel Haddo explains that he has at his command the power to burn up all the waters of the earth. "It would continue to burn while there was a drop of water on the earth, and the whole world would be consumed."[24] Like Fu Manchu, and like the arch-vampire in Hammer's *The Satanic Rites of Dracula,* megalomaniac Haddo is happy to destroy even himself in his pursuit of the ultimate power.

The hallucination that follows is a kind of Goethean Walpurgisnacht, inspired by the face of Margaret's immense sculpture of a faun. This statue had earlier collapsed onto her, necessitating an operation performed by her fiancé, but now it causes her to conjure visions of Pan himself, played, in a celebrated dream sequence, by the dancer Stowitz. Pan with his pipes presides over witches dancing around their cauldron in an orgy, which the makers of *The Devil Rides Out* went some way towards recreating. Haddo and Margaret observe all this from a distance, Haddo's hair combed up into two peaks like devil's horns. When Pan kisses Margaret on the neck, she wakes up; Haddo leaves his card and departs.

Unable to resist the power of his will, Margaret marries Haddo and sets off to Monte Carlo where, thanks to Haddo's magical influence, she wins a fortune playing roulette. Ingram having earlier obliged his audience with shots of Paris now takes us to another picturesque location, maintaining the interest and variety of his approach. But the climax of the film outshines— or should we say "out-shadows"?—all that. The imposing tower in which Haddo has built his laboratory is the prototype of many a subsequent villain's lair; and his stoking of the flames to facilitate his alchemical experiments has something of the grandeur of Benvenuto Cellini's account of the casting of his famous Perseus statue: "At this point there was a sudden explosion and a tremendous flash of fire, as if a thunderbolt had been hurled in our midst. Everyone, not least myself, was struck with unexpected terror."[25]

A superb shot of Haddo advancing towards the camera from Margaret's point of view gives Ingram the opportunity to explore, by means of uplighting, all the contours of Wegener's peculiarly gruesome features before he is sent off to be combusted in the fiery climax. The tower explodes in what would soon become a cinematic cliché, but which was a thing of novel and thrilling power when Ingram invented it.

CHAPTER FIVE

Ritual

Occultism is recognized more by its rituals than its results, and ritual has always been a significant element in its cinematic presentation. As I have already suggested, cinematic ritual has been cross-fertilized by opera, where ritual was dramatized rather more than it had been by the church alone. Verdi's *Requiem* (1874) brought the melodramatic language of opera to the Catholic Mass, but before that, magical ritual had long been a part of operatic tradition, with its invocations to both gods and devils. There are demonic evocations from the earliest days of opera, and these had become well-established by the seventeenth century. Purcell's *Dido and Aeneas* (c. 1688) contains a particularly impressive trio of witches who plan the destruction of the title characters:

> Wayward sisters, you that fright
> The lonely traveller by night,
> Who, like dismal ravens crying,
> Beat the windows of the dying,
> Appear! Appear at my command!

Much later in operatic history, another invocation, this time to summon the spirits of nuns who had not been faithful to their vows during life, caused a sensation at the Paris Opera, forming the central ballet scene of Meyerbeer's Grand Opera *Robert le diable* (1831). But the demonic tradition that would later characterize occult thrillers really began with Mozart's *Don Giovanni*. The chromatic power of Mozart's music, along with the sulfurous timbre of the trombones that announce the statue of the Commendatore come to life, made it a touchstone of the demonic for the nineteenth-century Romantics, out of whose tradition moving pictures evolved. E.T.A. Hoffmann was one of that opera's first important "Romantic" commentators, the music inspiring his story "Don Juan" (1813):

> Out of the dark night I saw demons stretch their fiery claws and loom menacingly over the lives of carefree mortals dancing merrily on the thin lid of a bottomless pit. The

conflict between human nature and the unknown, the terrible powers that confront man on every side and lie in wait for his ruin, took on a visionary intensity with the music.[1]

Hoffmann's description of the penultimate scene (nineteenth-century Romantics chose to overlook the optimistic sextet with which Mozart and his librettist, Lorenzo da Ponte, brought things to a close) pointed the way toward Dennis Wheatley and cinematic diabolism:

> Elvira and the girls flee, and to the accompaniment of terrifying chords that invoke the spirits of the damned, the awful marble Colossus enters and towers over Don Juan who seems reduced to the size of a pygmy. The ground quakes under the giant's thundering steps. Though the storm, through the thunder, through the howling of the demons, Don Juan cries his terrifying: "No!" and commits himself to his doom. The hour of destruction is come. The statue disappears, the room is filled with thick smoke out of which rise terrifying spectres. Don Juan, experiencing the torments of Hell, writhes in and out of the crowd of demons. Suddenly there is an explosion, as if a thousand bolts of lightning had all struck the same spot: Don Juan and the demons have disappeared without a trace! Leporello lies unconscious in a corner of the room.[2]

Stoker's *Dracula* may well have been partly inspired by *Don Giovanni*, with which it has many things in common, and the operatic element in Hammer's vampire films is certainly apparent in the ritualistic elements found in them. That Christopher Lee originally hoped to become an opera singer is also not without relevance with regard to his various Dracula performances. There are no rituals in the company's first Dracula film, but the high point of its sequel *Dracula—Prince of Darkness* is a lengthy resurrection scene, which Terence Fisher asked the actor, Philip Latham, to perform as a religious ceremony. Each of Latham's actions are carefully controlled: the removal of the funeral pall; the tying of the victim's feet with the rope that will hoist the corpse over Dracula's sarcophagus; the emptying of Dracula's ashes from the casket that has preserved them; the deliberate replacement of the lid on the casket after the ashes have been scattered; the careful placement of the knife which he uses to slash the victim's throat. There is no dialogue but rather a compelling collaboration between action and James Bernard's minimalistic score, which, initially through pure rhythm, builds up into a gigantic orchestral *tutti* as Dracula is finally reconstituted.

This scene began Hammer's increasingly occult presentation of the Dracula story, though the earlier *The Kiss of the Vampire* had connected different vampires with the occult in a much more overt manner. To defeat the coven of the undead, presided over by Noel Willman's Dr. Ravna, Clifford Evans' Prof. Zimmer performs an occult ceremony called "Corpus Diabolo Levitum." Complete with a magic circle, a grimoire, "the liquid and the horn," he intones the appropriate words to force the powers of evil to destroy themselves. Accordingly, an immense flock of bats appear and attack the human vampires at the chateau. "It worked!" Zimmer exclaims in relief and almost disbelief.

In *Dracula Has Risen From the Grave* (dir. Freddie Francis, 1968), Rupert Davies' Monsignor employs bell, book and candle to assist in a specifically Catholic rite of exorcism, spoken in suitably sepulchral Latin, against which a storm suggests the wrath not only of Dracula's unquiet spirit but also of the Almighty Himself. The whole thing is altogether more operatic in tone than the much grittier approach to the diabolic taken by *The Exorcist*, where Catholic rituals are employed but more in the manner of a violent police interrogation. The Devil is almost literally whipped out of Linda Blair's body, compelled "by the power of Christ" and lashings of holy water. *Taste the Blood of Dracula* also dwells on a ritual, being much more demonic than Hammer's previous attempts. In a ruined church, Dracula's blood is again reconstituted and drunk by his officiating "priest," Lord Courtley (Ralph Bates). As in *Dracula—Prince of Darkness*, care is taken over the regalia: three crystal goblets in a wooden carrying case, a phial of dried blood, Dracula's cloak, ring and seal, all of which Courtley manipulates with reverence.

Occultism far more strongly informs Hammer's two updates of their Dracula franchise, reflecting the occult revival of the time. In both films, Prof. Van Helsing is played by Peter Cushing, and in the first, *Dracula A.D. 1972* (dir. Alan Gibson), we are shown a close-up of his library, containing an array of suitably occult titles. These include, among others, A.E. Waite's *The Brotherhood of the Rosy Cross* (1928), Bernard Brommage's *The Occult Arts of Ancient Egypt* (1960), Rollo Ahmed's *The Black Art* (1967), Colin Wilson's *The Occult* (1971) and Moses Gaster's edition of *The Secret Grimoire of Turiel*. The ceremony that revives the count is presided over by Christopher Neame's Johnny Alucard, who invokes the names of several dangerous angels: Astaroth, Belberith, Belpheggor, Beelzebub and Ronwe. Alucard also wears black robes and is very obviously a Satanist, with Dracula as an emissary of the Devil rather than a mere vampire. "It was my will!" he insists, after his resurrection, which again reminds us of Crowley's definition of magic.

In *The Satanic Rites of Dracula*, there is no doubt about the Satanic goings-on. The title alone prepares us, and the film opens with a full-blown Black Mass: a human sacrifice, black candles, cowled figures, and an oriental High Priestess for good measure. Van Helsing compares the occult practices of the elderly businessmen and politicians who form the members of this demonic brotherhood with the Hellfire Club, adding, "Things do go bump in the night—quite often." In response to Denham-Dracula's insistence that he need not worry about what is happening at Pelham House, Van Helsing insists, "Evil begets evil. There is an unholy aura in this place, and it is not a question of a little occultism or a touch of mysticism, Mr. Denham. It is vampirism, and there's a host of damned souls at Pelham House."

Hammer had employed the Black Mass before, but always in period settings, thus distancing them from the hippie subculture of the late '60s and early '70s on which much of Hammer's latter-day appeal depended. A particularly impressive example of a period Black Mass is Dennis Price's attempt to entertain the dissolute Count Karnstein (Damien Thomas) in *Twins of Evil* (dir. John Hough, 1971). The impressive castle set allows for a grand magic circle surrounded by flaming torchères, along with a spectacular resurrection sequence in which blood from the sacrificed virgin drips over the corpse of the vampire beneath. This shrouded body then walks through swirling mist towards the terrified Karnstein; but it is the opening sequence of the film, featuring Peter Cushing's witchfinder Gustav Weil, in which we experience a style of invocation indebted to nineteenth-century operatic models. Weil is ostensibly praying to God to redeem "a child of the Devil": "We ask thee, in thy great goodness, to save her soul. We commend unto thee her earthly body and seek to purify its spirit." Harry Robinson's music for this scene is structured on a sequence of four notes, the first three of which are in fact an inversion of the famous "Dies Irae" sequence of the Requiem Mass. Though the "Dies Irae" was originally associated with the wrath of God, nineteenth-century Romantics, beginning with Berlioz in his 1830 *Symphonie fantastique,* increasingly employed it as a signifier of the demonic. By the time James Bernard echoed the sequence in his music for *Dracula Has Risen From the Grave,* the implication was simultaneously sacred and demonic, until its final appearance at the end of the film when it is placed in a major key to suggest unequivocally the triumph of good over evil. Robinson's re-arrangement of the first three notes of the "Dies Irae" in *Twins of Evil* are repeated three times, each repetition placed in successively higher pitches, with the fourth repetition expanding the intervals somewhat. The effect is rather more as though the Devil rather than the Almighty is being invoked, and we might usefully compare it to the summoning of Samiel, the devil in Carl Maria von Weber's 1821 singspiel, *Der Freischütz,* where the spoken invocation is accompanied by a simple rising chromatic scale in lower strings. *Satanic Rites'* modern-dress Black Mass finds its operatic equivalent in Nigel Finch's updated British television production in 1992 of Heinrich Marschner's 1828 singspiel *Der Vampyr.* Based on John Polidori's tale, which had inaugurated the modern vampire mythos in 1816, this production cast the original opera's coven of witches and ghosts as sophisticated, power-dressed Satanists.

Robes have always played an important role in magical rituals, but Hammer decided not to dress the participants of the Duc de Richleau's magical ceremony in *The Devil Rides Out* in the pajamas Dennis Wheatley describes in the original novel. Pajamas are deemed necessary in the novel as they are clean and uncontaminated, unlike everyday clothes, and "[h]uman impurities are bound to linger in one's clothes even if they have only been worn for a few hours, and it is just upon such things that elementals fasten most readily."[3] Christopher Lee in pajamas would indeed rather weaken his aura of authority, so Hammer retained his three-piece suit. The film's Satanists, however, wear loose-fitting purple robes, which are decorated with imagery derived from Lévi's *Transcendental Magic*, but according to Crowley, whom Wheatley wined and dined during his research for *The Devil Rides Out*, there are only three kinds of robe: the white and the black, "varied by the addition of various symbols," and "a Robe which few dare to wear. This Robe is of a rich silk of deep pure blue, the blue of the night sky." Purple, with its imperial connotations, was obviously regarded as more effective for the film, but a robe is more than merely a dramatic effect. Crowley explained that the magician's robe "is that which conceals, and which protects the Magician from the ele-

CHALK CIRCLE: **Christopher Lee, Paul Eddington, Patrick Mower and Sarah Lawson in *The Devil Rides Out* (dir. Terence Fisher, 1968).**

ments; it is the silence and secrecy with which he works, the hiding of himself in the occult life of Magick and Meditation." It is also "the 'aura' of the Magician."[4]

Though Hammer rejected pajamas, it did accurately realize Wheatley's description of the magic circle in Cardinal's Folly, the home of Richard and Marie Eaton:

> At last the broad chalk lines were drawn to the Duke's satisfaction, forming the magical five-pointed star, in which it was his intention that they should remain while darkness lasted.
> He then chalked in, with careful spacing round the rim of the inner circle, the powerful exorcism:
> In nomina Pa + tris et Fi + lii Spiritus + Sancti + El Elohym + Sother + Emmanuel + Sabaoth + Agia + Tetragammaton + Agyos + Otheos + Ischiros.[5]

This prayer is derived from Gérard Anaclet Vincent Encausse, aka "Papus" in his manual on *How to Fight Hexes*, as a "Plea against the wiles of evil spirits."[6] However, the film omits what Wheatley describes as the "curious and ancient symbols in the valleys and the mounts of the microcosmic star," such as the "Cabbalistic signs taken from the Sephirotic Tree; *Kether, Binah, Ceburah, Hod, Malchut* and the rest. But others, like the Eye of Horus, were of Egyptian origin, and others again in some ancient Aryan script."[7]

The Devil Rides Out was published during the ascendency of the Nazis in Germany, when the word "Aryan" was beginning to have undesirable connotations. So too was the ancient symbol of the swastika, which Wheatley introduces when de Richleau hypnotizes Simon Aron. Hammer's film version understandably substituted the swastika with a crucifix, which de Richleau places around Simon's neck. The misunderstanding that would no doubt have ensued was thus avoided, but Wheatley had anticipated this, having Rex van Run exclaim: "Fancy hanging a Nazi swastika round the neck of a professing Jew." De Richleau replies:

> My dear Rex! Do try and broaden your outlook a little. The swastika is the oldest symbol of wisdom and right thinking in the world. It has been used by every race and in every country at some time or other. You might just as well regard the Cross as purely Christian, when we all know it was venerated in early Egypt, thousands of years before the birth of Christ. The Nazis have only adopted the swastika because it is supposed to be of Aryan origin and part of their programme aims at welding together a large section of the Aryan race.[8]

Christopher Lee took considerable pride in having located a genuine incantation from the library of the British Museum, with which to vocalize Wheatley's unwritten Sussamma Ritual; it is spoken twice at times of imminent peril. "Hammer had always worried about the Church's reaction to the screening of the Black Mass," Lee recalled. "But we thought the charge of blasphemy would not stick if we did the thing with due attention to scholarship. I appointed myself black technical advisor, as well as playing a goody, and spent many hours in the British Museum guddling for Satanic trout, and came up with a useful catch, notably the genuine prayer of exorcism we used at the end."[9] The words are "Oriel Seraphim, Io Potesta, Zati Zata, Galatim Galata," which derive from the seventeeth-century *Grimoire ou la Cabale* by Armadel (its full Latin title is *Liber Armadel seu totius cabalae perfectissima brevissima et infallibilis scientia tam speculativa quam practiqua*). Now lodged in the Bibliothèque de l'Arsenal in Paris, it concerns how one may literally trap the Devil in a bottle:

> Uriel Seraphim, potesta, Io, Zati, Zata, Abbati, Abbata, Agla, Cailo, aila, I pray thee and conjure thee in the name of the Living God and by Him, thy Master and mine; by all the might of the Holy Trinity; by the virginity of the Holy Virgin; by the four sacred words which the great Agla said with His own mouth to Moses, Io, Zati, Zata, Abbata; by the nine heavens in which thou dwellest; and by the virtue of the characters said before, that thou appear to me visibly and without delay in a fair human form, not terrifying, without or within this phial, which holds water prepared to receive thee, in order than thou mayest answer what I desire to ask thee, and fetch and bring the book of Moses, open it, put thy hand upon it and swear truth while making me see and know clearly all that I desire to know; appear then, I conjure thee in the same of the Great God, Almighty Alpha, and be thou welcome in *galatim, galata, cailo, caila*.[10]

Lee also brought his experience of playing an ancient Egyptian priest in *The Mummy* to a later *Devil Rides Out* scene, when he adopts Egyptian hieratic poses ("The sign of Osiris slain" and "The sign of Osiris risen"), while summoning the spirit of the young woman, Tanith, who has been claimed by the Angel of Death as a consequence of his uttering the Sussamma Ritual. Blood and hair are burned in a crucible, but the novel makes clear that it is Tanith's hair and blood that are being burned. Wheatley describes how the blood is mixed with incense to form a paste from which de Richleau forms seven cones, each one coiled with Tanith's hair. These are then arranged around Tanith's body inside the magic circle, and lit, while de Richleau silently summons the girl's spirit. This gradually appears in the form of a faint blue light, which solidifies into a ball over the center of Tanith's body. In the film, de Richleau burns the hair, blood and, for good measure, salt, summoning her vocally, but instead of a ball of blue light, the film relies on James Bernard's magical use of differently tuned hand bells to suggest the materialization of Tanith's spirit.

The appearance of the Goat of Mendes earlier in the film arises not so much from a ritual as an orgy. In the novel, the participants are naked, but because of censorship restrictions, Hammer's actors are fully clothed. One imagines that Gwen Ffrangcon-Davies would hardly have agreed to have been filmed naked, "huge-buttocked and swollen, prancing by some satanic power with all the vigour of a young girl who had only just reached maturity,"[11] which is how Wheatley describes her role as Madame d'Urfé. But the Goat's manifestation is a marvelous approximation of Wheatley's description, even though it has only two, rather than the four horns specified in the text:

> Above rose the monstrous bearded head of a gigantic goat, appearing to be at least three times the size of any other which they had ever seen. The two slit-eyes, slanting inwards and down, gave out a red baleful light. Long pointed ears cocked upwards from the sides of the shaggy head, and from the bald, horrible unnatural bony skull, which was caught by the light of the candles, four enormous curved horns spread out—sideways and up.[12]

The final ritual in the book and the film is the Black Mass presided over by Mocata, at which the child, Peggy Eaton, is to be sacrificed in exchange for the soul of Tanith. Wheatley's biographer Phil Baker refers to "a recent academic book" that claims a Black Mass held on Boxing Day 1918, organized by Montague Summers, is "the earliest Black Mass for which there is reliable evidence,"[13] which is probably true, though hearsay suggests that they existed earlier, perhaps much earlier, as Huysmans' 1891 *Là-bas* implies, and there is really not a great deal of difference between Huysmans' description of an image of Christ with "a viral member projecting from a bush of horsehair"[14] and Wheatley's description of the Talisman of Set "set in the forehead of the Beast, laying it lengthwise upon the flat, bald, bony skull, where it blazed like some magnificent jewel which had a strange black centre."[15] The Talisman of Set is, in fact, the mummified phallus of Osiris.

Mocata's final attempt to sacrifice Peggy is foiled by the utterance of "a strange word—having five syllables," which the film substitutes with a repetition of the words Lee discovered for the Susamma Ritual. These have a devastating effect: "The whole chamber rocked as though shaken by an earthquake. The walls receded, the floor began to spin. The crypt gyrated with such terrifying speed that the occupants of the circle clutched frantically at each other to save themselves from falling."[16] The film dramatizes this faithfully, but not, of course, the separation of the Talisman of Set from the horns of the Goat as it is thrown "head downmost on the chapel steps" where it "dissolved in upon itself."[17] Wheatley finally describes the appearance of a "Lord of Light nearing perfection after many lives," who explains that the love the friends have for each other has saved them. The film omits all this. Instead, after he is told that Mocata is dead, Simon Aron simply says "Thank God." "Yes," de Richleau replies. "He is the one we must thank," at which point, James Bernard's once demonic main theme is placed in a major key in a section of transfigurative music that meant so much to him, he requested to have it played at his own funeral at Mortlake Crematorium. No such *deus ex machine* occurs in Huysmans' Black Mass at the end of *Là-bas*, though pandemonium of a different kind is indeed let loose:

> The place was simply a madhouse, a monstrous pandemonium of prostitutes and maniacs. Now, while the choir boys gave themselves to the men, and while the women who owned the chapel, mounted the altar caught hold of the phallus of Christ with one hand and with the other held a chalice between "His" naked legs, a little girl, who hitherto had not budged, suddenly bent over forward and howled, howled like a dog.[18]

Such cavortings informed the climax of Cyril Frankel's *The Witches* (1966), where an entire village assembles for demonic orgies under the auspices of their (lesbian) matriarch in the form of Kay Walsh's aging Stephanie Bax, who aims magically to transfer her highly educated mind into the body of a considerably less well-educated but much younger girl. The villagers crawl on all fours, writhe on the floor, cover themselves in dirt and dance to the hypnotically repetitive music provided by the film's composer, Richard Rodney Bennett.

All this bears little relation to the aims of magick as identified by Crowley, who describes "the Brothers of the Left Hand Path" as those "who have trampled Love in the race for self-aggrandizement."[19] In fact, Crowley denied the existence of the Devil altogether:

> The Devil does not exist. It is a false name invented by the Black Brothers to imply a Unity in their ignorant muddle of dispersions. A devil who had unity would be a God. [...] It is, however, always easy to call up the demons, for they are always calling you, and you have only to step down to their level and fraternize with them. They will tear you in pieces at their leisure.[20]

But this did not stop Crowley from raising the spirit of Choronzon, the Dweller in the Abyss, with the help of his associate Victor Neuburg. He explained in his *Confessions* that the Abyss "is filled with all possible forms, each equally inane, each therefore evil in the only true sense of the word— that is, meaningless but malignant, in so far as it craves to become real. These forms swirl senselessly into haphazard heaps like dust devils, and each such chance aggregation asserts itself to be an individual and shrieks 'I am I!' though aware all the time that its elements have no true bond." Choronzon apparently appeared to Crowley in many physical forms: "the form of myself, of a woman whom Neuburg loved, of a serpent with a human head, etc." His account of the materialization is very dramatic, Choronzon appearing in the form of a naked savage and attempting to tear out Neuburg's throat with "froth-covered fangs." Crowley identified himself with Choronzon, "so that I experienced each anguish, each rage, each despair, each insane outburst."[21]

This incident, or at least Crowley's account of it, informed another of Hammer's occult rituals in an episode from the TV series *Hammer House of Horror*. "Guardian of the Abyss" (dir. Don Sharp, 1980) stars John Carson as yet another screen version of Crowley, intent on raising the same demon. A scrying-glass is stolen from an antique shop. Rosalyn Landor, who played Peggy in *The Devil Rides Out*, appears doomed to become a sacrificial victim, but she in fact double-crosses the hero (Roy Lonnen). He thinks he is rescuing her, but ends up being sacrificed by the Satanists himself. He then transforms into Choronzon, whose demonic form gradually returns to Lonnen's features, all the better to infiltrate and presumably destroy society. All the occult *bric-à-brac* we might expect is here: a magic circle, arcane sigils, monks' robes, black candles, chanting, an inverted crucifix—even a Frankenstein reference when Lonnen, now inhabited by the demon, breaks the straps that secure him to the sacrificial slab.

"Guardian of the Abyss" was Hammer's last foray into black magic, its final feature film on the subject having been inspired by Wheatley's *To the Devil a Daughter*. "Inspired" is really the only word to use, as this highly imaginative and well-made occult thriller has very little to do with Wheatley's original novel, a fact that outraged the elderly author. But director Peter Sykes felt that the book was "unfilmable"[22] as it stood. The film's updated story concerns the birth of the demon Astharoth. Having ripped its way through its mother's stomach (Ridley Scott's *Alien* recapitulated these birth pangs in a somewhat more graphic manner in 1979), the infant demon is then to be slaughtered and reincarnated in the body of Catherine Beddows (Nastassja Kinski). Naturally, the girl's father (Denholm Elliott) attempts to prevent this, but he eventually loses his mind having been subjected to various psychic attacks by the presiding Satanist, the distinctly un–Christian Father Michael Raynor (Christopher Lee). His chosen method of protection is, as one would expect, a magic circle.

There are several rituals in this story. The film begins with a ritual, though a Catholic one, in which Father Michael is excommunicated for his heretical beliefs; but it is the final scene that is of most interest. It was shot inside the Dashwood Mausoleum at West Wycombe in Hertfordshire, a vast hexagonal burial ground enclosed by flint walls that are pierced with arches and rectangular openings, and decorated with Tuscan columns and Coade-stone vases. Inside are spaces for funeral urns and memorials, the whole standing in a commanding position atop West Wycombe Hill. It was built with funds left in 1762 by George Bubb Dodington, Lord Melcombe Regis, who was a friend of Sir Francis Dashwood, the most famous member of the Devil-worshipping Hellfire Club, the notorious caves of which form part of the nearby Dashwood estate; it thus provides an appropriately demonic backdrop to Father Michael's ceremony at the end of the film. He surrounds the central cenotaph, consisting of four columns and a marble urn, with a circle of blood to protect himself against Astaroth's demonic allies. In fact, this effectively lurid detail was an afterthought by Gerald Vaughan-Hughes, the film's uncredited script advisor, who was reminded by producer Roy Skeggs that they had "forgotten" about the blood that had been drained from the body of Catherine's surrogate mother, Eveline de Grass (Eva-Maria Meineke).[23] Earlier in the film, she pumps all the blood out of her own body in an effective scene, but one which seems originally to have been included merely for grotesque effect with no motivation.

Having just slaughtered the infant Astaroth, Father Michael now intends to resurrect him in the body of Catherine. Meanwhile, the demons are angry. Within the circle of blood, Father Michael is safe; but the ceremony in interrupted by the hero, John Verney (Richard Widmark), who throws one of the flints he finds on the hillside. Normally, this would have no effect, as flint is apparently the sacred stone of Astaroth (as the walls of the Mausoleum testify), but Verney has just used the flint to kill one of Raynor's disciples, and thus (somewhat illogically) the flint protects him. He is able to cross the circle of blood and dispatch Father Michael, rescuing the girl and saving the day—except that it is, in fact, all too late, as two drops of Astaroth's blood have already baptized Catherine, and the demon, like Choronzon in the body of the antique dealer, is ready to corrupt the world in human form.

Occult rituals in other films take place in less imposing environments. There are plenty of fake séance scenes to be found in suburban surroundings. Bryan Forbes' *Séance on a Wet Afternoon* (1964) begins with one, before the main title sequence, designed by Maurice Binder and accompanied by John Barry's raindrop prelude, evocatively summons the mood of the title of late afternoon suburban sogginess. The séance here is held by Myra Savage (Kim Stanley), a neurotic failure of a woman who persuades her husband (Richard Attenborough) to kidnap a schoolgirl and then contact the police, claiming to discover her whereabouts by psychic means. This, they hope, will make Myra into a world-famous medium. The film opens with the camera revolving around a candle burning in the middle of the séance table. Thus are we introduced to the faces of the bereaved family who hope to be comforted by Myra.

At the beginning of Peter Sasdy's *Hands of the Ripper* (1971), the camera also rotates around a table, in this case one that belongs to Dora Bryan's fake medium, Mrs. Golding, who is discovered to be exploiting the daughter of Jack the Ripper (Angharad Rees) as a "spirit voice." Though the medium is fake, Jack the Ripper's daughter really is possessed by the spirit of the world's most famous serial killer. Dr. Pritchard (Eric Porter), a psychiatrist, is fully convinced of the former fact, but it takes a while for him to accept the latter. He exposes Mrs. Golding by stepping on Anna's toes, which peep out from behind the curtain where she is hiding to whisper her spirit voices.

The cases of Myra Savage and Mrs. Golding curiously resemble one of the better-known exposures of the Society for Psychical Research in the 1930s. These concerned a medium, Mrs. Duncan, who, according to the historian of the Society for Psychical Research, Renée Haynes, also "wanted to make a living, and to be admired, rather than raise the standard of a new cult."[24] Mrs. Duncan faked ectoplasm by using cheesecloth, and in 1933 in Scotland, "'a little girl called Peggy' emerged from the cabinet. Someone grabbed her, the light was switched on, and there stood Mrs. Duncan."[25] In *Hands of the Ripper*, Mrs. Golding uses the same words ("a little girl") during her séance.

The delusions of spiritualism are also exposed in the opening scenes of Nick Willing's *Photographing Fairies* (1997). Horace Walpole's Gothick mansion, Strawberry Hill, stands in for the headquarters of the Theosophical Society, through which the initially disillusioned and unbelieving hero, Charles Castle (Toby Stevens), makes his way. As he does so, he passes a room in which various séances are taking place. We hear a medium asking if "Raymond" is there, a reference to Sir Oliver Lodge's well-known series of books about the "return" of his own Raymond after his untimely death in the First World War. *Photographing Fairies* thus begins with exposure of the exploitation and delusion of spiritualism in the wake of the mass bereavements caused by that conflict. (We encounter Edward Hardwicke's Arthur Conan Doyle at a lecture. His belief in fairies was only a part of his long-standing interest in spiritualism, which the rational character of Sherlock Holmes had only disguised.) As the plot unfolds, Castle comes to defend his own belief in fairies, and so the film as a whole stands in a curiously ambivalent position towards the subject.

Night of the Demon, Jacques Tourneur's 1957 adaptation of M.R. James' story "Casting the Runes," features another séance, which we are led to believe will be a farrago of nonsense. Its eccentric participants seem to confirm the disbelief of Dana Andrews' rational scientist Dr. Holden, especially when everyone is asked to sing "Cherry Ripe" to encourage the medium's spirit guide to appear; but things take a more sinister turn when the medium begins to speak with the voice of a Maurice Denham's Prof. Harrington, who was killed at the beginning of the film by the demon, which Tourneur, against his better judgment, was forced to include in his otherwise superb evocation of occult ambivalence.

In *The Masque of the Red Death* (dir. Roger Corman, 1964), Vincent

Price's Prince Prospero fancies himself a Satanist, believing that the Infernal Master will save him from the dreaded Red Death plague. Hazel Court, as his consort Juliana, also dedicates herself to the Devil, branding her bosom with his mark before experiencing a series of disturbing hallucinations. This all takes place in a small black cube of a room with scarlet-tinted windows, the culmination of Prince Prospero's suite of different colored rooms. Though these are derived from Poe's original story, Devil worship plays no part *in* that story. Corman's film combines the esthetic mood of Poe's writing with the demonic element that so often accompanied the work of the French decadents whom Poe inspired. In Corman's film, Prospero fails to realize until it is too late that it is Death, not the Devil, who has come to claim him, and the face of Death is Prospero's own. Juliana, meanwhile, has been killed by a hawk. The implications are entirely nihilistic and amoral. Death is the only certainty here. Corman's epilogue, echoing Ingmar Bergman's *The Seventh Seal* (1957), makes this plain, as the Red Death is joined by his variously colored colleagues in a final colloquy.

Sex also plays its part in cinematic occult ritual. As John Verney puts it in *To the Devil a Daughter*, 98 percent of occultists use their rituals as an excuse for sex, but there is always that "other two percent..." Indeed, Father Michael attempts to distract Verney from foiling his plans at the end of the film, by conjuring a vision of Catherine, stark naked and smiling. Sex is the great illusion as well as the great temptation, but it is also a means of generating psychic force. Invariably, movies use it an excuse merely for titillation, as we see in Vernon Sewell's *The Curse of the Crimson Altar* (1968), which betrays Tigon Film's past history as a purveyor of soft porn. Leather, whips, chains and feather-plumed headdresses accompany the psychedelic rituals that take place, even more incongruously, in the supposed cellars of Sir W.S. Gilbert's home Grim's Dyke, where the film was largely shot. "The Little Maids from School" it is not, but it is hardly any more terrifying than that.

In *Psychomania*, the empty room (more of a closet than anything else) in which Nicky Henson experiences the vision of a toad in a mirror along with a flashback sequence involving his mother (Beryl Reid) making a pact with the Devil, is one of the movies' oddest places of invocation. The mirror is another form of the kind of scrying glass Klingsor uses in *Parsifal*. Christopher Lee (who, had he been able to pursue an operatic career, would indeed have made a superb Klingsor) also uses a mirror in which to entrap the nobler aspect of the evil magician, Alquazar, whom he plays in *Arabian Adventure* (dir. Kevin Connor, 1979). His place of work is a cavern guarded by a fiery pit. Like "Snow White"'s wicked queen, Alquazar interrogates this mirror, and his better self is compelled to answer him with the truth. Crowley had his own explanation with regard to how this kind of thing is meant to work:

> There are a great many ways of acquiring power. Gaze into a crystal, or into a pool of ink in the palm of the hand, or into a mirror, or into a teacup. Just as, with a microscope, the expert operator keeps both eyes open through seeing only through the one at the eyepiece of the instrument, so the natural eyes, ceasing to give any message to the brain, the attention is withdrawn from them, and the man begins to see through the astral eyes.[26]

But mirrors might more straightforwardly be regarded as symbols of our divided consciousness—of our instinct rather than of our reason. This is why they appear in Jean Cocteau's *Orphée* (1950), where they give access to the underworld. "It is not necessary to understand," explains Orphée's Virgilian guide, Heurtebise (François Périer), "it is necessary to believe." Adorning their hands with magic rubber gloves, they pierce the glassy surface and, like Alice, enter the looking-glass world of María Casares' Princess of Death.

The scrying potential of mirrors appears in other guises. In *Dead of Night* (dir. Robert Hamer, 1945), Peter Cortland (Ralph Michael) gazes into a mirror and beholds a sinister room that is very different from what should be reflected back at him. The phenomenon eventually drives him insane, as giving in to instinct and over-indulgence in fantasy so often can. The same sort of thing happens in one of the stories in *From Beyond the Grave* (dir. Kevin Connor, 1974). David Warner plays Edward Charlton, who buys a mirror from Peter Cushing's sinister antiques dealer. When he gets it home, he too indulges in a séance, filmed like the one in *Séance on a Wet Afternoon*. This unfortunately awakens the spirit of a Satanist entrapped in the mirror world. It demands blood sacrifice, and much slaughter later, the infernal vision persuades Charlton to commit suicide, and then returns to the real world.

Hammer conflated Arabian and Western magic in the ritual scenes of *The Vengeance of She* (dir. Cliff Owen, 1968), and they form perhaps the most successful parts of this otherwise uneven production. Tormented by telepathic voices, the hapless Carol (Olinka Berova), who is in fact the reincarnation of Ayesha, seeks help from a Middle Eastern magician called Kassim (André Morell). He attempts to confront the magi of Kuma, priests of the eternal city where the immortal Killikrates (John Richardson) now rules after Ayesha's destruction at the end of the first film. The magi reject their former leader and decide to follow the evil Men-Hari (Derek Godfrey), a self-confessed Ipsissimus—the highest grade of magical adept, as Dennis Wheatley, who popularized the term, explained in *The Devil Rides Out* with regard to Mocata. A lavish temple set is furnished with an immense magic circle and pentagram protected by candles, priests brandishing caduceus wands, and priestesses who assume various hieratic poses. There is also a flaming censer and even a sword of Damocles suspended over a sacrificial virgin, who perishes at the climax of Men-Hari's ceremony.

Kassim constructs his own magic circle, but it is much smaller than Men-Hari's, as is his power to resist Men-Hari's magic. Kassim is fully aware of the dangers he faces from the magi: "Their skill lies in the understanding and the use of the human mind's deepest powers, magnified by ritual and by symbols, into a real living force for good or for evil." Men-Hari of course uses this power for evil, which manifests itself as a mist swirled by a violent wind and soon pushes the unfortunate Kassim over a balcony to his death.

A magic circle is traditionally regarded as offering protection for the magician from demonic forces raised outside it, as Crowley points out:

> Once the Circle is made and consecrated, the Magician may just not leave it, or even lean outside, lest he be destroyed by the hostile forces that are without. He chooses a Circle rather than any other lineal figure for many reasons; e.g.,
>
> 1. He affirms thereby his identity with the infinite.
> 2. He affirms the equal balance of his working; since all points on the circumference are equidistant from the centre.
> 3. He affirms the limitation implied by his devotion to the Great Work. He no longer wanders about aimlessly in the world.[27]

In an amusing variation of this belief, one of the three stories that make up *The Uncanny* (dir. Denis Héroux, 1977) features a magic circle, complete with pentagram, chalked on the floor of orphaned Lucy's (Katrina Holden Bronson) bedroom. Lucy's mother had been a witch, so she knows exactly what to do to revenge herself on her domineering, older stepsister, Angela, played by Chloe Franks, who had played a witch's daughter herself in *The House That Dripped Blood* (dir. Peter Duffell, 1971). Lucy entices Angela into the circle and then begins her incantation. Angela becomes smaller and smaller, like Alice in Wonderland. "You're not such a big girl any more!" Lucy laughs, as her black cat Wellington attacks the now mouse-sized Angela. In the end, Lucy simply stamps on Angela, crushing her into a "sticky mess," which she leaves for Angela's mother to be cross about and, not realizing the terrible truth, mop up.

When Chloe Franks played her witch daughter role in *The House That Dripped Blood,* her chosen form of magic was voodoo, using a figure of her father (Christopher Lee) carved from a wax candle. The film eschews ritual in favor of psychological exploration in a domestic setting, much as Victor Halperin's *White Zombie* (1932) does in a much more elaborately Gothic setting; but *The Plague of the Zombies* (dir. John Gilling, 1966) provided a full-blooded ceremony over which the masked figure of John Carson's Squire Hamilton prepares his voodoo figures to the accompaniment of James

Bernard's frantic native drumming. Distinctly less frenetic drumming, provided by a lank-haired John Carradine and one of his zombie cohorts, also accompanies the splendidly robed ceremony (stars and sigils) in *Voodoo Man* (dir. William Beaudine, 1944). Here, George Zucco causes a rope magically to knot itself as he assists Bela Lugosi's hypnotic transfer of the life-essences of various wandering women into the body of Lugosi's dead wife.

Voodoo Man is an unashamedly low-budget Monogram occult programmer; Robert Fuest's *The Devil's Rain* (1975) had a much larger budget and much grander pretensions. Unfortunately it was so unsuccessful that it virtually destroyed Fuest's career. Its incoherent plot (a Satanist in search of a book that lists the names of all the souls he has collected for the Devil) helped no one involved, but Fuest nonetheless brought some of the visual flair that he had lavished on his immensely successful Dr. Phibes films. The boarded-up church presided over by Ernest Borgnine's Satanist even features an organ with semi-circular keyboard rather like the instrument Phibes plays to such an effect. Borgnine performs several rituals in suitably scarlet robes ("Satan, ruler of the earth, king of the world!"), and the church is decorated with pentagrams which contrasts bizarrely with the way things are outside, for the church is situated in a Wild West ghost town, Redstone.

William Shatner is eventually sacrificed to the Devil by Borgnine's zombie-like congregation of lost souls, all of whom have lost their eyes; but Fuest certainly did not lose his, as the landscapes in this film are quite ravishing. Though photographed in color, they approach the intensity of Ansel Adams. The black-cowled figures that assemble in the dusty desolation of Redstone create an occult also echo Alain Resnais' figure grouping in *Last Year at Marienbad* (1961), while Borgnine, attired in red, is filmed from below against a blue sky, suggesting the manner of Leni Reifenstahl. More amusingly, though no less startlingly, Borgnine is even transformed into the Devil himself with resplendent ram's horns before torturing Shatner by burning a wax effigy of him. Alas, Fuest's visuals alone are unable to rescue this ill-conceived project, despite the apparent involvement of infamous Satanist Anton LaVey as both occult advisor and even bit player.

The use of magical ritual to attain power over others has obvious political connotations. Hitler, a movie fan, has inspired a great many films, which, as we shall see in the next chapter, have explored the nature of his "daemonic" will. But there are surprisingly few examples of the Wheatley-esque approach to Nazi occultism. It is often argued that Hitler had little personal interest in the occult beyond its symbolism as a tool of practical propaganda. Advocates of this interpretation often refer to a *Mein Kampf* passage which suggests that Hitler's adoption of the swastika was "esthetic" rather than occult:

> I myself, meanwhile, after innumerable attempts, had laid down a final form; a flag with a red background, a white disc, and a black swastika in the middle. After long trials I also found a definite proportion between the size of the flag and the size of the white disc, as well as the shape and thickness of the swastika. [...]
> In the midsummer of 1920 the new flag came before the public for the first time. It was excellently suited to our new movement. It was young and new, like the movement itself. No one had seen it before; it had the effect of a burning torch. [...]
> In *red* we see the social idea of the movement, in *white* the nationalistic idea, in the *swastika* the mission of the struggle for the victory of the Aryan man, and, by the same token, the victory of the idea of creative work, which as such always has been and always will be anti–Semitic.[28]

But this is to overlook not only the Nazi Party's evolution out of the *völkish* and occult-oriented Thule Society, but also Hitler's perennial interest in supposed supernatural forces, ranging from the mystical basis of his racist beliefs (in which Jews were not devils or vampires in a merely rhetorical sense), through his fascination with Wagnerian myth to his interest in homeopathy, vegetarianism and magic. Eric Kurlander refers to a speech Hitler gave as early as February 1920 in which he refers to the swastika as "the symbol of the sun. All of [the Aryans'] cults were built on light, and you can find this [...] cross as a swastika [...] carved into temple posts in India and Japan."[29]

Hitler may have distanced himself officially from occultism out of political expediency, but his personal commitment to supernatural ideas is no longer in any doubt. It is true, however, that the occult was far more of an obsession for Himmler, whose enthusiasm for it, according to Albert Speer, frequently irritated the Führer:

> What nonsense! Here we have at last reached an age that has left all mysticism behind it, and now [Himmler] wants to start all that over again. We might just as well have stayed with the church. At least it had tradition. To think that I may be some day turned into an SS saint! Can you imagine it? I would turn over in my grave.[30]

Paul Campion's *The Devil's Rock* (2011) is one of the few films to improvise imaginatively on the complicated subject of Nazi occultism. What starts out as a war movie turns into *The Third Reich Rides Out*, with magic circles, a shape-shifting demon from Hell and some entertainingly grisly murders, which one might usefully compare with Doré's illustrations to Dante's *Inferno*. Here, the general spirit of Wheatley's occult Second World War thriller *They Used Dark Forces* (1964) meets the low-budget appeal of Hammer's predominantly performance-led horror films, with Matthew Sunderland and Craig Hall carrying the whole affair with a gravitas worthy of Cushing and Lee. Sunderland plays an SS officer and member of the secret occult society, the Germanenorden. The Nazis have succeeded in raising a shape-shifting demon from Hell to use as a super-weapon against the Allies, but the demon isn't

SS-Circle: Matthew Sunderland and Craig Hall in *The Devil's Rock* (dir. Paul Campion, 2011).

particular as to whom it consumes and has devoured all but Sunderland's SS officer on the secret base in one of the Channel Islands.

We are also informed that Hitler is already in possession of the Spear of Longinus (a myth given spurious credibility by Trevor Ravenscroft's *The Spear of Destiny* [1972]), and very nearly acquired the Ark of the Covenant (but was presumably foiled by Indiana Jones). With the help of a grimoire, which looks as though it has been stained with tea to make it look somewhat unconvincingly much older than it obviously is, the demon is again called up. As in *The Devil Rides Out*, a double-circle is drawn in chalk by the SS officer, who, spattered with his and other men's blood, presides over a ceremony within a triangle rather than the seal of Solomon, the whole protected by candles. Unwittingly involved in these occult goings-on is Hall's commando, who has been sent to the island merely to blow up a gun emplacement. Just as the illusory phantoms of Peggy and Tanith appear to lure Marie and Rex from the magic circle in Wheatley's book, here the demon takes the form of the commando's dead girlfriend, in a failed attempt to lure him away from his magical protection. The demon is unaware that this commando is in possession of the words of a charm from the grimoire, which ultimately saves him. The SS officer is less fortunate.

Chapter Six

Willpower

Mocata's definition of magick in Hammer's *The Devil Rides Out* derives from Crowley's *Magick in Theory and Practice*:

> **Magick**
> **is the Science and Art of causing Change to occur in conformity with Will.**
> (*Illustration*: It is my Will to inform the World of certain facts within my knowledge. I therefore take "magical weapons," pen, ink, and paper; I write "incantations"—these sentences—in the "magical language," i.e., that which is understood by the people I wish to instruct; I call forth "spirits," such as printers, publishers, booksellers, and so forth, and constrain them to convey my message to those people. The composition and distribution of this book is thus an act of
> **Magick**
> by which I cause Changes to take place in conformity with my Will.[1]

Ritual is only one way of focusing this force, and films that aim to explore it do so in a variety of ways. Eyes being the windows of the soul, as well as the principal organ on which film depends, willpower is often shown to be working by means of ocular close-ups, as we often see in Dracula films. To emphasize the hypnotic effect of Dracula's eyes in his 1931 film adaptation, Tod Browning shone two pencil beams into Bela Lugosi's eyes. Unfortunately, these lights did not always meet their mark, revealing that they were projected onto him, rather than emanating from him. Close-ups of Christopher Lee's bloodshot orbs required no such trickery; but the most unnerving and powerful close-ups are really those of Boris Karloff in *The Mummy* (dir. Karl Freund, 1932): His eyes gaze at the viewer with compelling force from their dark, desiccated sockets, like dreadful flowers from a bottomless swamp.

It is the power of the will that makes *The Cabinet of Dr. Caligari* an occult horror film. Caligari is more than just a fairground huckster. He is a magician who, again like Klingsor, is able to compel others to do his bidding by psychic means. Conrad Veidt's Cesare is, like Kundry, a somnambulist, and both are raised from their sleeping states by the power of their evil masters. "Herauf! Herauf! Zu mir!" Klingsor sings at the opening of Act II of *Parsifal*. "Dein Meister ruft dich..." ("Arise, Arise, To me! Your Master calls you.") Wagner's stage direction specifically alludes to the fact that Kundry "seems asleep" and "moves like one awaking." She longs to return to her death-like sleep: "Schlaf.... Schlaf ... tiefer Schlaf.... Tod!" ("Sleep ... sleep ... deepest sleep ... death!"), but Klingsor's will is too strong for her to resist, just as Cesare cannot resist Caligari. Kundry enslaves the Knights of the Grail, but is saved by Parsifal who resists her charms. Cesare is sent to dispatch Caligari's enemies, but manages to avoid murdering the heroine (Lil Dagover) and abducts her instead. The camera is, however, much more interested in Veidt's eyes—staring, black-rimmed portholes of lunacy—than those of Krauss, who plays Caligari, and this is because Cesare's eyes are the conduits of Caligari's will. As the title of Siegfried Kracauer's book *From Caligari to Hitler* suggests, it is appropriate to see the infamous Führer as another kind of magician with a similarly demonic pair of eyes. Dennis Wheatley was unable to resist combining his tried and tested occult formula with Nazism, though *They Used Dark Forces* (his main text on the subject) in fact refers to Hitler's adversaries Gregory Sallust and a Jewish occultist called Malacou, who use black magic in their struggle against the Third Reich. However, as Wheatley's biographer Phil Baker points out, "[E]ven on the cover and blurb, the emphasis has slipped to the Nazis and their involvement with the occult."² Indeed, Wheatley presents Hitler as the Cesare to the Devil's Caligari:

THE EYES HAVE IT: Boris Karloff in *The Mummy* (dir. Karl Freund, 1932).

> The Devil's emissary who, for so many years, possessed by the spirit of Evil, had done his work in the world so well, had, at last, gone to join his Infernal Master.³

Kracauer, while avoiding Wheatley's sensationalism, nonetheless regarded the succession of German films about hypnotic tyrants made during the Weimar Republic as both a prediction and manifestation of the nation's political destiny:

> *Caligari* was too highbrow to become popular in Germany. However, its basic theme—the soul being faced with the seemingly unavoidable alternative of tyranny or chaos—exerted extraordinary fascination. Between 1920 an 1924, numerous German films insistently resumed this theme, elaborating it in various fashions.⁴

Among these, Kracauer mentioned Murnau's *Nosferatu* ("a blood-thirsty, blood-sucking tyrant figure"[5]), Lang's *Dr. Mabuse—der Spieler* ("an unscrupulous mastermind animated by the lust for unlimited power..., Dr. Mabuse hypnotizes his presumptive victims"[6]) and the return of Conrad Veidt in Paul Leni's *Wachsfigurenkabinett* (the title echoes *Caligari's* Cabinet), in which there are three tyrants, initially reduced to wax figures: Harun-al-Rashid, Ivan the Terrible and Jack the Ripper. Kracauer traces a direct line of descent from these films to Leni Riefenstahl's *Triumph des Willens* (*Triumph of the Will*) in 1935. Just the title of this film indicates the importance of willpower, and Riefenstahl's technique amplifies the "magical" qualities that helped to create and sustain the Third Reich's glamor and influence.

> To substantiate this transfiguration of reality, *Triumph of the Will* indulges in emphasizing endless movement. The nervous life of the flames is played upon; the overwhelming effects of a multitude of advancing banners or standards are systematically explored. Movement produced by cinematic techniques sustains that of the objects. There is constant panning, traveling, tilting up and down—so that the spectators not only see passing a feverish world, but feel themselves uprooted in it. The ubiquitous camera forces them to go by way of the most fantastic routes, and editing helps drive them on. [...]
>
> The film also includes pictures of the mass ornaments into which this transported life was pressed at the Convention. Mass ornaments they appeared to Hitler and his staff, who must have appreciated them as configurations *symbolizing the readiness of the masses to be shaped and used at will by their leaders* [italics mine].[7]

Kracauer concludes that *Triumph des Willens* is "the triumph of a nihilistic will. And it is a frightening spectacle to see many an honest, unsuspecting youngster enthusiastically submit to his corruption, and long columns of exalted men march towards the barren realm of this will as though they themselves wanted to pass away."[8] To compare this with the seduction of the Semitic Simon Aron by Mocata in *The Devil Rides Out* might seem trivial (the millions of Jews who suffered at the hands of Hitler were not, after all, mere entertainment), but it is certainly true that history is more often the result of illusion and irrational forces than their opposites. The theater and ritual of Nazi propaganda has often be allied to Wagnerian techniques, and *Parsifal,* with its anti–Semitic subtext disguised by some of the most ravishingly beautiful music ever composed, has been claimed by some as a kind of Black Mass itself. This was certainly the view of Robert W. Gutman, who regarded *Parsifal* as a perversion of the Eucharist, dedicated to a "sinister god." This is debatable if exploring the work purely in its own terms, but interpretation becomes more complex when allied with Wagner's so-called "Regeneration" essays, which he regarded as significant supplements to the ideological program of *Parsifal*:

Wagner ended [his essay] "Know Thyself" ("*Erkenne dich selbst*") of 1881 with a mystically phrased observation; only when his countrymen awakened and ceased party bickering, would there be no more Jews, a "great solution" (*"grosse Lösung"*) he foresaw as uniquely within the reach of the Germans if they could conquer false shame and not shrink from ultimate knowledge (*"nach her Überwindung alter falschen Scham die letzte Erkenntnis nicht zu scheuen"*). *Parsifal* showed the way. The shattering "*Erkenntnis*" that came to the hero in the magic garden would be Wagner's final revelation to his countrymen. "Germany, awake!" ("*Deutschland erwache!*") was the slogan under which Hitler brought the *"grosse Lösung"* to reality.[9]

Parsifal is also about a great deal more than anti–Semitism; it has much to say about compassion, empathy and psychological integration. But the inversion of sacred symbols central to the rituals of black magic can be found in Wagner's final work. Seen from Wagner's perspective, Klingsor is obviously the villain of the piece, and the Christian knights are the heroes. Klingsor is destroyed, as is his presumably Judaic accomplice Kundry, who is troublingly "redeemed" by death. However, viewed from a contrary perspective, the situation might well be reversed. Debussy identified Klingsor as the only "human" character in the work.[10] (His flawed character is consumed by the will to power—a quality that unites us all.) And the Temple of the Grail has indeed been decorated with swastikas in some productions, though Syberberg took a more balanced approach when including a single Nazi flag as one of many other flags through which Parsifal and Gurnemanz must pass on their way to the temple in his 1982 film version of *Parsifal*. There is, after all, a considerable difference between a work of art and its reception history.

It is to be expected that film directors should be enthralled by the charismatic willpower so often exploited by politicians. Crowley believed that magical transformation was the product of "fascination": "This consists almost altogether in distracting the attention, or disturbing the judgment, of the person whom it is wished to deceive." He claimed to have mastered the power of invisibility—a kind of confidence trick rather than an actual method of physically "disappearing." Then he continued (frustratingly without further elucidation), "There are, however, 'real' transformations of the Adept himself which are very useful."[11]

Film is the artform of charisma *par excellence*, persuading us to believe in an illusion. In this sense, it is even more a demonic artform, *par excellence*. It is a necromancer, reviving the long-dead and summoning ghosts. Consisting of no more than shadows, everything about it is unreal, and yet it is somehow so much more convincing than a theater filled with living actors. This was certainly the view of director Thorold Dickinson, who regarded film as "unique, so much more capable of imagination than the theatre, visually speaking."[12]

Conrad Veidt played one of the most infamous examples of daemonic charisma in the title role of *Rasputin Dämon der Frauen* (dir. Adolf Trotz, 1932), though curiously without the dramatic power he lent to Cesare. The overriding impression of Lionel Barrymore in *Rasputin and the Empress* (dir. Richard Boleslawski and Charles Brabin, 1932) is of a lecherous old man; but Rasputin also inspired three rather more compelling evocations of demonic willpower. Christopher Lee, master of the vampiric gaze, starred in *Rasputin the Mad Monk*. Historically, the film is hopelessly inaccurate and, as was the case with Hammer's low-budget attempts to re-create the splendors of ancient Egypt in various damp British sandpits, the atmosphere of Imperial Russia is distinctly unconvincing, particularly with the insertion of a ball scene from another film with more money to spare. But Lee's performance is quite another matter. Director, Don Sharp, who devoted several long close-ups to Lee's evocative eyes, began to feel that his leading man might well have developed a genuine hypnotic power.[13] When Lee was a boy, he was also personally connected, even if only tenuously, with this famous story, having been introduced to Rasputin's assassin, Prince Youssoupoff:

> I was once actually hauled out of bed to meet two men, and shooed downstairs in my dressing-gown, admonished to rub the sleep from my eyes because I would want to remember I'd met them. Well, I do remember them now—Prince Yusupov and the Grand Duke Dmitri Pavlovich—though I was trundled back to bed without being told that they were two of the assassins of Rasputin.[14]

Lee regarded Rasputin as one of the best roles he had been given up to that time, but explained that the film could not show the death scene as they wanted to do it because Youssoupoff, who was still alive in 1966, would never have allowed it.

> Surely it is unique in an actor's life to have met Rasputin's assassins as a boy, to have played the part on screen in 1965, and to have met Rasputin's daughter Maria in 1976 (who said I had his "expression"). Finally, in 1977, I visited the Yusupov palace on the Moika canal in St. Petersburg, and went down to the actual basement room where the murder took place.[15]

There is no suggestion of black magic in *Rasputin the Mad Monk*, despite Rasputin's palatial residence being, in fact, the re-dressed set for *Dracula— Prince of Darkness*, with which it was made back to back; but Rasputin *is* shown to possess mystical healing powers. It is really the strength of Rasputin's will that is the justification for the film, and that is due entirely to Lee's screen charisma. The historical Rasputin insisted, "I myself am a simple man and don't deal in hypnotism,"[16] though Youssoupoff claimed, "Rasputin's hypnotic power was enormous."

> I felt a strength enter me in a warm flow and take hold of my entire being, my body grew numb, and I tried to speak but my tongue would not obey me. Only Rasputin's eyes shone before me—two phosphorescent beams. And then I felt awaken in me the will to resist the hypnosis. I realized I had not let him subordinate my will completely.[17]

Whatever power Rasputin actually had in this area, he was certainly able to achieve results, alleviating, as he did, the Tsarevitch's hemophilia, and consequently exerting a disastrous influence over the Tsarina Alexandra.

If Lee's gaze was the power behind his *Rasputin the Mad Monk* performance, Tom Baker's Rasputin in *Nicholas and Alexandra* (dir. Franklin J. Schaffner, 1971) depended on his mordant sense of humor. When he first meets Alexandra, Baker's Rasputin tells a joke:

> I knew a woman [...] who was so afraid of strangers that she bought herself a pinewood box and lived in it. Then one day, her husband nailed the lid on, dug a hole and dropped her into it. "Ivan, don't," she cried. "I only want to make you happy," he said. "I know, but Heaven's full of strangers. Let me out."

This approach is hardly in Christopher Lee's line. Baker's eyes are also of a very different quality to Lee's imperious gaze. They persuade rather than

RASPUTIN WHO?: Tom Baker as Rasputin in *Nicholas and Alexandra* (dir. Franklin J. Schaffner, 1971).

command, but both manifest the will and its intent to effect change. The legend of Rasputin's prolonged death agonies adds another element of demonic appeal to the story, linking it with vampire mythology—the kind of thing that happens in *Dracula Has Risen From the Grave*. (The customary stake through the heart fails to kill Lee's undead count, because the person who put it there is an atheist.) Similarly, Rasputin's alleged poisoning, multiple shootings and other mutilations at the hands of Youssoupoff and his accomplice suggest there was something otherworldly, even immortal about him; but again, *Nicholas and Alexandra* remains ambivalent on the subject.

Ambivalence was retained in *Harlequin* (dir. Simon Wincer, 1980), a modern-dress version of the Rasputin story starring Robert Powell as Gregory Woolf, whose name echoes Rasputin's first name, Grigory, while also suggesting his character. The high-powered political couple Woolf visits are also suitably called Nick and Sandra Rast ("Rast" is "Tsar" backwards). Their leukemic son is Alex, so it's all rather obvious that he fulfills the role of Tsarevitch Alexei. The film differs from the other two Rasputin films not only in being set in modern-day Australia but also by showing a considerable amount of supernatural phenomena beyond faith-healing. Not all of that can be comfortably explained by means of conjuring or hypnosis: Alex develops the psychic ability to move the marbles of his solitaire board, and at a party he cures an elderly woman of her toothache, a cymbal is made to fly through the air, embedding itself in the wall, and a piano levitates, echoing the famous phenomena caused by the Victorian spiritualist D.D. Home. An image of Woolf's face miraculously appears on a kitchen floor tile, and he even levitates after escaping from prison (a feat that is never explained). But far from being an emissary of the Devil, Woolf ultimately proves to be on the side of the angels. He aims not only to heal the sick child of the Rasts' loveless union but also to convince David Hemming's Nick that the real demonic forces at work are those of the politicians and their spin doctors, who are far greater magicians than Woolf himself. As he puts it himself to the chief *eminence gris*, Doc Wheelan (Broderick Crawford), "Perhaps I should make a grown man vanish at sea," which is exactly what was done to one of Doc's unwanted political rivals.

The ambivalent nature of Woolf's portrayal at first errs on the side of the demonic. He appears as a clown at Alex's birthday party, echoing Damien's birthday party in *The Omen*. Woolf blows up an imaginary balloon and pretends to burst it, at which moment a thunderclap resounds from a gathering cloud. Here, Wincer seems to be referencing the *Night of the Demon* scene in which the Crowley-inspired Satanist, Julian Karswell (Niall MacGinnis), also dressed as a clown, is found entertaining at another children's party. To persuade the ever-skeptical John Holden that his magic is real, Karswell summons a storm. There is no elaborate ritual—just a pinch of the nose and a moment of concentration, and it's done. A storm duly arrives. Later in *Harlequin,* Woolf apparently appears in the form of a bird, echoing the Satanic raven that announces death and disaster in *Damien—Omen II* (dir. Don Taylor and Mike Hodges, 1978). But Alex's explanation that Woolf "came in through the television" also anticipates the form of entry used by the spirits in *Poltergeist* (dir. Tobe Hooper, 1982).

Powell had famously played Christ in Franco Zeffirelli's television series *Jesus of Nazareth* in the 1970s, and so brought a Messianic connotation to his modern-day savior in *Harlequin.* Woolf's costume and makeup signal deliberately unnerving impressions. He wears black nail varnish, and changes from a white to a more a stylized grey robe, the combined effect of which blends Satanic transvestitism in the manner of Hermann Göring, and with more traditional monastic associations, anticipating the Jedi of *Star Wars.* He also appears in everyday casual dress and, on other occasions, camp leathers with decorated eyebrows. Again, eyes are shown to be emissaries of the will. When Woolf and Alex amuse themselves by unnerving a security guard, they hum together in the back seat of a car, and cause the windscreen to shatter. The camera accordingly zooms into their eyes during this exercise of applied Magick.

Rasputin's scandalous exploits with women (his daughter claims his fully erect penis was 13 inches long[18]) is also echoed by the film. Woolf wills a housemaid to strip naked before him and his influence over her causes her to fall on her knees before him, just as Janet Suzman's Alexandra does before Tom Baker's Rasputin. Rasputin's infamous death is also updated. Woolf knows that he will be assassinated, but nonetheless attempts at the last moment to persuade Nick to forswear the forces of political evil. He fails and is shot. Appearing to be dead, he revives only to be shot again with an M16 rifle wielded by a security guard. Modern weapons cannot disguise the historical allusion. The final image of the film suggests that Alex has absorbed Woolf's personality: his eyebrows, arches of the will's temple, are similarly decorated.

Rasputin also informed Archie Mayo's 1931 Warner Brothers' adaptation of George du Maurier's novel *Trilby,* which carried the much more exciting title of its evil protagonist, *Svengali.* Made in the same year that Universal released Bela Lugosi's *Dracula,* it starred John Barrymore in the title role, and the two performances reward close comparison. Both had their hypnotic eyes enhanced by pencil spotlights, Barrymore's hitting the mark more consistently than in Lugosi's case, it has to be said. Indeed, as an evocation of

SVENGALI **John Barrymore in the title role of** *Svengali* **(dir. Archie Mayo, 1931).**

the power of will to effect change, Barrymore's performance is even more impressive than Lugosi's. True, he lacks the sinister intonation of Lugosi's elongated vowels, but this is more than compensated for by the incredible effect of his visual impact. Foreshadowing the blood-red contact lenses that were to be increasingly exploited by Christopher Lee's makeup artists in successive Hammer Dracula films, not to mention the blank white orbs of the resurrected dead in Terence Fisher's *The Earth Dies Screaming* (1964) and Gilling's *The Plague of the Zombies*, Barrymore also wears lenses which, together with the pencil spotlights and atmospheric backlighting, create a truly otherworldly impression. Svengali is later presented sitting down, with the shadow of a stuffed bird (surely echoing Poe's Raven) behind him. The close-up of him from below creates a sense of Zeus on his throne—or perhaps a demonic version of Abraham Lincoln in the Washington Memorial. When Seth Holt came to direct Hammer's *Taste of Fear* (1961), the corpse of Mr. Appleby (Fred Johnson) was posed in a similar manner. (The shock is so great for Susan Denberg's Peggy Appleby, who thinks her father is still alive, that her wheelchair falls into the swimming pool as she makes her escape.)

But Barrymore is by far the more imposing sedentary nemesis. With his pointed beard, long, greasy hair and bushy eyebrows (all derived from du Maurier's original illustrations for the novel in which he looks even more like Pan), he is a combination of that pagan god, Eisenstein's Ivan the Terrible, Rasputin and Mephistopheles.

The film's most impressive demonstration of willpower occurs midway, when a sweeping outward zoom takes us away from Svengali's blank, staring eyes, through the window of his room and out, far across the roofs of Paris. The sound of wind on the soundtrack suggests the power of his will as it seeks out Trilby, asleep in her bed far away, but this is no obstacle for Svengali, whose influence awakens her and forces her to visit him. The success his hypnosis has in transforming the tone-deaf Trilby into a famous soprano, the world at her feet and riches in Svengali's pocket, is indeed a kind of Pygmalion story, but the manner in which all this is presented suggests the kind of black magic we encounter in more overtly occult entertainments. A later hypnosis sequence would not have been out of place in a Dennis Wheatley adaptation: Svengali's face is plunged in dark shadow and his eyes are again illuminated. Lugosi's Dracula never looked so positively Satanic as this.

Du Maurier himself was very much a part of the esthetic movement at the turn of the nineteenth century. (*Trilby* appeared in 1894, only three years before Stoker's *Dracula*.) The character of the artist Joe Sibley was said to have been based on both James McNeill Whistler, whose dictum of "Art for Art's Sake" as represented by his *Nocturne in Black and Gold—The Falling Rocket*, caused critic John Ruskin to accuse him of flinging a pot of paint in the public's face. On the continent at this time, particularly in Paris where *Trilby* is set, Symbolist artists were challenging the Impressionists, and the Decadent movement was oxymoronically gaining strength. A pertinent visual reference to this esthetic is suggested towards the end of *Svengali,* when the almost somnambulistic Trilby, now a celebrated diva, adorned in tiara, jewels and fur, awaits her sinister Pygmalion in a coach. Her passive, doll-like face, framed with such delicate extravagances, brings to mind the work of the Belgian symbolist artist Fernand Khnopff, who regularly exhibited in Paris—particularly his 1900 pastel "The Silver Tiara."

Du Maurier's portrayal of Svengali has been justly criticized as an anti–Semitic parody, a quality Barrymore tones down; in fact, his pathos inspires a degree of sympathy with the character. But there is no doubt that Svengali is both Jewish and malevolent. Du Maurier creates a powerful stereotype here:

> He would either fawn or bully, and could be grossly impertinent. He had a kind of cynical humour, which was more offensive than amusing, and always laughed at the

wrong thing, at the wrong time, in the wrong place. And his laughter was always derisive and full of malice. And his egotism and conceit were not to be borne; and then he was both tawdry and dirty in his person; more greasily, mutedly unkempt than even a really successful pianist has any right to be even in the best society.[19]

Svengali is also quite able to smarten himself up when he has the money, but despite the fur-collared coats, evening dress and theatrical conducting-costume, he never manages to assimilate himself into society. He is forever the untrustworthy, demonic outsider.

The year 1931 was a bad time to be a European Jew. Hitler was appointed German chancellor two years later, and in this context, *Svengali* acquires extra significance, especially when compared to the infamously appalling Nazi blockbuster *Jud Süss* (1940). Director Veit Harlan's film is a sophisticated production, performed with panache and with high production values, both of which are used to promote its unsavory anti–Semitic message. It is based on the eighteenth-century historical figure Süss Oppenheimer, the treasurer of the Duke of Wurtemburg. Süss corrupts the duke and brings the community into civil conflict. Not all versions of this story are anti–Semitic. Leon Feuchwanger's novel of the same name definitely was not. Neither was the English film version starring Conrad Veidt in the title role. But Joseph Goebbels insisted that the story be interpreted along Nazi Party lines. Thus, in Harlan's film, Süss is finally hanged in a spectacularly barbaric dénouement, and the audience is assured that this is the right and proper outcome not just for Oppenheimer but for all Jews. Ferdinand Marien's performance as Süss is a remarkably powerful interpretation. He was forced against his better judgment into playing the role by Goebbels; it damaged his subsequent career and may have contributed to his early death in a car accident, which has often been interpreted as suicide. His Süss begins as a sinister, very still and silky moneylender. He later shaves off his beard, side ringlets and caftan and assimilates himself into high society rather more successfully than Svengali; this also had its propaganda point: Jews, like vampires, might seem "normal," but this, the film argues, is where they are most "dangerous." With raised eyebrow and steady gaze, Marien's Süss obviously continues the Svengali stereotype, if less melodramatically. Süss uses his will just as much as Svengali to achieve his aims. He corrupts, flatters and exploits the innocent in every way but an overtly supernatural one. Nonetheless, an occult mood hovers over Harlan's film.

A similar continuum operates in Riefenstahl's *Triumph des Willens,* in which ritual and willpower combine in an explosive manner. This account of the 1935 Nazi Party Rally at Nuremberg not only presented Hitler as a kind of Wotan, descending from the clouds at the beginning of the film as he flies to the capital of "old" Germany, but also contains one of the strangest sequences in any propaganda film, which today indeed looks like the arcane ceremony of a magical cult. The sequence in question concerns the assembled 52,000 workmen who carry spades rather than rifles; and in the almost hypnotized ecstasy of their antiphonal responses to one another, they are far more unnerving than the film's other scenes of geometric military might.

"Here we stand," they chant. "We are ready to carry Germany into a new era. GERMANY!"

A close-up of an individual follows.

"Comrade," he asks, "where are you from?"

The comrade replies with a slow movement of his head to the right, a gesture so often used in horror films to suggest some form of controlled malevolence, but here, presumably, intended to be almost beatific. The fanatical comrade, profoundly expressive of "Sehnsucht" or "yearning," which the Nazis so ruthlessly hijacked from Romanticism, replies, "From Friesland."

And thus the interchange continues with others from Bavaria, Kaiserstuhl, Pomerania, Königsberg, Silesia: "From the coast; from the Black Forest; from Dresden; from the Danube; from the Rhine, and from the Saar."

That this list finishes with a conjunction suggests that the whole thing has been carefully scripted and stage-managed as a kind of chorus, seemingly with nothing spontaneous about it. The rhythms of the words have all been carefully considered, leading up to the infamous exclamation of "One people, One Führer, One Reich, One Germany!" Riefenstahl makes sure that one of her most imposing shots of Hitler, photographed from below to emphasize his godlike status, accompanies the words, "One Führer." Hitler poses thoughtfully, perceived by his devotees as His Messianic Majesty. He is also presented in slightly softer focus than the workmen, with the light behind him, casting his face somewhat in shadow, thus deifying him further.

The occult mood increases as the men describe their work. "We are all at work together," exclaims the wide-eyed fanatic. And a stichomythic exchange between individuals and the chorus, as in a Greek tragedy, ensues:

SOLO: And we in the furnaces.
CHORUS: In the furnaces.
SOLO: And we in the quarries.
CHORUS: In the quarries.
SOLO: We are reclaiming the North Sea.
SOLO: We are planting trees.
SOLO: We are building roads.
CHORUS: From village to village. From town to town…

They then break out into a marching song, after which flags are lowered to symbolize the fallen of the First World War; but presently these flags are raised aloft, their swastika symbols fluttering like Frankenstein Monsters imbued with sinister life. The chorus leader exclaims, "You are not dead. You are alive. You are Germany!" and Riefenstahl again inserts her brooding shot of the Führer. The sequence is endlessly fascinating and seems to form the core experience of the film as a whole. Here indeed is the Triumph of the Will, which can even overcome death. It is a kind of Black Mass offered up to a secular devil, who was regarded at the time as a Wagnerian god, his power generated by ritual.

Crowley explained the power of ritual in *Magick in Theory and Practice*:

> There is a single main definition of the object of all magical ritual. It is the uniting of the Microcosm with the Macrocosm. The Supreme and Complete ritual is therefore the Invocation of the Holy Guardian Angel; or, in the language of Mysticism, Union with God.[20]

Regardless of one's metaphysical beliefs (or lack of them), it is possible to make an analogy with Nazi ritual here, the German people being the Macrocosm, seeking union with the *person* of Hitler, the Microcosm. On an individual level, the process might be reverse: the microcosmic German citizen seeking union with the macrocosmic Nazi gods. To achieve this, "magickal" ritual served the Nazis well. Without such displays as the Nuremberg rallies, the propaganda films of Riefenstahl and the skillful use of propaganda, such a union would never have been achieved in the way it was. Crowley, no friend of democracy himself, regarded the Weimar Republic as the product of a misuse of magical principles. *Magick in Theory and Practice* was published in 1924, before Hitler's rise to power, but his comments on the magical nature of politics now seem prescient:

> One must find out for oneself, and make sure beyond doubt, *who* one is, *what* one is. This done, one may put the Will which is implicit in the "why" into words, or rather into One Word. Being thus conscious of the proper course to pursue, the next thing is to understand the conditions necessary to following it out. After that, one must eliminate from oneself every element alien or hostile to success, and develop those parts of oneself which are specially needed to control the aforesaid conditions.
>
> Let us make an analogy. A nation must become aware of its own character before it can be said to exist. From that knowledge it must divine its destiny. It must then consider the political conditions of the world; how other countries may help it or hinder it. It must then destroy in itself any elements discordant with its destiny. Lastly, it must develop in itself those qualities which will enable it to combat successfully the external conditions which threaten to oppose its purpose. We have had a recent example in the case of the young German Empire, which, knowing itself and its Will, disciplined and trained itself so that it conquered the neighbours which had oppressed it for so many centuries. But after 1866 and 1870, 1914! It mistook itself for superhuman, it willed a

thing impossible, it failed to eliminate its own internal jealousies, it failed to understand the conditions of victory, it did not train itself to hold the sea; and thus, having violated every principle of

MAGICK

it was pulled down and broken into pieces by provincialism and democracy, so that neither individual excellence nor civic virtue has yet availed to raise it again to that majestic unity which made so bold a bid for the mastery of the race of the man.[21]

There are many true and apocryphal stories about Crowley's involvement in military intelligence against Hitler during the Second World War—that he suggested the "V" for Victory sign to Churchill as a magical symbol to counteract the swastika, that he worked for Ian Fleming, that he falsified Hitler's astrological birth charts, etc.; but there is little doubt that he also understood the "magickal" aspect of Nazi ritual and propaganda. Even if one perhaps sensibly strips away the literal and metaphysical, one is still left with the psychological reality of effecting change by means of the will. Despite Riefenstahl's insistence that *Triumph des Willens* was a prayer for hope and peace, it is hard to see, in the cult-like trance of its participants and effect on German audiences, that anything other than the triumph of the will-to-power was being expressed.

Science fiction films have also explored the demonic aspect of the will. Eyes, once again, are the chosen medium. In *Village of the Damned,* the eyes of the Midwich Cuckoos literally glow with malevolent intent, demonstrating, at least within the context of the film, that looks really can kill. *Village of the Damned* is also a modern reworking of the ancient incubus myth, which might be explained in psychological terms as an expression of the fear of parenthood we also encounter in films such as *Rosemary's Baby* (dir. Roman Polanski, 1968), *I Don't Want to Be Born* (dir. Peter Sasdy, 1975), *Demon Seed* (dir. Donald Cammell, 1977), *Eraserhead* (dir. David Lynch, 1977) and *Alien* (dir. Ridley Scott, 1979). Impregnation, reproduction, gestation and birth are all potentially—if not inherently—horrifying. No mother knows exactly what kind of creature will emerge from her womb. A deformed baby, or even a perfectly normal one rejected for various reasons by a mother, can provide the basis for all manner of horrors. (Birth under any circumstances is a traumatic experience for the baby at least, which is, after all, born crying. Martin Heidegger's sense of our being "thrown into the world" reminds us that no one gives their consent to be born.)

Crowley also experimented with the idea of magickal birth in his 1923 novel *Moonchild,* though in that case the creation of a homunculus imbued with a lunar spirit is not treated as a horror story but rather as a manifestation of occult eugenics:

> He imagined his desired Moon-soul, afloat in space, vehemently spurred towards the choir of sympathetic intelligences whom it could hardly fail to perceive, by reason of the intensity of the concentration of the magical forces of the operators upon the human idea.[22]

Moonchild has yet to be filmed, though some of its themes did find their way into the screenplay of Julian Doyle's 1998 film *Chemical Wedding* (see below). Much earlier, however, Otto Rippert's film serial *Homunculus* combined the disturbing proto-Nazi ideals of artificial insemination and the triumph of the will. Lotte H. Eisner described the character of Homunculus as "a kind of Führer" who can "split his personality at will."[23] As one might expect, Kracauer goes even further, arguing, "[T]he film foreshadows Hitler surprisingly. Obsessed by hatred, Homunculus makes himself the dictator of a large country, and then sets out to take unheard-of revenge for his sufferings. Disguised as a worker, he incites riots which give him, the dictator, an opportunity to crush the masses ruthlessly." Homunculus is finally dispatched by a bolt of lightning, reversing the process that brought Frankenstein's creation to life many years before. Kracauer also draws a parallel between this film's immense popularity during the First World War and the lectures given by German philosopher Max Scheler around the same time, which attempted to explain why Germany was so hated across the world:

> The Germans resembled Homunculus: they themselves had an inferiority complex, due to an historic development which proved detrimental to the self-confidence of the middle class. Unlike the English and the French, the Germans had failed to achieve their revolution and, in consequence, never succeeded in establishing a truly democratic society.[24]

Under these circumstances, it was perhaps inevitable that a triumph of the will was necessary to compensate for such psychological insecurity. Fritz Lang's films concerning the master criminal Dr. Mabuse continued this approach.

Demonic will, coupled with monstrous birth, forms a trope in many occult fantasies. In *The Omen*, Damien, born of a jackal, develops a truly demonic will, which is able to murder or inspire suicide at a glance, like the Midwich Cuckoos before him. Whereas the Midwich horrors force a villager to turn a shotgun on himself, Damien persuades his nanny to hang herself from the bedroom window during his birthday party. But the murders that propel the narrative are mere milestones on his path to mastery. "What is good?" asks Friedrich Nietzsche in his book *The Antichrist*. "All that heightens the feeling of power the will to power, power itself in man."

> What is bad?—All that proceeds from weakness.
> What is happiness?—The feeling that power *increases*—that a resistance is overcome.[25]

Nietzsche's consequent assault on Christianity, which he perceived as exactly the kind of weakness he laments here, was certainly not a form of Satanism: The title of the book is ironic, but it is also quite specific in its opposition to Christianity as an idea. However, the Antichrist of *The Omen* is just as much in pursuit of power as anyone else, even though Damien's means to that end are rather more spectacular and successful than they are for the rest of us. Nietzsche anyway regarded murder as a particularly crude manifestation of the will-to-power, which is put to much better use through sublimation. In fact, he regarded the most powerful people to be those who lived by themselves, uninterested in exerting power over anyone, so complete is their mastery over themselves; but such people would have made a much less exciting film. For Crowley, "Everything's a magical phenomenon, in the long run. But war's magic, from the word jump."[26] If human activity is the product of will, and magick is "merely" the application of enhanced will to achieve non-causal change, he might well have been right.

Evocations of pure will naturally require some form of symbolism. In "Ligeia," Poe claimed to be quoting lines by Joseph Glanvill:

> And the Will therein lieth which dieth not. Who knoweth the mysteries of the will with its vigour? For God is but a great will pervading all things by nature of its intentness. Man doth not yield himself unto the angels, nor unto death utterly, save only through the weakness of his feeble will.

When Roger Corman adapted the story for *The Tomb of Ligeia*, he employed a black cat to suggest Ligeia's vengeful will as it prepares to inhabit the body of Lady Rowena, Ligeia's successor. Similarly, in Hitchcock's *Rebecca* (1940), the powerful will of the absent, because deceased, Mrs. De Winter is evoked not only through Mrs. Danvers, her devoted housekeeper, but even more through Manderley, the house Rebecca once inhabited, and seemingly still does in another form. In Freddie Francis' *The Skull* (1965), Hitchcock's ideal of "pure cinema" is approached to evoke the apparently demonic will of the Marquis de Sade, which lives on in his skull. Unlike *The Omen* and *Village of the Damned*, the protagonist of *The Skull* is unseen throughout, though *symbolized* by the Skull itself. Francis emphasizes this symbolism by occasionally placing the camera behind an enlarged model of the skull's eye sockets, effectively shooting scenes from the Skull's point of view. The ghastly relic even levitates a biography of itself, bound in human skin. (This latter detail is oddly reminiscent of the edition of Hitler's *Mein Kampf*, apparently bound in human skin, which Himmler had presented to his mistress Hedwig Potthast. Certainly the Sadean-occult context of the film echoes that of the Third Reich.[27]) The Skull compels its new owner, Prof. Maitland (Peter Cushing), to steal the statue of a demon. It subsequently places itself and the statue inside a pentagram. It glows in the dark and floats around Maitland's home, its obsessive nature enhanced by Elisabeth Lutyens' ostinati patterns, which characterize the single-minded purpose of its murderous spirit.

Occult fantasy usually regards the will as an independent force, able to inhabit, unchanged, different hosts. In *The Witches*, Stephanie Bax (Kay Walsh) aims to transplant her own soul into the body of a much younger girl, Linda Rigg (Ingrid Boulting), but the ceremony is interrupted by Joan Fontaine's school mistress Gwen Mayfield, and Stephanie dies before she is able to enact the required ritual sacrifice. Stephanie does, however, have time to explain her plans to Miss Mayfield:

> All my life I have tried to push my brain to the limit; to get all the ideas and the reach out of it and put them at the service of mankind. [...] Only now, that the end of my life is in sight, do I feel that I am really learning. If only I could live a second lifetime, or just another 50 years—oh, the things I could do for the world.

Showing Gwen an antique grimoire, she recites her translation of the magical rhyme it contains:

> Grow me a gown
> With golden down
> Cut me a robe
> From toe to lobe
> Give me a skin
> For dancing in.

The implication here is that everyone is merely a skin for the will to "dance" in. This is somewhat different from a Faustian pact to gain extra time, or the portrait of Dorian Gray, which takes upon itself the burden of the years. In *The Mephisto Waltz* (dir. Paul Wendkos, 1971), a world-famous concert pianist, Duncan Ely (Curt Jurgens), is dying and aims, like Stephanie Bax, to preserve his genius by transferring his soul into the body of music journalist Myles Clarkson (Alan Alda). Ely remarks that Clarkson has "Rachmaninoff hands," but the Rachmaninoff reference seems inappropriate, as Jerry Goldsmith's elaborate *Mephisto Waltz* soundtrack is entirely structured around Franz Liszt's famous warhorse of that name, which is also the arrogant and insufferable Ely's party-piece. Goldsmith virtually reinvents the work by filtering it through a series of avant-garde techniques, such as the use of dramatic string glissandi and tone clusters associated with composers Krzysztof Penderecki and Witold Lutosławski, as well as electronic instruments and other special effects. He also often distorts the sound by means of reverberation, or even playing the music backwards during the mixing process. *The Mephisto Waltz* was released two years before *The Exorcist* and five years before *The Omen*, for which Goldsmith won an Oscar for Best Score, a highly unusual achievement for a horror film. Goldsmith's *Mephisto Waltz* score was therefore among the first to ally such extreme avant-garde techniques with the emerging new wave of occult shockers with which I will be dealing in Chapter Eight.

Because the score plays such an integral part in this film, it is useful to explore it a little more. The main title introduces the initial open fifths of Liszt's piece and juxtaposes them with the celebrated medieval "Dies Irae" chant, which is first presented by ecclesiastic tubular bells against a disorientating string glissando. Berlioz had first demonized the "Dies Irae" in the final movement of his *Symphonie fantastique* of 1831. Before then, this plainchant sequence had none of the Romantic terror with which Berlioz invested it. Subsequently, however, the opening four notes of the "Dies Irae" chant increasingly became a kind of musical shorthand for the demonic.

When Myles becomes Duncan Ely, he also becomes more amorous, as do the dancers in Nikolaus Lenau's poem (the inspiration of Liszt's piece) when under the influence of the Devil's music. Liszt's "amoroso" section is hence the perfect accompaniment to such a transformation. So too is the repeated use of the "Dies Irae," which is either played by bells or punctuated by bells during Duncan's funeral (a ceremony replete with decadent peacock feathers, a grandiose casket and sinister mourners). It also accompanies the various nightmare dream sequences and the grisly deaths yet to come. None of this musical symbolism would have been possible without Berlioz's demonization of the "Dies Irae" and the Romantic cult of the Mephistophelean hero, which Liszt's piece celebrates.

The film's occult premise could be taken as a metaphor for how unpleasant highly successful people in the world of the arts can be. The various party scenes demonstrate all too realistically the kind of sniping indulged in by the *cognoscenti*, regardless of the fact that, here, they are all Devil worshippers as well. Such a hothouse atmosphere is nothing if not willful, and in Fred Mustard Stewart's original novel, Ely has the *Sadducismus Triumphatus* of Joseph Glanvill on his library shelves,[28] to remind the reader of Poe's attribution of the opening quotation of "Ligeia" to Glanvill, even though Poe more than probably made it up himself. Stewart's novel is a musical update of "Ligeia," with the added twist at the end that Clarkson's wife, realizing what has happened to her husband, decides to repeat the ritual and transplant her own soul into the body of Ely's Satanic daughter, with whom Ely, in Myles' body hopes to continue his incestuous relations.

> She didn't believe in transmigration of souls, but she had to admit to herself that Myles had somehow become Duncan Ely on the night Ely had died, almost as if Ely's soul had entered Myles' body. That was the only logical explanation of the "new" Myles

whose personal habits were so strangely different, whose memory was so strangely bad, whose sexuality was suddenly triple forte and who could play the most difficult pieces in the piano repertoire like a seasoned master.

But of course, that wasn't a logical explanation. It was a completely illogical explanation.[29]

This process also provides the basis for Bram Stoker's 1903 *The Jewel of Seven Stars*, an ancient Egyptian variation on "Ligeia" in which the spirit of an ancient Egyptian queen takes over the daughter of an Edwardian archaeologist who has discovered her tomb. The story has been thrice filmed; Hammer's updated adaptation *Blood from the Mummy's Tomb* (dir. Seth Holt and Michael Carerras, 1971) is the most successful. Here, the name of the queen becomes Tera, and an occult ceremony is necessary to make the transference of her soul into the body of Margaret Fuchs (Valerie Leon) complete. Christopher Wicking's screenplay makes quite clear the element played by willpower in this process of reincarnation: "She would lie as if dead in her coffin," says Mark Edwards' Tod Browning, as he reads from Prof. Fuchs' research notes, "willing her body into some abstract metaphysical state." Tera's will grows stronger throughout the course of the story and ultimately appears to have triumphed over the body of her identical host, though some ambiguity remains in the final shot: Is it Margaret or Tera's eyes staring out through the hospital bandages? Whichever it is, the will behind them is trapped, and the staring eyes of Margaret-Tera provide an ironic response to Karl Freund's overwhelming close-ups of Karloff's Imhotep. The ambivalent nature of magick itself is also reflected in Tera's observation that good things are "useless without their opposites."

A similar process, though achieved in a quite different manner, occurs in *Chemical Wedding*, in which the personality of Aleister Crowley usurps the body of Simon Callow's Dr. Oliver Haddo, a university academic whose mother must presumably have been reading Somerset Maugham during her pregnancy. But there are non-genre films which also explore the nature of the will and the magical process of artistic creativity. Among these is Cocteau's *Orphée*, in which he brilliantly symbolizes the process of poetic inspiration by having Orphée (Jean Marais) tune into abstract messages on a car radio. Communication, according to Crowley, is a magical act in itself:

> It is my Will to inform the World of certain facts within my knowledge. I therefore take "magical weapons," pen, ink, and paper; I write "incantations"—these sentences—in the "magical language," i.e., that which is understood by the people I wish to instruct; I call forth "spirits," such as printers, publishers, booksellers, and so forth, and contain them to convey my message to those people. The composition and distribution of this book is thus as act of
> **MAGICK**
> by which I cause Changes to take place in conformity with my Will.[30]

The ultimate cinematic expression of this process might well be Jack Gold's *The Medusa Touch* (1978), in which Richard Burton plays a writer and ex-barrister with the power to will catastrophes simply by thinking about them. The presence of Lee Remick as his psychiatrist (who eventually attempts to murder him) helps to connect this film with *The Omen*, in which she also starred. (Michael J. Lewis' score with its ostinati is also reminiscent of Jerry Goldsmith's *Omen* music.) *The Medusa Touch* is, indeed, a kind of remake of *The Omen*, being a series of will-induced murders and catastrophes, but with rather more to say about the nature of evil and humanity. Burton's character, John Morlar, attacks the hypocrisy of the establishment, its injustice and violence, its wars and institutions; but he begins with the unloving authority of his nurse and parents, all of whom he wills to their destruction. He prays to the Devil to finish off his ghastly Irish nanny (just as Damien will do to his), and causes a car to push his parents over a cliff. Throughout the film, Gold inserts close-ups of the boy's (and later Burton's) eyes to indicate the source of this power: Morlar's indomitable will, which survives brain damage and, perhaps like Ligeia, even death.

In Morlar's diaries, the police detective assigned to investigating his murder reads: "The Walls of Jericho fell to the power of thought, so what is the meaning of impossibility?" Utlimately, Morlar causes the walls of a great cathedral to fall on the assembled multitudes of the church and state, but not before he has dispatched his schoolmaster (willing the immolation of Hammer Films' favorite location of Oakley Court, which stands in for his school), encouraged a complaining neighbor to throw herself out of the window, induced a heart attack in the judge who overrode his defense of a client, traumatized a genial palmist (Michael Hordern), caused his unfaithful wife to be killed in a car crash, and demonstrated his magickally destructive ability to his skeptical psychiatrist, make an airplane fall from the sky and crash into a tower block, in an astonishing premonition of 9/11. "We're all the Devil's children," he insists. "We find out what powers the sun and we make bombs of it. We create wealth and we become obsessed with greed. We achieve power and we go mad. We always destroy." It is indeed a fairly accurate portrait of the human species, regardless of magick.

Chapter Seven

Return of the Magi

So far, we have encountered Klingsor, a wicked magician created by a musical wizard, and seen how Crowley inspired a host of cinematic Satanists. The figure of the magus is somewhat more complex, however: He is more ambivalent and has his roots in the arcane symbolism of tarot. The original French name for the first of the 22 tarot trumps is "Le Bateleur" or "The Juggler," and later packs have renamed this "The Magus." As Richard Cavendish explains, referring to the *fin de siècle* French occultist Gérard Encausse (Papus), this card is a symbol of "creative power, will and intelligence."[1] The characteristic gesture of the Magus shows one hand pointing to the heavens and the other towards the earth:

> "Man with one hand seeks for God in heaven," Papus said, "with the other he plunges below, to call up the demon to himself, and thus unites the divine and the diabolic in humanity."
>
> The conclusion can be drawn, though not everyone would draw it, that man, made in the image of God, potentially is God: that God is man raised to his highest power.[2]

Cavendish also explained,

> because the Juggler unites the divine and the diabolic, and is shown in the old packs as a trickster, there are sinister possibilities in the card. The Juggler has all the confident strength, determination and self-centredness of youth setting out to master the world, using his body and his will and intelligence as weapons. He can be egotistical, brutal and ruthless, abusing his powers for his own selfish ends. The magician can be a black magician. Evil, as well as good, has its root in the divine.[3]

This is the key to understanding the appeal of the magus figure in popular culture: His ambivalence is the source of his fascination. The magus can be found across a range of genres, from science fiction–fantasy and crime detection, to mythology and spy drama. The long-running appeal of the BBC television series *Doctor Who* is largely due to the magical aspects of the Doctor's nature. With his sonic screwdriver (an updated wand) and his ability to travel through time, he is portrayed as the heroic opposite of his own shadow: The Master. (In the *Ring* cycle, Wagner similarly has Wotan refer to himself as "Licht-Alberich": the benevolent aspect of "Schwarz-Alberich," the evil dwarf who is the villain of the piece.) This magus aspect of the Doctor is unfortunately entirely absent from Peter Cushing's two attempts at the role for the big-screen, in what are perhaps his least successful performances. This at first seems unexpected from an actor who made so many horror films, but on closer analysis, one realizes that Cushing excelled in the application of reason even when dealing with the highly unreasonable. There was little that was mystical about his interpretations even when fighting the supernatural forces of evil or reveling in the appliance of science. Fighting a vampire for Cushing's Van Helsing is always a matter of fact, not belief or magic, just as building a creature when playing Frankenstein was, with the exception of *Frankenstein Created Woman*, more a matter of materialism than mysticism. (Even the soul in that latter film is dealt with as an object rather than a mystical force.)

During his tenure of the role on television during the 1970s, Tom Baker's Doctor Who was but one aspect of the occult revival that pervaded British culture in that decade, and it is significant that he was awarded the role largely on the strength his appearance as the black magician Koura in *The Golden Voyage of Sinbad* (dir. Gordon Hessler, 1973). Baker's expressive eyes were frequently shown to be channeling the magical will of this magician. This, together with his earlier role as Rasputin in *Nicholas and Alexandra*, confirmed his ability to create the magickal ambivalence required of a magus.

In *Star Wars*, the magus figure of Obi-Wan Kenobi (Alec Guinness) is also aware of this interdependence, and understands the ambivalent nature of The Force: "It's an energy field created by all living things. It surrounds us and penetrates us and binds the galaxy together." Control of the Force depends, like any other kind of magick, on the correct application of the will ("Feel the Force"). As with magick, how the Force is applied can work for good or evil. Crowley had in fact defined the now-famous *Star Wars* Force long before, in *Book Four*. "Every intentional act is a Magical Act," he explained. "By 'intentional' I mean 'willed.'" Magickal force is, according to this view, no different in its application from any other kind of force, and can fail if inappropriately employed:

> There may be failure to apply the right kind of force, as when a rustic tries to blow out an electric light. There may be failure to apply the right degree of force, as when a wrestler has his hold broken. There may be a failure to apply the force in the right manner, as when one presents a cheque at the wrong window of the bank. There may be a failure to imply the correct medium, as when Leonardo da Vinci found his masterpiece fade away. The force may be applied to an unsuitable object when one tries to crack a stone, thinking it a nut.[4]

One year before the release of *Star Wars*, Gerry Anderson's TV series *Space: 1999* had also experimented with the magus figure. In "New Adam New Eve" (dir. Charles Crichton, 1976), Guy Rolfe plays a cosmic magician who actually calls himself "Magus." A crystal embedded in his brain allows him to convert the sun's energy into immense psychic force. In the past he has been Simon Magus, who attempted to buy supernatural power from the apostles Peter and John. He has also been Merlin and Nostradamus and the Magician who contended with Moses in Egypt. He offers the inhabitants of Moonbase Alpha a new Garden of Eden. Like a kind of mystical zookeeper, he selects four of them and pairs them off. His previous attempts at playing God have resulted in hideous mutants who long for death but whom he will not permit to die. In this, he resembles the mad scientist in H.G. Wells' story *The Island of Dr. Moreau*. We might thus also claim Charles Laughton's performance of Dr. Moreau in 1932's *Island of Lost Souls*, not only as a premonition of the terrible medical experiments that were soon to take place in Nazi Germany, but also as another manifestation of the magus figure, for Laughton's Moreau has performed the ultimate conjuring trick:

FÜHRER OF LOST SOULS: Charles Laughton as Dr. Moreau stares us down past Richard Arlen and Kathleen Burke in *Island of Lost Souls* (dir. Erle C. Kenton, 1932).

> I started with plant life in London 20 years ago. I took an orchid and upon it I performed a miracle. I stripped 100,000 years of slow evolution from it and I had no longer an orchid—what orchids will be in 100,000 years from now.

And now he has applied the same approach to animals, out of which he has created hybrid Beast Men, the lost souls of the film's title. "Do you know what it means to feel like God?" he asks, his face eerily up-lit. But eventually his creations cease to believe in this god of vivisection. His question "What is the Law?" is no longer answered as he had previously commanded. The Beast Men take the law into their own hands. "Do What Thou Wilt Shall be the Whole of the Law" is now their credo, but without Crowley's important but often overlooked qualification, "Love is the Law, Love under Will." Moreau is, indeed, a mirror image of Crowley.

In the very different world of crime detection, the Magus qualities of Sherlock Holmes, particularly in the romantic interpretation of him by Jeremy Brett in the Granada television series, elevate his character from mere logician to a mystic (again, a quality that is entirely absent in Cushing's interpretation of the role in both Terence Fisher's *The Hound of the Baskervilles* [1959] and in his TV performances of the role). There is also an element of the demonic about him, for Holmes is, after all, a drug addict, and his entire existence is dependent upon crime. He loathes the mundane nature of existence. He requires what he opposes to give his life meaning. Brett was keen to capitalize on the mystical nature of the character, as, for example, in his poetic delivery of lines when contemplating a red moss rose in "The Naval Treaty" (dir. Alan Grint, 1984):

> "There is nothing in which deduction is so necessary as in religion," said he, leaning with his back against the shutters. "It can be built up as an exact science by reason. Our highest assurance of the goodness of Providence seems to me to rest in the flowers. All other things, our powers, our desires, our food, are really necessary for our existence in the first instance. But this rose is an extra. Its smell and its colour are an embellishment of life, not a condition of it. It is only goodness which gives extras, and so I say again: we have much to hope for from the flowers."[5]

These curious lines, which also derive from Conan Doyle's own longstanding interest in mysticism, have a direct reference to what Arthur Edmund Waite had to say about the Juggler-Magus tarot card. Significantly, they are quoted at the very beginning of John Fowles' 1965 novel *The Magus*:

> On the table in front of the Magus are the symbols of the four Tarot suits, signifying the elements of natural life, which lie like counters before the adept, and he adapts them as he wills. Beneath are roses and lilies, the *flos campi*, and *lilium convallium*, changed into garden flowers to show the culture of aspiration.

Doyle cannot have been referring to Waite's book, which didn't appear until 1911, eight years after "The Naval Treaty" was published. But Doyle, like Waite, was a Freemason with an active interest in the occult, so it is quite possible that Holmes' mystical reverie over the moss rose has some extra significance. Waite's reference to "I am the flower of the field, and the lily of the valleys" from "The Song of Solomon" in *The Bible* suggests not only the marriage of Christ with his spouse, the Church, but also that the path of aspiration is also that of love.

Perhaps the most overt personification in popular culture of the tarot's Magus card appears in Guy Green's 1968 film adaptation of *The Magus*. In this, Anthony Quinn plays the mysterious Maurice Cochis, ostensibly a multimillionaire master of ceremonies on a Greek island, where Michael Caine's selfish schoolteacher, Nicholas Urfe, is subjected to a series of bizarre masques and role-plays to teach him the importance of love over lust, of compassion over selfishness and of the courage to confront life's hazards in the name of freedom. During the surreal trial scene towards the end of the film, Conchis appears in the costume of the Tarot's Magus, wearing the large, floppy hat that Richard Cavendish describes as being shaped like a figure 8 lying on its side. He also wears a robe emblazoned with the signs of the tarot's minor arcana: cups, swords, batons and coins (or in this case pentagrams). He is fully the image of Fowles' "astrologer-magician."[6] Divided into opposing halves of red and white, the robe also symbolizes the opposing elements in the psyche, which must find balance and equilibrium.

The quotation from Waite's *The Key to Tarot*, which opens the novel, begins: "The Magus, Magician, or Juggler, the caster of the dice and mountebank in the world of vulgar trickery." This is a concise description of the role Conchis plays in the story; but, as his name suggests, Conchis is also a personification of Urfe's conscience, as well as a kind of Crowley figure, presiding over miracles, for which Fowles provides rational explanations, without ever fully explaining who Conchis actually is. His symbolic role is obviously what matters, the naturalistic explanations being part of the hoax, as it were. Both the novel and the film inhabit the realm of magical realism, presenting fantastic events in a naturalistic context. In the novel, Conchis refers to himself as Prospero,[7] the magician of Shakespeare's *The Tempest*. Urfe is therefore the equivalent of Caliban, who rages at his own reflection, locked, as he is, in his own corrosive selfishness. Urfe's name, particularly its original French spelling of Urfé, echoes Orpheus (Orphée), and like Orpheus, he too must descend into the underworld to find his own Euridice.

Urfe has rejected the only woman who really loves him (Australian Alison in the book, French Anne, played by Anna Karina, in the film) and loses her, not by looking back (as Orpheus famously did) but by *going* back to Conchis' island where he has become infatuated with Julie (Candice Bergen), an

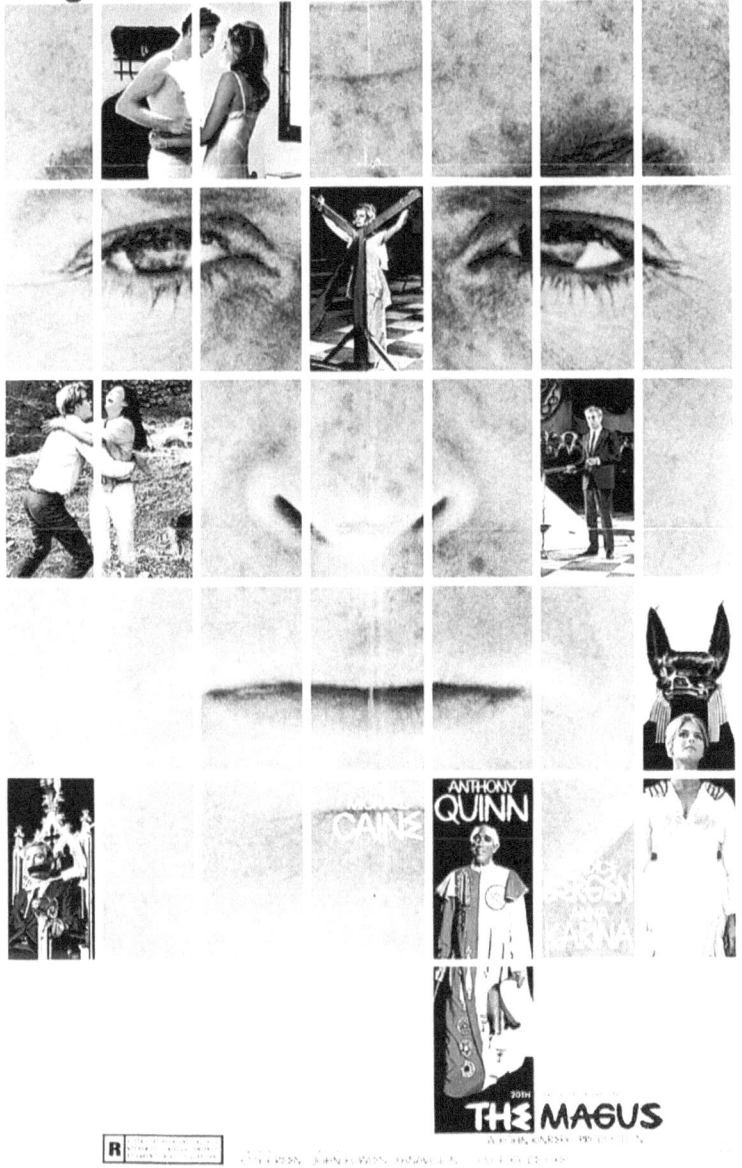

MAGUS **Poster for** *The Magus* (dir. Guy Green, 1968).

actress supposedly hired by Conchis to play the role of a young woman called Lily.

This is a test he fails, but there are others he passes. The first involves the casting of dice, the traditional role of the Juggler. Conchis suggests that instead of war, which men use to prove their manhood, it would be much more efficient to instead throw a pair of dice and, if unlucky, bite on a suicide capsule. Nicholas agrees to throw the dice and is unlucky, but in the end refuses to finish the game. Conchis congratulates him, explaining that one of the dice was loaded anyway:

> "Patriotism, propaganda, professional honor, *esprit de corps*—what are all those things? Cogged dice. There is just one small difference, Nicholas. On the other table these are real." He put the remaining teeth [capsules] back in the box. "Not just ratafia in coloured plastic."[8]

This is Nicholas' first lesson on the overriding importance and value of freedom—the ultimate ideal. When Conchis catches an octopus with what it thinks is food but is not, he observes, "You note reality is not necessary. Even the octopus prefers the ideal."[9] The film shows us the octopus being speared but unfortunately does not include the comment, thus losing its significance. This is a problem with the film in general, despite the fact that Fowles wrote the screenplay. In many ways, the tighter construction of the screenplay helps illuminate the novel, but in other ways it is like playing the whole of Wagner's *Ring* cycle without any of the words.

Conchis has another story to tell. During the Second World War, he was the mayor of his island village. When three Greek freedom fighters killed some German soldiers, the Nazis took revenge by threatening to execute 80 villagers. Conchis was offered an impossible choice. If he executed the resistance fighters, the villagers would be saved; but when one of the fighters shouted, "Eleutheria!" (the Greek the word for "freedom"), Conchis realized that this was more important than anything else. He had the freedom to choose. No matter how he chose, he would be condemned as a German collaborator, but he chose to die in the name of Eleutheria. Instead, he was subjected to a worse fate by the Germans, who shot everyone but him, which is why Conchis arranged his own "death" (Nicholas has already seen his tombstone) and assumed a different persona.

The Nazi episode is really a way of explaining Nicholas' own dilemma. His selfishness has resulted in the suicide of his girlfriend Alison-Anna. He therefore has one death on his conscience already. Conchis has 80, but the extremity of Conchis' situation is really only a way of emphasizing and illuminating Nicholas' own guilt. During the trial scene, Nicholas realizes that he, like Conchis before him, has the freedom to choose, to forgive, to relinquish, and he thus resists his desire to whip Julie in revenge for her part in the charade. (This scene, with Julie bound to a flogging frame, presents an interesting parallel with the party scene in *Theatre of Death* [dir. Sam Gallu, 1967], in which Christopher Lee's theater director, a similar kind of magus figure, rehearses his latest sketch, "The Witches of Salem." Under the hypnotic influence of Lee's Philippe Darvas, Jenny Till's Nicole advances towards Lelia Goldoni's Dani with a red-hot poker, and we are persuaded that a theatrical illusion is soon to become horrific reality.)

Freedom, as perceived by Fowles, is the only reality: the freedom of chaos, or hazard, as he terms it. There is no plan. All is hazard, and the imposition of a plan or a meaning on chaos is the cause of all our suffering. The Nazis claimed they were imposing order but were in fact presiding over demonically organized chaos (all those neatly typed lists of condemned Jews) with catastrophic results. It is unorganized hazard that Fowles regards as true freedom. In this, *The Magus* is a distinctly Nietzschean text. It promotes the benefits of facing up to the reality of life. Conchis praises individualism, freedom, life and, most important of all, joy. This is what the smile of the statue at the end of the film signifies:

> That is the truth. Not the hammer and sickle. Not the stars and stripes. Not the cross. Not the sun. Not gold. No *yin* and *yang*. But the smile.[10]

Our aim should therefore be the pursuit of total freedom, which has always been the aim of magicians, and this is why in both the book and film Conchis raises his arms aloft in the Yr rune gesture, made famous by the German symbolist artist Fidus (Hugo Höppener) as a symbol of light and life. (The Magus of *Space: 1999*'s "New Adam New Eve" also makes this gesture, for he, like Conchis, is at one with the universe and with universal light.) But Fowles realizes that total freedom is not enough. We must love ourselves before we can love anyone else. This is something Nicholas patently does not do. Balance, therefore, is the key to success; that balance symbolized by the Magus gown we see Conchis wearing in the film's spectacular trial scene.

There is an illuminating parallel here with Crowley's famous dictum, "Do what thou wilt shall be the whole of the law. Love is the law. Love under will." Life is something inflicted on us without being given any real choice. Fowles explores this in distinctly psychedelic fashion when Conchis hypnotizes Nicholas. (Appropriately, Fowles compares the process to the relationship between Svengali and Trilby.) The result is a mystical experience of union—a very Nietzschean state of affairs in which there is no good and no evil, but instead a balance of opposites. Nicholas realizes that he has been enchanted into wanting sexual satisfaction, but never into wanting love; and love is essentially an irrational mystery. Conchis explains that in his youth he studied medicine and believed passionately in reason, but he learns that rationality is not enough. "I preferred the mystery of birds' voices to any scientific explanation of it,"[11] he explains. Again, reason and the irrational belong together in balance: Conchis has been both a doctor and an artist.

The film ends with the smiling statue and with a symbol that is not in the novel: Anne's paperweight, the good-luck charm she will not travel without. It is now passed on to Nicholas, who finally understands: It represents the integrated self behind the layers of life's onion:

> It says that right at the very heart of things there's something not spoilt—unbetrayed. Everything I'm not and the world's not. ... It's the core.

When Nicholas picks the paperweight up from its place beneath the smiling statue, he attains the balance he has been seeking throughout all the strange events of the masque and his life before it. He has freedom, but he also understands the necessity of loving himself and allowing others to love him. He loses Anne, but gains himself. The film's quotation from T.S. Eliot's *Four Quartets* underlines this insight:

> We shall not cease from exploration,
> And the end of all our exploring
> Will be to arrive where we started
> And know the place for the first time.

Guy Green's direction has received a great deal of unjust criticism; but the film's faults are more the fault of Fowles' screenplay, which has difficulty condensing the novel's complexity into just under two hours' screen time. Michael Caine, who gives an excellent performance as Urfe, called it his worst film, confessing that he didn't understand what it was about. According to Green's son Michael, Green himself was unsure, and Fowles was unwilling to elucidate. Visually ravishing as it is, it resembles the way in which Visconti's *Death in Venice* (1971) addresses the naturalistic superficialities of Thomas Mann's novella, while not so convincingly addressing the philosophical bedrock on which those superficialities rest. The naturalism of both stories is in fact illusory. In the case of *The Magus*, the naturalism is a deliberate lure to draw us into what is really an entirely allegorical world. Fowles teases the reader much as Conchis teases Nicholas into believing that there will be a conventional explanation at the end of the story. Nicholas wastes most of his energies in wanting to find out who Conchis really is and why he is doing all this, when he should be thinking about *what* he is doing, which is to expose Nicholas to himself. The voyage of self-discovery is an internal journey, and Conchis is therefore a mythical rather than a kind of Bond villain. It is not too extreme to think of him as God Himself. Fowles was originally going to call the novel *The Godgame,* a term he retained to describes the masques and improvisations on the island.

> NICHOLAS: OK. I'll play. I'd just enjoy it more I knew what it was all about.
> CONCHIS: Man has been saying that for the last ten thousand years, but the one common feature of all the gods he has said it to is that not one has ever returned an answer.
> NICHOLAS: But why me?
> CONCHIS: Why anyone? Why anything?
> NICHOLAS: I said I'll play, but not unless I know the rules.
> CONCHIS: Then, my friend, this world is not for you.

Released in December 1968, *The Magus* has much in common, both stylistically and thematically, with Patrick McGoohan's TV series *The Prisoner,* in particular that series' final episode, "Fall Out," directed by McGoohan and first aired in February 1968. It is tempting to consider if *The Prisoner might* have inspired some of the imagery of *The Magus,* or if the similarities are merely an example of synchronicity. Both are certainly very much products of their time. Both *The Magus* and "Fall Out" feature a trial scene in which their respective protagonists sit on dais-mounted thrones. In *The Magus,* Conchis puts Nicholas on trial. In *The Prisoner,* Kenneth Griffiths performs the role of judge. The penny-farthing wheel symbol of *The Prisoner* is echoed by the eight-spoke wheel symbol in *The Magus.* Even the paperweight that symbolizes "the core" in *The Magus* has its equivalent in "Fall Out," where it takes the form of a clear glass sphere, which smashes, somewhat after the manner of the snow globe during the opening sequence of Orson Welles' *Citizen Kane* (1941). All three "spheres" represent psychological integration. At the end of "Fall Out," McGoohan's Number Six at last confronts the mysterious Number One, whom he has spent the entire series attempting to unmask, but Number One is revealed to be himself, just as Prince Prospero in Roger Corman's *The Masque of the Red Death* discovers that Death wears his own face at the end of the story. Given the philosophical context of *The Prisoner,* which is primarily an allegory about freedom and individuality, this final revelation suggests that we are all our own prisoners. How much freedom will we allow ourselves? How courageous are we in confronting it? How much is our identity dependent upon it? Those viewers who were confused, even outraged by the final *Prisoner* had been led to expect some kind of James Bond apotheosis, in keeping with the naturalistic expectations of the series, in which the surreal elements were presented as "other"—a mystery requiring resolution. (Anthony Quinn's Conchis plays up to the Bond aura of *The Magus* by wearing the uniform of all Bond villains: a Nehru suit.) McGoohan's aim, however, was to undermine such expectations—partly in defiance of his previous screen persona in *Danger Man,* where he did inhabit a conventional spy drama. By playing with the audience in this manner, he attains the status of another magus, that "mountebank in the world of vulgar trickery," as Waite describes this tarot card.

The Magus' trial scene is a splendid visual paraphrase of its source material in the novel, which Green sets up as an hallucination induced by a drug injected into Nicholas by Conchis. In the novel, Fowles ironically draws a comparison between Conchis and Aleister Crowley when describing Nicholas' response to the occult imagery he employs:

> Huge backswept horns, left their natural colour: amber glass eyes; the only ornament, a fat blood-red candle that had been fixed between the horns and lit. I wished I could speak, for I badly needed to shout something debunking, something adolescent and healthy and English; a "Doctor Crowley, I presume." But all I could do was to cross my knees and look what I was not—unimpressed.[12]

In *The Prisoner,* Number Six similarly sits with nonchalant crossed legs; and Nicholas' desire for adolescent rebellion in Fowles is voiced in *The Prisoner* by Alexis Kanner's top-hatted teenager, who sings "Dem bones" in an attempt to debunk the whole of the society's rules, regulations and taboos, which are represented by the jury behind him. Fowles' Satanic goat features on Tom Adams' front cover design of the original edition of the novel, and the trial scene of Green's film splendidly realizes it, along with all the other occult imagery of the various masks worn by the participants:

> Next to Conchis appeared, from behind the bird-head and pregnant belly, a slim middle-aged woman. She was wearing a dark-grey suit; a headmistress or a business woman. The jackal-head, Joe, was dressed in a dark-blue suit. Anton came, surprisingly, from behind the pierrot-skeleton costume. The succubus from Bosch revealed another elderly man with a mild face and pince-nez. The corn-doll was Maria. The Aztec head was the German colonel, the pseudo–Wimmel of the ridge incident. The vampire was not Lily, but her sister; a scarless wrist. A white blouse, and the black skirt. The crocodile was a man in his late twenties. He had a thin artistic-looking beard; a Greek or an Italian. He too was wearing a suit. The stag-head was another man I did not know; a very tall Jewish-looking intellectual of about forty, deeply tanned and slightly balding.[13]

The stag-head implies Herne the Hunter; the crocodile head, the Egyptian god, Sobek. The film also shows what Fowles describes as an African "folk-horror," a woman with a beaked white head (a kind of fish-bird-woman), and Anubis, the Egyptian god of the dead, who appears during one of the novel's earliest masque scenes. All these are of course archetypes, no more than elaborate set dressings for the drama of Nicholas' moral drama.

As these mythological characters are unmasked, earlier lines of dialogue are spoken, serving as evidence against Nicholas:

> "Why did you cast me as the traitor?"
> "If it hadn't been for you and your damned games, she'd be alive"
> "I fear you are deceitful, Mr. Urfe."
> "Marriage is for mice, Melin, not men."
> "To hell with Anne."
> "You'll never see me again. Never again."
> "'Eleutheria!'—Freedom."

The first line was originally spoken by Nicholas to Conchis, and refers to the fact that he is a traitor to himself. The second is the accusation Nicholas made to Conchis, whose masques involving Lily-Julie enticed Nicholas back to the island, his lust causing him to abandon Anne. The third is delivered by Lily in her role as an Edwardian lover of Conchis' youth, and again refers to his self-deceit. Nicholas delivers the fourth line to his colleague Melin at the Lord Byron School on Phraxos where he works, and again explains his inability to commit to genuine love. He also said, "To hell with Anne," and Anne, prior to the suicide his callousness causes, spoke the penultimate line. Freedom speaks for itself. Nicholas' character is finally revealed to him, by a computer, as "a familiar type of male parasite. His only law is his own pleasure. His only morality is his own good. He is a machine for self-gratification, not a human being." Shallow, vain, ego-centered, he is also a liar. The computer that delivers this analysis concludes by recommending that Nicholas should be sterilized. "There is no hope for him." "Except," Conchis laughs, "as an actor, of course." The irony here is that actors (and we have been watching them hard at work for the past 90 minutes) tell lies to reveal the truth, just as novelists do. Nicholas eventually discovers that true freedom is meaningless without love.

The film version of *The Magus* is therefore not only visually compelling, but also perfectly coherent if one accepts the stylistic parameters it sets for itself. (Reading the novel first also helps.) The naturalism is a lure, as is the promise of a logical explanation. The real action takes place on an allegorical level; everything else is demonstrated to be an illusion. Indeed, the final scene in a hotel bedroom is revealed to be no more than a film set with false walls— another trick of Conchis. When Nicholas picks up the paperweight that has been left beside the smiling statue, he too smiles, for he now understands himself. He has become his own magus.

A rather more negative interpretation of the magus figure can, of course, be found in Hitler, the ultimate trickster, who presided over the devastating masque of the Second World War. Hypnotist and mountebank, Hitler lured his nation to dwell on a magic island of illusion, not to enlighten, as Conchis does, but to confirm existing prejudices and fears. Hitler achieved the seemingly miraculous through the strength of his own will, the power of his rituals and the demagoguery of his mythical persona.

One non-fiction work which seems to present a parallel universe to Fowles' novel is Albert Speer's *Inside the Third Reich*. Like Nicholas Urfe, the ambitious, well-educated but distinctly self-centered Speer found himself in thrall to the Führer, whom he grew to love and who was loved by Hitler in return. The homosexual implications, no matter how sublimated, are hard to overlook, but Hitler inspired infatuation from men and women alike. ("Do you love Maurice?" asks Lily in the middle of Green's film. "We all love him. So deeply.") Speer wrote for many in his account of Hitler's seduction:

> His persuasiveness, the peculiar magic of his by no means pleasant voice, the oddity of his rather banal manner, the seductive simplicity with which he attacked the complexity of our problems—all that bewildered and fascinated me.[14]

Few films have explored Hitler the magus as convincingly as Hans-Jürgen Syberberg's *Hitler—Ein Film aus Deutschland* (1977). In part two of this cinematic tetralogy, Hitler appears in particularly demonic form:

> Like a vision at a Black Mass in back of Wahnfried [Wagner's villa at Bayreuth]. From the opened grave of Richard Wagner, Hitler (played by Heinz Schubert) emerges in a Roman toga: he is the colour of a corpse as he comes out of hell, as in Doré's Dante illustration.[15]

Emerging from the mythic aura of Wagner's music dramas (particularly *Rienzi*, the music of which Syberberg calls for at this moment), Hitler, a denizen of Hell, breaks through into the modern world. Part four explains the consequences of his magical mass-deception of the German people:

> The words "magic" and "myth" and "serving" and "ruling," "Führer," "authority," are ruined, are gone, exiled to eternal time. And we are snuffed out. Nothing more will grow here. An entire nation stopped existing, in the diaspora of the mind and the elite. The New Ones were deigned, developed, the New Man is here. The Plague of materialism has won in the East and West! Congratulations![16]

By exploiting the symbols, aspirations and magic of German Romanticism, Hitler's Magus ironically destroyed them for all time.

CHAPTER EIGHT

Theological Horror

In 1971, Hammer Films, which had jolted the horror genre back to life in Britain in 1957 with *The Curse of Frankenstein*, were still prolific, producing (some might say with dangerous complacency) traditional, Gothic costume dramas such as *Countess Dracula* (dir. Peter Sasdy), starring Ingrid Pitt as a blood-drenched Hungarian hag who sacrifices virgins to keep her young and beautiful. In *Twins of Evil*, Peter Cushing starred as a Puritan vampire hunter in a Gothic never-never land (the inevitable Black Park, so often exploited by Hammer for its sylvan shudders). There was a sex change involved in *Dr. Jekyll and Sister Hyde* (dir. Roy Ward Baker), but the setting was Victorian London, as it was for *Hands of the Ripper*. The only two Hammer films with a contemporary setting that year were a big-screen version of the popular TV sitcom *On the Buses* (dir. Harry Booth) and *Blood from the Mummy's Tomb*. Regarding the latter, Chris Wicking's decision to update Bram Stoker's Edwardian setting picked up on the trend for horror films with contemporary settings, which began with *The Mephisto Waltz* in 1970 and helped Richard Donner's *The Omen* become what Mark Gatiss has called "the first horror blockbuster."[1] Contemporary settings and a much more realistic agenda revitalized a genre sated with period settings, melodramatic monsters and a style of moviemaking that was becoming all too predictable.

Alas, Hammer failed to adapt to the wind of change, making only a few contemporary horror films such as *Dracula A.D. 1972* and *The Satanic Rites of Dracula*. Hollywood, however, was unflinching in its approach to the possibilities of what one might term supernatural realism, and it was to the occult rather than traditional Gothic that such films looked for their inspiration.

William Friedkin, who directed *The Exorcist* (1973), took his supernatural theme seriously, claiming that the film "strongly and *realistically* [italics mine] tries to make the case for spiritual forces in the universe—both good and evil. ... It's about real people in a real street in a real town. ... I knew that this was going to be—or needed to be—something more than just

115

another horror film. This had to be a realistic film about inexplicable events."[2] He thus changed horror films forever. William Peter Blatty's 1971 novel, on which the film was based, did, however, allow for a more fluid interpretation of the supposedly demonic events, stressing, almost to the point of exhaustion, the possible psychological, psychiatric, psychotic and paranormal possibilities, which Friedkin's sensationally graphic visualizations somewhat cancel out. Blatty's screenplay also strengthens the demonic explanation, which is treated with more ambivalence in the novel. Even the film's most lurid moment—the 360-degree rotation of the head of the possessed girl, Regan, which is hard to explain in any way other than supernaturally in the film—is marked by distinct ambivalence in the novel. It occurs at the very end of Part II, where it is briskly described, and carefully set up with as many references to incoherence and uncertainty as Blatty can manage: Regan's mother Chris, exhausted, her vision "blurring, unfocused," somewhat inebriated and overwhelmed by the horrific sight of her daughter masturbating with a crucifix, shrinks back "in incredulous terror as *she thought* [italics mine] she saw hazily, as if in an undulating fog, her daughter's head turning slowly and inexorably completely around on a motionless torso."[3] What made audiences shriek with visceral horror in movie theaters would, in the novel, hardly stand up in a court of law as evidence of anything other than extreme psychological distress.

On the side of the believers, Blatty has the exorcist, Lancaster Merrin, express the opinion that "perhaps Satan—Satan, in spite of himself—somehow serves to work out the will of God,"[4] which is pretty much what Goethe has Mephistopheles say in *Faust*. For Merrin, matter "was still evolving and destined to be spirit that at the end of time would join with Christ, the 'Omega Point.'"[5] But Blatty balances this by making Chris a non-believer, and by having Merrin's assisting exorcist, Father Karras, struggle with his loss of faith. Immense physical strength, telepathy, psychokinesis, poltergeists, speaking in tongues, levitation—nearly all the so-called "occult" activity of the novel is subjected to exhaustive psychological analysis (what Father Karras calls "logical doubt"[6]) and is argued as being quite possible in purely psychological terms, motivated by repressed emotions, buried guilt, unresolved resentments: "the limitless abilities of the mind."[7] The novel is as much a treatise on *interpretation* as anything else, and its "meaning" is surely that God is Love, even for an atheist, for while it is quite possible to live without God, it is pointless to live without Love. For Merrin, demonic possession is any kind of behavior that diminishes our self-respect and encourages despair. One doesn't have to believe in God or the Devil to recognize how important it is to guard against such corrosive states of mind, which so often lead to evil actions. Merrin sees possession "most often in little things...: in the senseless, petty spites and misunderstandings; the cruel and cutting word that leaps unbidden to the tongue between friends. Between lovers. Between husbands and wives."[8] Even "demons" crave Love: "It is sweet in the body! I feel," are the words, played in reverse, which Karras has captured on a tape recorder from the apparently possessed Regan's lips. "Let us warm in the body. Do not [unintelligible] from the body into void."[9] These words seem to be the voices of other entities, but can we be sure of anything where the subconscious is concerned? Such ambivalence, along with the inspired idea of having Father Karras both a Jesuit priest and a psychiatrist, is what makes the story so much more "modern." So too are Blatty's opening quotations—the unsettling conversation of two mafiosi, delighting in unspeakable torture, and the simple words DACHAU, AUSCHWITZ, BUCHENWALD.

Many involved with this new wave of horror regarded realism as the key to their success. *Omen* screenwriter David Seltzer remembered that his aim was "to do something preposterous and it's going to look real." Gregory Peck, who brought, in Seltzer's words "a straight face" and "incredible dignity"[10] to *The Omen*, said, "If we can convince them with this shit, we all deserve Oscars!"[11] The demonic goings-on in the household of Peck's ambassador to the Court of St. James had been foreshadowed in a 1975 episode of Brian Clemens' British television series *Thriller*, "Nurse Will Make It Better," in which Patrick Troughton warmed up for his role as Father Brennan the following year. In "Nurse Will Make It Better" (dir. Shaun O'Riordan, 1975), he plays Lyall, a similarly tormented adversary of the Devil. Instead of the walls of his grubby bedsit being plastered with newspaper clippings, as in Father Brennan's case, Lyall has placards announcing, "The End is Nigh." And whereas Father Brennan is impaled by a lightning rod before he can stop the Antichrist, Lyall successfully takes on the evil nurse Bessie (Diana Dors). Dors' performance looks back to Bette Davis' incarnation as the crazed child carer of Hammer's *The Nanny* (dir. Seth Holt, 1965).

Nurse Bessie is an emissary of the Devil amidst the tragedy that has beset the home of an American diplomat in England: The diplomat's spoiled and headstrong daughter has broken her back in a riding accident and proves to be such a difficult patient that she has driven away all her other nurses. Bessie now appears like a sulfurous, wart-faced, pipe-smoking Mary Poppins, miraculously curing her charge in return for her soul and also the "conversion" of other members of the family to her satanic point of view. The dénouement has Lyall holding up a Bible to his adversary, who promptly makes it burst into flames. Snatching a sword from the wall, he strikes Bessie with it. "Pain can be such a pleasure in my world," she smiles back, transforming the sword into a snake. (Christopher Lee's Father Michael in *To the Devil a Daughter* does the same trick with Denholm Elliott's telephone wire.) This is really the only "magickal" thing to happen in "Nurse Will Make It Better." The weapons used against Bessie are entirely Christian (in fact, the only symbol we see is the crucifix), and no one summons her; she merely appears from nowhere.

In *The Omen*, Billie Whitelaw's demonic nurse, Mrs. Baylock, carried on where Bessie left off. Mrs. Baylock is an apostate of Hell, devoted to Damien. *The Omen* is similarly a theological rather than occult horror film. This is even more the case in the second sequel *Omen III—The Final Conflict* (dir. Graham Baker, 1981), which updates Christ's nativity and the Massacre the Innocents in terms of the Second Coming. (In contrast, Ken Russell's *The Devils* [1971] falls into the category of psychological horror, the extreme violence and perversions it presents being entirely the result of sexual repression and politico-religious oppression: There is very little that is purely "spiritual" going on in *The Devils*, still less "occult.")

Following Sir James Frazer's distinction between "magic" and "religion," which I mentioned in the introduction, theological horror does not summon demonic forces. There is no magic in *The Omen*. Good and Evil are presented as supernatural forces in no need of human mediation. Consequently, there is no ritual until the very end, and even that fails, the forces of evil proving triumphant in the morally uncertain 1970s. As in *The Exorcist*, "evil" appears from nowhere and only appeals to the Power of Christ, via Christian priests, can remove it. Quite the opposite happens in *The Kiss of the Vampire* where Noel Howlett's Father Xavier is very much a marginal figure who merely follows the orders of the magus, Prof. Zimmer. God and the Devil are obviously involved, but not the church. This is even more the case in Hammer's *The Devil Rides Out*.

In *The Exorcist*, there are no pentagrams, no magic circles, no "occult" paraphernalia: only the cross and the Bible. There is no attempt at exorcism at all in *The Omen*. The Devil makes his appearance, wreaks his havoc, and the only manual to deal with the menace is the Book of Revelation. Even this fails, despite taking place in a church, as Ambassador Thorn is shot before he can ritually slay Damien on the altar with specially provided knives. Seltzer's approach to the Catholic Church in *The Omen* is also more in line with the opinion of the medieval Cathar heretics, who regarded it as the church of Satan, who had created the world and all its suffering. In her history of the Cathars, Zoé Oldenbourg described the heretics' view of the Church of Roman as "the Great Beast, the Whore of Babylon; and none who remained obedient to her could hope to be saved. Everything appertaining to this

"You'll See Me in Hell, Mr. Thorn": Patrick Troughton (Father Brennan), discusses the Antichrist on London's Embankment with director Richard Donner and Gregory Peck (Senator Robert Thorn) during filming of *The Omen* (dir. Richard Donner, 1976).

Church was wicked and blasphemous. Her sacraments were not only worthless in themselves, but a snare set by the Devil, since they led men to believe that wholly material rites and mechanical gestures could bring them salvation."[12]

Seltzer's *Omen* screenplay has Damien handed over to Senator Thorn by a Roman Catholic priest, Father Spiletto (Martin Benson). Supposedly an orphan, Damien is in fact the product of a satanic birth from a jackal, presumably presided over by the very same priest. The action appropriately begins in Rome, the seat of the so-called Whore of Babylon. Patrick Troughton's Father Brennan, whom Thorn encounters in London, is also a Roman Catholic priest, present at the Rome hospital when Damien was born, and has now recanted from his satanic affiliation. He recites the Nostradamus-style poem Seltzer has written for him: "From the eternal sea he rises/Creating armies on either shore," but it is not just from the "eternal sea" of American politics from which the Antichrist rises, it is also from the political and materialistic world of the Catholic Church.

John Carpenter's *Prince of Darkness* (1988) provides another example of this theological approach to horror, in which Donald Pleasence's Catholic priest takes on the "concentrated essence of evil" that is contained in a sinister canister in the bowels of a derelict church. This swirling green soup is apparently as evil as the sacred Host of Catholic communion is supposedly "good," but all this has very little to do with the magickal thinking of occultism, in which "good" and "evil" have, after all, little meaning. (Carpenter is anyway more interested in body horror, for which the theological premise is merely a pretext.) "The great forces cannot be described as either good or evil," Richard Cavendish explains, even though "they have a good and an evil side, or in occultists' terms a positive and a negative aspect."[13] Crowley puts this in a more amusing and graphic fashion, insisting that there is "no enmity between Right and Left, Up and Down, and similar pairs of opposites."

> These antitheses are real only as a statement of relation; they are the conventions of an arbitrary device for representing our ideas in a pluralistic symbolism based on duality. "Good" must be defined in terms of human ideals and instincts. "East" has no meaning except with reference to the earth's internal affairs; as an absolute direction in space it changes a degree every four minutes. "Up" is the same for no two men, unless one chance to be in the line joining the other with the centre of the earth. "Hard" is the private opinion of our muscles. "True" is an utterly unintelligible epithet which has proved refractory to the analysis of our ablest philosophers.[14]

Friedkin realized that if one really wanted secular 1970s audiences actually to believe the theological premise he was offering, he would need a wholly new approach, not only to the way in which *The Exorcist* was shot but also to how the soundtrack was used. Realizing that the traditional language of film music (predominantly tonal, with discordant elements viewed from within the context of that tonality) would no longer be adequate for this purpose, he understood that the emerging art of sound design could achieve much more realistic and atmospheric effects than music. *The Exorcist*'s sound design is far more significant than the relatively brief musical excerpts it channels, principally from the back-catalog of Penderecki. Penderecki was approached by Friedkin to score the film but he declined, feeling that horror films were beneath him.[15] Friedkin approached Lalo Schifrin, who provided music of Pendereckian style, with some echoes of Bernard Herrmann's score for Hitchcock's *Psycho*. Schifrin's music was originally commissioned to accompany the film's six-minute trailer, and it was largely responsible for the overwhelming impact those six minutes had on audiences and studio executives; but Friedkin later rejected the rest of Schifrin's score in favor of Penderecki, using extracts from a variety of his works including *Polymorphia, Kanon for Orchestra and Tape*, his 1960 String Quartet and *The Devils of Loudon*, as well as works by Hans Werner Henze and Anton Webern, consequently enlarging the audiences of these composers no end. Identifying precisely which pieces appear at what moment is a beguiling pastime but not particularly helpful in explaining how they contribute to the film, for all these pieces adopt similar (and now very familiar) *avant-garde* effects such as the use of tone clusters (sometimes moving through a *glissando*), fragmentary *pizzicato* effects and aleatoric elements, which from the point of view of the majority of the film's audience are, quite frankly, interchangeable from one piece to the other. It is the disorientating effect of such techniques (particularly so in their original 1970s context, when such sounds were less familiar to movie audiences than they are today) that is more to the point.

The film opens with a typically *avant-garde* cluster effect. Significantly there is no extended main title sequence—another important way in which the film distances itself from Hollywood norms to proclaim its "reality"; but this soon segues into a Muezzin call, not only indicating the opening location of Northern Iraq but also suggesting something of the Biblical nature and "otherness" of the events about to unfold. Just as Friedkin famously fired guns on-set to startle his actors and thereby create realistic emotional responses, so too does he exploit contrasts of light and darkness on screen and stark contrasts of sheer decibels on the soundtrack to assault the sensibilities of the audience. (Street noise, metallic hammering and wind effects are contrasted with the interior of a museum room, which is accompanied only by the sound of a ticking clock.) Friedkin always highlights the details of his ambient soundscapes, making mundane sound effects (footsteps, truck engines, bells on a cart) serve the dramatic function of a traditional film score, and inverts our musical expectations, having, for example, no music at all for the shots in which Max von Sydow walks though the ruined temple. Only

THE POWER OF CHRIST: **Max von Sydow as Father Merrin in *The Exorcist* (dir. William Friedkin, 1973).**

when he looks at the sunlit demon statue does Penderecki's music really make itself felt. It returns for the shot in which von Sydow confronts the demonic statue that his archaeological dig has uncovered.

As we fade to an establishing shot of Georgetown, where the remainder of the action takes place, snarling dogs (again suggesting the story's struggle with evil) are mixed with the music before it is entirely removed and we return to purely ambient sounds: cars outside Ellen Burstyn's study, the sound of her pen against paper and then the "demonic" scratching from the attic, which she at first puts down to rats. Such use of sound design, and only minimal use of musical sounds, plays a significant role in creating the impression that the film is a presentation of documentary evidence rather than carefully manipulated fantasy.

Burstyn plays Chris MacNeil, a movie actress; and by opening the film with scenes showing her acting in a film that is being made (a Warner Brothers film—just like *The Exorcist*), Friedkin is able to give the impression that the action that follows these scenes is, by contrast, not like the film we observe being made at the outset: *The Exorcist* is really happening. Even the policeman who investigates the goings-on in Burstyn's apartment is a film enthusiast and asks for her autograph. The implication is that the film world lies beyond the narrative and events of *The Exorcist* itself.

As Burstyn walks back from the day's shoot, Friedkin inserts a brief extract from Mike Oldfield's *Tubular Bells*, the closest thing to main title music the film offers (though no titles are shown on screen against it). *Tubular Bells* had only just been released in 1973, and it not only aids the sense of the film's self-conscious contemporaneity, but also contributes to the demonic mood: The main theme of Oldfield's piece does indeed contain the principal intervals of the "Dies Irae" chant, which, either consciously or not, are improvised upon in the opening phrases of Oldfield's theme. However, Friedkin fades this out fairly soon before noise from a jet plane obliterates it completely. We briefly glimpse Jason Miller's Father Damien Karras being consoled by another priest and overhear that he fears he has lost his faith.

Friedkin now cuts to a subway, a shrieking train exploiting the famous "Lewton Bus" effect, so-called after producer Val Lewton's 1942 film *Cat People* (dir. Jacques Tourneur) where it was first used. No music could be as startling as this sound. As Karras walks down a shabby street and enters his mother's antiquated apartment, Friedkin allows the ambient sound of car horns, footsteps, youths playing on top of a car, the rustling of keys, the distorted voices speaking various languages emerging from a radio, to create the mood of depression, loneliness and alienation. This removes the need for music altogether (though most earlier filmmakers would no doubt have relied on an atmospheric cue to support a sequence without dialogue such as this).

The film's priests are presented as spiritual "cops," no doubt to make the film's theological context more believable, modern and urban. ("You're the best man we've got," one of them tells Father Karras.) Friedkin also introduces "realistically" strong language during a distraught phone call made by Burstyn's Chris, which had a great deal more power to shock in 1973 than it does now. After the supernatural is briefly brought to the fore by an incident with the *planchette* of an ouija board, the demonic noises recur in the attic. Chris investigates, taking with her a candle, which might be seen as a rather more traditionally Gothic symbol, to heighten the sense of expectation here. The expectation is fulfilled by the sudden appearance and high-pitched vocal register of Chris' odd-job man. There is nothing demonic about him, but the candle does flare up as he speaks, suggesting that demonic forces are making their presence felt.

In his introduction to *The Exorcist*'s 25th anniversary DVD edition, Friedkin argues that if one believes the world to be an evil place, the film will confirm that beliefs. But if we believe that good triumphs over evil, we will be getting close to what he tried to convey in the film. A non-believer's view of *The Exorcist* is that it is a very well-made movie, which uses a variety of sophisticated sound devices to create a mood of supernatural expectation and physical horror. Throughout the film, sound montage takes the place of the music we might otherwise expect: Throughout Father Karras's dream sequence, in which he observes his mother emerge from a subway (surely a symbol of Hell), ambient, though electronically manipulated sound is used, not music. When Regan is given her series of unpleasant medical tests in hospital, Friedkin emphasizes naturalistic hospital noises (clanking bars around the bed, the whirring and clicks of monitoring equipment, the rustling of clothing and sheets). These all lead to the truly terrifying *martellato* noises of the X-ray machine itself, which sound fully as demonic as the rats in the attic, and are actually far more frightening than anything Penderecki's music could have summoned.

The strong language continues during Regan's subsequent and increasingly lewd scenes on her bed at home, as the Devil takes over more of her body and soul; and, again, the fully focused ambient sounds are all that Friedkin needs to support the illusion of realism. Throughout the film, Penderecki's music and that of his *avant-garde* colleagues is employed really only as a means of transition from one scene to the next. The atonality is meant to build the mood of unease, which may not necessarily have always been Penderecki's original intention. Arnold Schoenberg, godfather of the New Music, aimed to convert traditional dissonances into "higher consonances," and even saw the comic potential of serial style (his own brand of organized atonality) in his opera *Von Heute auf Morgan*. It might very well be argued, therefore, that films such as *The Exorcist* have undermined the aims of the *avant-garde* by attaching a significatory function to music that it might not originally have had. In this respect, Hollywood has always employed dissonance, no matter how advanced, from within the context of a tonal perspective. Not even Schoenberg could alter that, as his unproductive interview with Irving Thalberg about scoring MGM's adaptation of Pearl S. Buck's novel *The Good Earth* demonstrated all too well.[16]

The manipulated breathings, gurgles and vocal gymnastics of the possessed Regan (voiced by Mercedes McCambridge) are quite "musical" enough on their own to allow Friedkin to dispense with orchestral support. Exploiting recording technology, after the manner of the experiments in *musique concrète* first pioneered by Pierre Schaeffer in the early 1940s, create a highly effective "demonic" ambience, which Jerry Goldsmith had to compose for *The Mephisto Waltz*. Friedkin had McCambridge's voice reversed, multi-tracked, superimposed, distorted and mixed with animal noises in ways that would have been familiar to Schaeffer. The man responsible for realizing these effects was Mexican Foley artist Gonzalo Gavira, who also used an old leather wallet with credit cards inside it to create the effect of Regan's famously rotating head. Penderecki's music is only used to signal specifics, such as the extract from *Polymorphia* to emphasize the words HELP ME which appear on Regan's chest. Note clusters also underscore the iconic image of von Sydow arriving in the fog at the apartment (an image itself modeled on Magritte's surrealist painting "The Empire of Lights").

Most significantly of all, I think, there is no music at all during the exorcism itself, reversing entirely the received wisdom, which originated with Max Steiner, that fantasy requires music to aid the suspension of disbelief. Only McCambridge's manipulated voice and the sounds of crashing furniture are needed to create this illusion of supernatural reality. The silence of the central moment of the exorcism—Regan's levitation—makes the effect much more believable and simultaneously much more supernatural. The priest's combined reiteration "The power of Christ compels you" provides a linguistic rather than musical *ostinato*, serving the same function as the *ostinati* James Bernard used to punctuate *The Devil Rides Out*'s magic circle scenes. Here, however, the effect is realistic as opposed to Bernard's much more melodramatic approach.

Tubular Bells makes its third and final appereturns at the end of the film, the end title sequence proper employing Hans Werner Henze's rather more tonal Fantasia for Strings to usher us out of the film's reality and back to our own. As Friedkin put it, "People actually believed what they saw on the screen,"[17] and this was in no small part due to the inventive sound design. One might say more accurately, they believed what they heard on the soundtrack.

The following year, Alberto De Martino cashed in on *The Exorcist*'s success with his own *L'Anticristo*, which covered much the same ground: A possessed woman levitates and spits green vomit, causes furniture and oil paintings to move of their own accord, etc., etc. Once more, it is up to a priest, rather than the psychiatrist, to exorcise her; but the major difference here is the much more pronounced Catholic context of this film. It was shot in Rome, with ecclesiastic architecture and imagery apparent everywhere. We begin with a religious procession in which statues are dressed, women crawl in abasement before them, kissing the floor, and the sick, halt and lame pray for miraculous cures. Eucharist is performed: A priest blesses the wafer and eats it, then drinks the wine, and Ennio Morricone increases the ecclesiastic mood by placing the organ at the center of his score for the film.

The toad imagery of *Psychomania* returns here in a flashback to the previous life of the paralyzed heroine, Ippolita Oderisi (Carla Gravina). In her former life, she was a condemned witch, having been impregnated by the Devil in a satanic ceremony in which a toad's head is pulled, with much blood, from its body and then inserted into her mouth. Ippolita is later seen wearing a snakeskin belt and a dressing robe, the paisley design of which also resembles serpentine scales—hence an allusion to Eve's tempter in the Garden of Eden. A magic circle proving inefficacious at containing her, Ippolita is finally exorcised by George Coulouris' priest, using the power of Christ rather than occultism. Closing shots of St. Peter's Basilica set the final Catholic seal on this extreme form of theological horror film.

The Omen (1976) took a rather different approach. Friedkin and Blatty (and probably De Martino) were seriously committed to discussing the idea of demonic possession; the writer and director of *The Omen*, though playing their story with a straight face, were not. No overtly supernatural happenings occur in this film, which is basically a series of bizarre and horrific deaths, the cumulative effect of which is to suggest that the Devil is responsible, but which Donner insists were only coincidences. Donner's opinion is that Gregory Peck's character is actually insane.[18] Jerry Goldsmith's *Omen* score is much more in evidence (and far more traditional in style) than the brief musical excerpts that appear in *The Exorcist*, but his approach to the music differs from horror tradition in that the majority of the cues are actually based on the film's love theme. The impressive demonic chant that opens the proceedings has, however, the greatest impact: It is a satanic reworking of the opening bars of Mozart's "Requiem," as well as (according to Goldsmith) a conscious attempt to recapture some of the momentum of John Williams' energetic ostinato for *Jaws* (dir. Steven Spielberg, 1975).[19] Following the convention that Satanism inverts the symbolism of the forces of good, Goldsmith's "Ave Satana" chant is the acoustic equivalent of an inverted crucifix, for if we compare the base line that opens Mozart's piece with Goldsmith's chant, we see that the ostinato of *The Omen* begins in the same way, but after D, F, and E it returns to F rather than Mozart's movement to G. By using this Mozartian model and combining it with his own setting of the satanic text ("Sanguis bibimus, corpus edimus, tolle corpus Satani, Ave Satani! Ave Versus Christus!" ("Drink the blood, eat the flesh, raise the body of Satan, Hail Satan! Hail the Antichrist!"), Goldsmith powerfully inverts the sacred connotations of the Requiem Mass to create a musical Black Mass. Two years later, he subtitled the soundtrack recording of *Damien: Omen II* exactly that.

Goldsmith's love theme has certain things in common with Francis Lai's romantic melody for *Love Story* (Dir. Arthur Hiller, 1970), and thus launched the decade of New Hollywood. Both are characterized by the interval of a sixth. Lai's "Where Do I Begin?" is little more than a rumination on a minor sixth, whereas Goldsmith's marginally more elaborate love theme encompasses the interval of a major sixth. The echo is perhaps deliberate, enforcing realism by branding the film as a mainstream Hollywood product, as opposed to a less believable traditional horror film. Goldsmith is also careful to echo his major sixth with the minor seventh of the piano solo that introduces the demonic chant. The oscillating two-note motif of the latter (A-flat to B and back again) echoes the melodic contour of Lai's "Where Do I Begin?" and the troubled Romantic connotation it brings with it is emphasized by its conjunction with romantic scenes between *Omen* stars Gregory Peck and Lee Remick. The love affair between their characters is under threat just as was that between Ryan O'Neill and Ali MacGraw.

We are asked to believe that the Devil of *The Omen* has been incarnated in a boy called Damien (Harvey Stephens), coincidentally the same name as the *Exorcist* priest who, very briefly at the end of that film, is similarly possessed, before he plunges to the pavement. Goldsmith signifies the demonic nature of the dog who compels Damien's nurse to hang herself (Damien is perhaps not quite old enough to compel her to do this entirely by himself), with a throbbing synthesized *ostinato*. Sound effects also play their part here, notably the at-first cheerful screeching and then terrified screaming of the children who witness the horror. Goldsmith employs *avant-garde* effects such as string *glissandi* but nothing as advanced as Penderecki, mostly relying on *ostinato* rhythms to connote the demonic element at work in the action sequences. These, such as the cue for the ride to the church, the Windsor Safari Park sequence when Katherine Thorn's car is attacked by Satan-sensitive baboons, and the build-up to the impalement of Troughton's priest, all palpably derive from the driving *ostinati* of the "Dance of the Adolescents" in Stravinsky's *Rite of Spring* (1913).

Other set pieces dispense with music altogether, reprising Freidkin's approach. The dispatch of Mrs. Thorn by her demon child was later borrowed by Stanley Kubrick in *The Shining* (1980), a film that also features a boy purposefully pedaling a squeaking tricycle. Goldsmith announces Katherine Thorn's imminent demise with a female choir, but then allows the wheels of Damien's tricycle to provide the acoustic momentum required during what follows. Silence is also a powerful tool here: The slow-motion shot of a plummeting goldfish bowl is mute before the bowl smashes on the floor at the correct speed. By dispensing with music at this moment, Goldsmith and Donner are able to suggest a greater sense of realism, echoing the techniques of *The Exorcist* but, crucially, from within *The Omen*'s rather more traditionally melodramatic context. Later in the film, tried and tested conventions return for the highly Gothic scene in the Etruscan cemetery at Cerveti. This terrible place contains the grave of Damien's canine mother, and here Goldsmith employs *col legno* strings (another macabre effect first codified by Berlioz in his *Symphonie fantastique*). Flutter-tongued flutes (previously heard to underline the anxiety of the hospital scenes in which Katherine pleads with Robert not to let her son kill her) are also apparent. The sound effects function much as one would expect them to do in such a context: The crickets stop chirping, a disturbing wind rises, and the hounds of Hell start barking. The *ostinati* Goldsmith lays under these are also conventional enough and perhaps even unnecessary under such an acoustic barrage.

Goldsmith's use of the choir at his disposal adds an extra element of Gothic frisson, inverting the heavenly choir convention of previous Hollywood Biblical epics. Particularly effective is his instruction for the choir to whisper rather than sing during the scenes in which Thorn is pursued by a demonic dog. Goldsmith elaborated on his choral inventiveness in *Damien: Omen II,* in which the choir imitates the sound of the carrion crows, which replace the various hounds of Hell of the original film as the Devil's heralds.

Apart from the desire to reinvent the horror film and consequently to gather a new audience for the genre, *The Omen* might also be interpreted as a response to the revival of Cold War anxieties, which are more often associated with 1950s science fiction films. By placing the Devil's child at the center of the world of politics "From the eternal sea he rises/Raising armies on either shore," Donner's film seems to reflect an anxiety felt at that time that those who lead us are leading us into damnation rather than delivering us from evil. To make this subtext more apparent, greater realism was no doubt considered necessary. The soundtrack was crucial in helping to place the film in the mainstream—not merely a "horror" film, but the kind of entertainment we regard as being parallel with, rather than opposed to, reality.

CHAPTER NINE

Theosophy

Theosophy exerted a powerful influence on music and poetry at the turn of the nineteenth century. Poet W.B. Yeats, painters Piet Mondrian and Wassily Kandinsky and composer Alexander Scriabin all responded to theosophy. It also fascinated the children's writer Francis Hodgson Burnett, whose Gothic novel for children *The Secret Garden* (1911) is in some ways a theosophical reworking of the Biblical Garden of Eden. Instead of Adam and Eve, we have Archibald Craven and his wife, who enjoy a walled Secret Garden at their Yorkshire home, just as Burnett enjoyed hers. Craven's wife is killed when she falls from a branch in the garden, and we understand why Burnett chose the particular surname for her protagonists, as "Craven" also means "defeated" or "overwhelmed." Expelled from Paradise, Archibald becomes truly as miserable as sin. His son Colin is a weak, sickly specimen, and everyone believes he will soon die. Rejected by his father, he is spoiled by privilege, and lives alone in his own quarters; but when the orphaned Mary comes to live in her uncle's gloomy establishment, his situation begins to change. Mary hails from mystic India, where Blavatsky ultimately transferred the headquarters of her Theosophical Society, and it is Mary who will cure the unfortunate Colin, not by conventional scientific medicine but by means of "magic." The magic here is entirely natural and "as white as snow,"[1] being the magic of growing seeds in the open air. Mary and Colin set about reclaiming the Secret Garden, locked up years ago by the grieving Archibald. They are helped by Dickon, a Pan-like figure at one with animals and the natural rhythms of life. Time and again, Burnett refers to the process of life itself as Magic with a capital M.

> Fair fresh leaves and buds—and buds—tiny at first but swelling and working Magic until they burst and uncurled into cups of scent delicately spilling themselves over their brims and filling the garden air.[2]

Cured of his largely hysterical illness by such pantheistic infusions of natural magic, Colin eventually gives a speech that sums up the "scientific" quest of theosophy to unlock the mystical and unifying powers of the universe:

"The great scientific discoveries I am going to make," he went on, "will be about Magic. Magic is a great thing and scarcely any one knows anything about it except a few people in old books—and Mary a little, because she was born in India where there are fakirs. I believe Dickon knows some Magic, but perhaps he doesn't know he knows it. He charms animals and people. I would never have let him come to see me if he had not been an animal charmer—which is a boy charmer, too, because a boy is an animal. I am sure there is Magic in everything, only we have not sense enough to get hold of it and make it do things for us—like electricity and horses and steam. ...

"When Mary found this garden it looked quite dead," the orator proceeded. "Then something began pushing things up out of the soil and making things out of nothing. One day things weren't there and another they were. I had never watched things before and it made me feel very curious. Scientific people are always curious and I am going to be scientific. I keep saying to myself, 'What is it? What is it?' It's something. It can't be nothing! I don't know its name so I call it Magic. ... Everything is made out of Magic."[3]

Agnieska Holland's 1993 film adaptation of the novel opens with a powerfully "mystic" shot of India, featuring scarlet sands and the Taj Mahal, and these nicely implant the theosophical resonance of the story without over-emphasizing it. Ignored by her selfish and materialistic military parents, young Mary watches exotic entertainments with elephants and rajahs but is never allowed to join in the fun. Lonely and alienated, she is desperately in need of magic too. In the novel, the parents are killed by plague. In the film, an earthquake does the damage, and as a consequence, Mary finds herself transplanted to rainy Yorkshire. A friendly robin, surely an emissary of the divine, eventually shows Mary the door that gives access to the garden—a true "Door in the Wall"—and with Dickon's help, the garden is brought back to life. Stop-motion photography emphasizes the "miracle" of blooming flowers which transform the place into a paradise where animals and humans live in harmony, not unlike the domain of Montsalvat in Wagner's *Parsifal*.

The shutters in Colin's room are pulled down. Light floods into his dreary, airless room and soon he is being wheeled outside. By now, the garden is festooned with roses, which ramble over the Gothic arches of this Temple of Nature. Colin presents a condensed version of his speech in the novel about making "great discoveries," but the film devotes more time to an interesting ritual that is not present on the page. Dancing around a fire in the garden one night, the children perform a rhythmical chant calling for the return of Colin's father, who has traveled abroad to escape his grief. Mystical orientalisms in the music here remind us of the film's brief prologue, and the spell does indeed have the desired effect. Archibald "hears" the voices of the children and his dead wife calling to him and is compelled to come home. Life, health and, more importantly, love return to the once gloomy house. "The magic worked!" Colin whispers. And who is to say that it cannot work in the real world as well?

Unfortunately, theosophy was also one of the many seeds of Nazi race theory. These later germinated in the pages of the "racial-economic" magazine *Ostara*, which was very probably read by the young Adolf Hitler. *Ostara* was edited by the mystical and racist writer Jörg Lanz von Liebenfels, later to be much admired by Rudolf von Sebottendorf, who founded two racist sects which eventually mutated in the NSDAP. The historian of Nazi occultism, Nicholas Goodrick-Clarke, explains:

> From July 1908 until the end of the First World War, Lanz managed to write no less than seventy-one issues himself. Their stock themes were racial somatology, anti-feminism, anti-parliamentarianism and the spiritual differences between the blond and dark races in the fields of sexual behavior, art, philosophy, commerce, politics and warfare, and caste law derived from the Hindu codes of Manu. The First World War was eventually documented as an eschatological phase of the Manichean struggle between the blonds and the darks.[4]

Another of the magazine's contributors, Harald Grävel von Jostenoode, "outlined a thoroughly theosophical conception of race and a programme for the restoration of Aryan authority in the world. His quoted sources were texts by Annie Besant, Blavatsky's successor as leader of the international Theosophical Society at London, and Rudolf Steiner, the Secretary General of its German branch in Berlin."[5]

This, in turn, influenced Lanz, whose ideas had evolved from Madame Blavatsky's evolutionary theories, which he quoted in *Die Theosophie und die assyrichen "Menschentiere"* (*Theosophy and the Assyrian "Man-Beasts"*). Lanz exploited "the materials of modern theosophy, as he had already done in the cases of archeology and anthropology, in order to substantiate his own neo-gnostic religion."[6] Like Blavatsky, Lanz believed in the myth of the lost continents of Lemuria and Atlantis, that humanity once had a third eye and supported a racial explanation of the Fall of Man. According to Lanz, "[T]he fourth root-race of Atlanteans had divided into pure and bestial subspecies, corresponding to the early anthropoids and the anthropomorphic apes. The fateful mistake of the former's descendants, the fifth root-race of Aryans or *homo sapiens*, had been persistent interbreeding with the latter's descendants."[7]

Modern Atlantology, derived from Plato's writings, was pioneered by the American politician Ignatius Donnelly (1831–1901) in his 1882 book *Atlantis: The Antediluvian World*. The following year, A.P. Sinnett, an Anglo-Indian journalist, published *Esoteric Buddhism,* in which he supposedly recorded the revelations he had received from his Mahatma teacher. Atlantis was of particular interest to Sinnett, who wrote of "cataclysms of either fire or water," destroyed civilizations, "degenerate fallen remnants" of once advanced human races and, most worrying of all, "sub-races."[8]

The publication of Blavatsky's magnum opus *The Secret Doctrine* (1888) propelled these ideas to a much wider audience. Her theory, apparently revealed to her by telepathic means from spiritual sources in Tibet (though rather more likely from Sinnett), equated each Race or "Round" with a particular continent or region. Hence, the first race lived in the Imperishable Sacred Land, of which "very little can be said."[9] The second race were the Hyperboreans, who dwelt on the land "which stretched out its promontories southward and westward from the North Pole." It was apparently "a real Continent, a *bona-fide* land which knew no winter in those early days ... the *land of the Gods*, the favorite abode of Apollo, the god of light." Lemuria formed the continent of the third race, a land mass that stretched "from the Indian Ocean to Australia ... now wholly disappeared beneath the waters of the Pacific, leaving here and there only some of its highland tops which are now islands."[10]

Atlantis was the home of the fourth race; the fifth, our present state, emerged from North America. The sixth is due in South America and by the time we attain to the seventh, continents will no longer be necessary as we will have developed into pure spirit. Blavatsky thus describes the progress of humanity as mystical evolutionism, in which inferior strains will be weeded out and perfection attained. These ideas proved to be very attractive to later right-wing racist ideologists. While Blavatsy's supporters continue to maintain that such interpretations are a perversion of her program, what are we to make of a statement such as this?:

> Here the *inferior* Races, of which there are still some analogues left—as the Australians (now fast dying out) and some African and Oceanic tribe—are meant. "*They were not ready*" signifies that the *Karmic* developments of these Monads had not yet fitted them to occupy the forms of men destined for incarnation in higher intellectual Races.[11]

Any idea of perfecting the human race necessarily requires the eradication of what is seen to be imperfect, with consequences now all too well known. The position of Blavatsky's theories on the lunatic fringe unfortunately inspire Nazi policy via the work of deranged adherents such as Lanz, whose eccentric fantasies would certainly have made promising material for a Boris Karloff "mad scientist" thriller:

> Lanz claimed that these early beings had possessed extraordinary sensory organs for the reception and transmission of electrical signals. These organs bestowed the powers of telepathy and omniscience upon their owners but had atrophied into the supposedly superfluous pituitary and pineal glands in modern man owning to the miscegenation

of the god-men with the beast-men. However, Lanz claimed that a universal programme of segregation could restore these powers to the Aryans as the closest descendants of the god-men.[12]

Another cultural development in early twentieth-century Germany that contributed to later Nazi ideology was the Germanenorden. As we have seen, Matthew Sunderland's SS officer in *The Devil's Rock* is a member of this order, which he claims was created by Hitler. It was not. The Germanenorden had emerged in the years prior to the First World War from various sources, particularly the anti–Semitic periodical *Hammer,* edited by a Saxon miller called Theodor Fritsch and a Magdeburg official, Hermann Pohl. These individuals eventually formed the first Germanenorden lodge in 1911, with Pohl as Master and Fritsch as Grand Master. Its symbol was a swastika superimposed on a cross, an emblem later adopted by the Thule Society and, stripped of the cross, the NSDAP. Goodrick-Clarke's reliable description of Germanenorden rituals is almost a parody of a Dennis Wheatley fantasy:

> The ceremony began with soft harmonium music, while the brothers sang the Pilgrims' Chorus from Wagner's *Tannhäuser.* The ritual commenced in candlelight with brothers making the sign of the swastika and the Master reciprocating. Then the blindfolded novices, clad in pilgrimage mantles, were ushered by the Master of Ceremonies into the room. Here the Master told them of the Order's Ario-Germanic and aristocratic *Weltanschauung,* before the Bard lit the sacred flame in the grove and the novices were divested of their mantles and blindfolds. At this point the Master seized Wotan's spear and held it before him, while the two Knights crossed their swords upon it. A series of calls and responses, accompanied by music from *Lohengrin,* completed the both of the novices. Their consecration followed with cries from the "forest elves" as the new brothers were led into the grove of the Grail around the Bard's sacred flame.[13]

The concept of superhumans with psychic powers can be traced beyond theosophy to one of that movement's most formative influences, the novels of Edward Bulwer-Lytton, later Lord Lytton, who was much admired (and plagiarized) by Madame Blavatsky. His science fiction novel *The Coming Race* (1871) describes a subterranean society of superhumans who channel a mystical force called Vril. According to the German rocket engineer Wernher von Braun this idea lay behind the Nazis' so-called Vril Society, dedicated to developing psychic powers for the Nazi war effort. The attraction of such a fantasy is obvious, and the Nazis were certainly fantasists, but the evidence for this claim is otherwise non-existent. Certainly, if Vril did exist, those without its power would surely have cause for concern. As Bulwer-Lytton's hero expresses it:

> [T]he more I think of a people calmly developing, in regions excluded from our sight and deemed uninhabitable by our sages, powers surpassing our most disciplined modes of force, and virtues to which our life, social and political, becomes antagonistic in

proportion as our civilization advances—the more devoutly I pray that ages may yet elapse before there emerge into sunlight our inevitable destroyers.[14]

Hermann Rauschning's celebrated volume *Hitler Speaks* (1940) implies that Hitler had a glimpse of the terrifying New Man. He gave his seal of approval to Raushning's book, and may well have claimed such a thing, but there is no denying that these ideas derived from Bulwer-Lytton in the first place.

The combination of superhuman powers, racist supremacy and the powerful esthetics of the Third Reich inevitably found its way into horror films. *The Frozen Dead* (dir. Herbert J. Leder, 1967) has Dana Andrews as a Nazi scientist, experimenting with cryogenics: Nazis on Ice, but with the grisly severed head of Andrews' daughter's best friend thrown in for good measure. (The latter echoes the idol-head of Baphomet supposedly worshipped by the Knights Templar, providing the film with yet more "occult" resonance.) Even more pertinent to Bulwer's theme is *Shock Waves* (dir. Ken Wiederhorn, 1977), in which Peter Cushing finds himself washed up, in more ways than one, on a remote island at the mercy of the zombie stormtroopers his Nazi character helped to develop:

B-MOVIE BAPHOMET: Jean (Anna Palk) examines Elsa Tenney's (Kathleen Breck) severed head, kept alive in *The Frozen Dead* (dir. Herbert J. Leder, 1966).

> We Germans developed the perfect weapon: a soldier. He was capable of fighting under any conditions, adapting to any environment or climate—equally at home in the Russian winter or in the African desert. They were the most vicious and bloodthirsty of all the SS divisions. The group under my command was designed for the water, to man submarines which would never have to surface. We created the perfect soldier from cheap hoodlums and thugs and a good number of pathological murderers and sadists as well. We called them "Der Todenkorps"—the Death Corps, creatures more horrible than any you can imagine. Not dead, not alive but somewhere in between.

Syberberg also addresses the mystical element that informed so much of the Nazi mythos in his Hitler film. The character of the Ice Cosmologist in Part Two, "(The German Dream)," played by Peter Lühr, appears soon after Hitler rises from the tomb of Richard Wagner. Wearing dark glasses and pushed in his wheelchair by a disciple, he articulates, to the accompaniment of Wagner's *Lohengrin* prelude, the eccentric theories of the Nazi World Ice theory:

> New breeds will arise, giant plants and giant animals, giant men. But only these giants, the race of the supermen, the lords of the earth, will have the strength, after the struggle with the legendary, cunning dwarfs and lower races, to survive the imminent destruction of the earth or at least hold it up for a millennial civilization, like Plato's legendary Atlantis of yore.[15]

To this, the disciple (Rainer von Artenfels) adds the following, echoing Rauschning's Hitler quotation regarding the terrifying quality of the New Man:

> We are going to change the world. And if we are human beings, then those cannot be called human beings, "animals" would be too kind, "subhumans" and "repulsive vermin" too flattering, for that nest of vipers that we are stamping out underfoot. I am afraid, for I have seen the New Man. I shall be acknowledged as the greatest or perish, cursed and damned by all for all time.
> We are going to create the New Man.
> ... There shall be men of a master race, raging prophets full of holy madness, full of providence in the spirit of the struggle between the world-blaze and the world-ice, securing solely their survival in the cosmos, courageous in their solitude, full of self-discipline, achieving their own completion. With souls, Nordic, ethical, as echoes of remote past worlds and a golden future.[16]

Emphasizing the German mystical tradition, which the Nazis harnessed to this theosophically derived racial fantasy, Syberberg places a three-dimensional model of the famous black stone of Dürer's woodcut "Melancholia" at the end of his vast tetralogy, accompanying the image with these words:

> Black Stone, Lapis Lapidi, Stone of Light, *lux ex coelis,* fallen from Lucifer's crown. The Grail, the Kaaba, the Golden Fleece from the Tree of Life, fallen from the stars, the rise and end of the stars, part of the treasure of Delphi, from the legacy of Apollo, the

sun god, brought to the gardens of the Hesperides, and granting eternal life to the gods and those who want to be like the people in the land of the Hyperboreans in Monségur. Do you remember? The Holy Vessel of the Grail, in which the blood flowed that night, the true, pure blood. Orient, Mohammed, Middle Ages, and Christianity together. King Arthur's court and Richard Wagner once again. Richard Wagner! A Black Stone fallen from the sky to the earth with eternal yearning for the heavens, for the paradise lost, of the angels, the paradise that bears the guilt for the sin of the world, when Eve and Adam were guilty.[17]

Here, in summary, are all those Romantic yearnings of the German soul, nourished by Wagner and theosophy, exploited and betrayed by the Arisophists and the Nazis.

But the occult agenda of theosophy has other cinematic tributaries, and these bring us more firmly into the realm of science fiction. Evolution depends on birth, but what if the process endangers the survival of the parents? John Wyndham understood this anxiety:

> By a dichotomy familiar to us all, a woman requires her own baby to be perfectly normal, and at the same time superior to all other babies. Well, when any of these women concerned is isolated from the rest with her own baby, it is bound to become more strongly borne in upon her that her golden-eyed baby is not, in relation to the other babies she sees, quite normal.[18]

This passage from *The Midwich Cuckoos*, articulates the ambivalence of parental ambition; but, as we have seen, it also articulates the greater ambivalence of giving birth—the fear that one might indeed be engendering monsters. Mary Shelley mythologized this anxiety in *Frankenstein*, but Wyndham presents the anxiety in a modern, naturalistic context, articulating exactly the fear that Hitler was supposed by Rauschning to have felt on encountering his simultaneously desired "New Man." After the children have caused the deaths of several Midwich inhabitants, the anxiety about them reaches a critical level:

> At present, we are conceding them all the privileges of the true *homo sapiens*. Are we right to do this? Since they are another species, are we not fully entitled—indeed, have we not perhaps a duty—to fight them in order to protect our own species? After all, if we were to discover dangerous wild animals in our midst our duty would be clear.[19]

The children certainly have no qualms about doing exactly this against those humans who threaten them: "We are responsible for defending ourselves," the boy, Eric, explains. "As you apparently have not grasped it, I will put it more plainly. It is that if there is any attempt to interfere with us or molest us, by anybody, we shall defend ourselves."[20]

The whole point of *The Midwich Cuckoos* rests on this evolutionary dilemma, brilliantly realized in the film adaptation *Village of the Damned*, in which the "otherness" of the children is articulated by presenting them as a kind of parody of the Aryan ideal imagined by the Nazis, with blonde hair, piercing eyes, seriousness, superiority of intellect, implacable will, ruthlessly applied. The sequel *Children of the Damned* (dir. Anton Leader, 1964) elaborates this theme in a more complex manner. Here, the children are unnerving, but not quite so obviously threatening. Indeed, they are shown to be just as frightened by adults as the adults are frightened of them. With the intention of politicians to exploit their powers for the Cold War, they have good reason to be afraid. Though the scientist played by Alan Badel eventually comes to regard these children as a threat to humanity due to their superior intellect, the children themselves explain that although they don't know why they are here, they do know that they represent humanity as it will become after centuries of evolution: In Blavatsky's terms, they are a foretaste of the sixth and possibly seventh Round of our development. By destroying them, the politicians and the military under their command are in fact destroying themselves. The anti-war message is made clear by the fact that their destruction is caused by a casual accident: a screwdriver falling on a switch that sets off the destruction.

In *Quatermass and the Pit* (dir. Roy Ward Baker, 1967), what originally appears to be a Nazi weapon unearthed in the London Underground station at Hobbs Lane is revealed to be a spaceship, which now holds the dead bodies of locust-like Martians. These creatures' genetic manipulation of the brain capacity of early humanoids has a great deal in common with Blavatsky's theory that "higher" races descended from the superior magical minds of the ancient Atlanteans. These people were, as she put it, "a nation of wicked *magicians*,"[21] an idea that eventually found expression in the films *Atlantis, the Lost Continent* (dir. George Pal, 1961) and *Warlords of Atlantis*, both of which present the Atlanteans in Blavatskyian terms as the possessors of immense psychic powers. In the former, Zaren (John Dall) has enslaved his fellow Atlanteans to mine crystals with which he plans to construct a giant death ray that will make him master of the world. In *Warlords of Atlantis*, the Atlanteans are revealed to be Martians who have crash-landed on Earth. Traveling inside a fully equipped meteorite, they were seeking a suitable planet on which to relocate their population, but they were diverted from their course and plunged in the Atlantic Ocean. Unable to propel themselves back out into space, they have directed the destiny of humanity, providing them with the knowledge to develop nuclear weapons, which will do the job for them. Screenwriter Brian Hayles brought together various strands of Atlantean theory to his screenplay for this film:

In my mind, Atlanteans are a very passive people. They do not wish to fight or kill, but they'll *use* anyone who comes under their power, who can be of use to them, as a means to their end. They never employ violence themselves. They use other people's violence, when necessary. They live by their occult and hypnotic powers over minds inferior to their own elite intelligence. Edgar Cayce's hypnotic theories claimed that Atlantis was powered by what they called "the terrible crystal." The crystal form gave them the energy to survive, but not sufficient power to rise from the sea.

In my script, the top Atlanteans use the power of a crystal helmet to enable Charles, the scientist played by Peter Gilmore, to look into the future. Yes, the Atlanteans are a master race and it's interesting to note that Nazis, such as Himmler, were convinced that that Atlantis and Atlanteans really existed. This theory I worked on about the Great Flood, advanced by the German, Horbiger—his beliefs were taken up by Himmler in his fanatical determination to prove that Germans were the only pure Aryan race on earth ... the only race to be descended directly from the Atlanteans! ... Therefore, it's a fascinating fact that it was the Nazis who pushed scientific and military technology to its utmost, resulting in rocket warfare, atomic bombs and so on. The Atlanteans would have admired the German race and its promotion of scientific development as one of their own kind. By making the Nazis create a world-dominating power, the Atlanteans would think *we* were creating the energy to help them take off again.[22]

The inconvenient truth that disturbs Hayles' theory is that it was, of course, the U.S.A. who beat the Nazis to the atomic bomb; but Hanns Hörbiger's World Ice Theory did put forward the idea that the Earth was originally orbited by more than one moon, and that the eventual collapse of these moons onto the Earth's surface was the cause of the Great Flood and the destruction of Atlantis. Himmler's interest in Atlantis as the origin of the pure Aryan race (it was claimed that the German people were descendants) is also well documented. He did believe that the Nordic race "came directly down from heaven to settle on the Atlantic continent."[23] Despite his professed irritation with Himmler's mystical ideas, Hitler was also bound to have been interested in anything that supported his racial program. In *Mein Kampf,* he disturbingly provided the blueprint for what Hayles describes in *Warlords of Atlantis*:

> The progress of humanity is like climbing an endless ladder; it is impossible to climb higher without first taking the lower steps. Thus, the Aryan had to take the road to which reality directed him and not the one that would appeal to the imagination of a modern pacifist. The road of reality is hard and difficult, but in the end it leads where our friend would like to bring humanity by dreaming, but unfortunately removes more than bringing it closer.
>
> Hence it is no accident that the first cultures arose in places where the Aryan, in his encounters with lower peoples, subjugated them and bent them to his will. They then become the first technical instrument in the service of a developing culture.
>
> Thus, the road which the Aryan had to take was clearly marked out. As a conqueror he subjected the lower beings and regulated their practical activity under his command, according to his will and for his aims. But in directing them to a useful, though arduous

activity, he not only spared the life of those he subjected; perhaps he gave them a fate that was better than their previous so-called "freedom." As long as he ruthlessly upheld the master attitude, not only did he really remain master, but also the preserver and increaser of culture.[24]

Hayles even incorporated an equivalent of "the ruthless Nazi classification of the people under their domination," by having his Atlanteans categorize their prisoners according to intelligence and brain-wave type: Alpha people, such as the Atlanteans, Atsil and Atraxon (Cyd Charisse and Daniel Massey), Delta people (Doug McClure's marine engineer, Greg) and Thetas—"potential thugs."[25] "We are a Master Race," Atsil explains. "We control. We manipulate. We of the red planet will not soil our hands with blood." Atraxon adds, "The ruling class must always survive."

Stripped of its appalling social and humanitarian crimes, the Nazi program really does resemble a sci-fi B movie, built on exactly this kind of irrational fantasy, which in turn was derived from Sinnett's slender volume and Blavatsky's considerably heavier occult Bible. Blavatsky's worldview has an ironic twist, for her Atlanteans (Himmler's supposed Ur-Aryans) abused their powers and ended up destroying themselves and their continent. Hitler's admiration of Wagner's *Ring* cycle is similarly ironic, for he seemed to overlook the fact that the ruthless pursuit of power, manifested in the cursed ring of the Nibelung, results in the destruction of civilization. Just as Wagner liked to repeat himself ("Wagner treats us as if—he says something so often—till one despairs—till one believes it,"[26] wrote Friedrich Nietzsche), so too Blavatsky's *Secret Doctrine* quotes her earlier thoughts on the subject in *Isis Unveiled*:

> The conflict came to an end by the submersion of the Atlantis, which finds its imitation in the stories of the Babylonian and Mosaic flood. The giants and magicians "... and all flesh died ... and every man." All except Xisuthrus and Noah, who are substantially identical with the great Father of the Thlmkithians in the *Popol-Vuh,* or the sacred book of the Guatemaleans, which also tells of his escaping in a large boat like the Hindu Noah Vaivasvata.
>
> If we believe the tradition at all, we have to credit the further story that, from the intermarrying of the progeny of the hierophants of the island and the descendants of the Atlantean Noah, sprang up a mixed race of righteous and wicked. On the one side the world had its Enochs, Moseses, various Buddhas, its numerous "Saviours," and great hierophants; on the other hand, its "*natural* magicians" who, through lack of the restraining power of proper spiritual enlightenment, ... perverted their gifts to evil purposes...[27]

Blavatsky's censure of power-hungry Atlantean magicians provides us with a metaphor, at least, of Nazi hubris. Hitler's dream of a Triumph of the Will is also echoed in Hayles' screenplay:

ATRAXON: Think, Aitkin. What you now call science was once condemned as magic, yet it is only the understanding and control of the natural order. Mind over matter.

Half an hour into *The City Under the Sea* (dir. Jacques Tourneur, 1965), Vincent Price's Captain explains how he arrived at a similar dilemma. The past inhabitants of this underwater city were rather like Atlanteans—masters of technology with an advanced pumping system and flashing lights to prove just how civilized they were before a volcano sank their citadel. Like the stranded Martians in *Warlords of Atlantis*, these people lived an underwater existence for a while; but eventually they died. Only the Gillmen survived, "the half-men: pathetic remnants of a great nation." Racism thus appears once more. *The City Under the Sea* was very loosely based on Poe's poem of the same name and Price quotes (inaccurately) one of its lines, explaining that these Gillmen think he is "Death looking gigantically down from my tower." Price's Captain was in fact the leader of a Cornish smuggling gang. Escaping from the excise men, he and his men made their way through coastal tunnels and discovered the ancient, abandoned city, where they were trapped and became immortal due to an "imbalance of oxygen, brought on by the presence of the volcano." They have also grown sensitive to ultraviolet light, which would kill them, and so they can never return to the surface. The volcano eventually obliges with an eruption, this culminating catastrophe also echoing the film's generally Atlantean credentials.

Theosophy also lies behind the Cthulhu mythos of H.P. Lovecraft. As he writes in "The Call of Cthulhu" (1928):

> Theosophists have guessed at the awesome grandeur of the cosmic cycle wherein our world and human race form transient incidents. They have hinted at strange survivals in terms which would freeze the blood if not masked by a bland optimism. But it is not from them that there came the single glimpse of forbidden aeons which chills me when I think of it and maddens me when I dream of it.[28]

In its violent paganism, Lovecraft's evocation of the world as it was when ruled by "the Great Ones," with Cthulhu at their head, also has a distinctly Nietzschean tone:

> The time would be easy to know, for then mankind would have become as the Great Old Ones; free and wild and beyond good and evil, with laws and morals thrown aside and all men shouting and killing and revelling in joy. Then the liberated Old Ones would teach them new ways to shout and kill and revel and enjoy themselves, and all the earth would flame with a holocaust of ecstasy and freedom.[29]

Lovecraft's work has inspired several adaptations for both the large and small screen, the most interesting of which, at least from a visual point of view, is Daniel Haller's *The Dunwich Horror* (1970). Haller's previous employment as art director on Roger Corman's Poe films in the 1960s ensured that he found a convincing way of suggesting the invisible emanations of evil that are summoned at the end of the film by Dean Stockwell's Wilbur Whateley. The tentacled horror of Cthulhu makes a brief appearance before being sent back to the lower depths, but it is Wilbur's otherworldly brother who is of most interest, being the product of a coupling between Mrs. Whateley and something not of this earth. The scenes in which this monstrosity is born prefigure the conception and horrific birth scenes in Peter Sykes' *To the Devil a Daughter.* We are not shown anything quite so graphic as the latter's depiction of Isabella Telezynska's Margaret, with her legs tied together so that the Antichrist is forced to burst through her stomach, but two ancient crones standing by Mrs. Whateley's bed assure us that this is no normal birth. Kept locked in an upstairs room like an extra-terrestrial Mrs. Rochester, this creature, after much door-rattling, eventually breaks free, and it is here that Haller's visual imagination comes to the fore. Accompanied with unnerving sound effects, Haller filters reversed "negative" imagery through truly psychedelic colors, which could well have been inspired by Lovecraft's story "The Colour Out of Space":

> All the farm was shining with the hideous unknown blend of colour; trees, buildings, and even such grass and herbage as had not been wholly changed to lethal grey bitterness. The boughs were all straining skyward, tipped with tongues of foul flame, and lambent trickling of the same monstrous fire were creeping about the ridgepoles of the house, barn, and sheds. It was a scene from a vision of Fuseli, and over all the rest reigned that riot of luminous amorphousness, that alien and undimensioned rainbow of cryptic poison from the well—seething, feeling, lapping, reaching, scintillating, straining, and malignly bubbling in its cosmic and unrecognisable chromaticism.[30]

Haller's effect is first used when we are shown the world through the eyes of Mrs. Whateley, who languishes on her asylum bed, having long ago been driven insane by the birth of her cosmic horror. We see the Dunwich doctor and the local university professor enter her room from Mrs. Whateley's point of view, their negative images soaked in vivid violet and sepulchral scarlet. A ghoulish green then complements the blood tones, transmuting into awful orange against the green, before bleeding back to blue, red and purple. The colors continue to change in this manner, with a coruscating effect rarely seen in film before, brilliantly suggesting the crazed workings of Mrs. Whateley's brain with the psychedelic imagery of the time in which the film first appeared.

Haller brings the effect back during the escape of the cosmic horror from its bedroom. (Could it really have been withheld by a wooden door?)

Wilbur has meanwhile taken his sacrificial victim to the abandoned ruins of the old Cthulhu Temple on the Whateley estate, and there he indulges in a fairly conventional ritual involving much waving of a knife and a goblet, extravagant hand gestures, billows of incense smoke, and invocations of unpronounceable Lovecraftian coinages read out from the notorious *Necronomican* "Bible" propped on his victim's stomach. These incantations "open the gateway" and let loose the Old Ones to repossess the Earth: "Brother of Darkness! Leave your prison and help me bring the Old Ones through!" he commands. "Brother of my blood—my soul—I summon you!"

Whatever it is that bursts through the upstairs bedroom door, Haller makes sure we think it to be the most horrible thing we can imagine, precisely by revealing nothing in clear detail. It seems to be all mouth, but thereafter becomes an invisible force. It sets fire to the Whateley house and sees the world much as Mrs. Whateley did on her asylum bed—in vividly colored negative images. As it moves down a dirt track, its heartbeat pounding on the soundtrack, it raises spectral dust. It causes a dried riverbed to rehydrate, it kills the Christian couple who were previously hostile to Wilbur, and gradually makes its way to the scene of the sacrifice. Without Haller's psychedelic shots, this somewhat loose adaptation of Lovecraft's tale would have considerably less interest and significance, but they successfully suggest the extra-dimensional entities of Lovecraft without recourse to unconvincing literalism—something Lovecraft always avoided. However, as we shall see in the next chapter, psychedelic imagery was by no means confined to Haller's vision of *The Dunwich Horror.*

CHAPTER TEN

Psychedelia

Aldous Huxley's 1954 study of the effect of mescaline in *The Doors of Perception* describes how this drug affects our perception of color:

> Mescaline raises all colours to a higher power and makes the percipient aware of innumerable fine shades of difference, to which, at ordinary times, he is completely blind. It would seem that, for Mind at Large, the so-called secondary characters of things are primary. Unlike Locke, it evidently feels that colours are more important, better worth attending to than masses, positions, and dimensions. Like mescaline takers, many mystics perceive supernaturally brilliant colours, not only with the inward eye, but even in the objective world around them. There are certain mediums to whom the mescaline taker's brief revelation is a matter, during long periods, of daily and hourly experience.[1]

Huxley describes these drug-induced moments of revelation as "Artificial Paradises."[2] ("A rose is a rose is a rose. But these chair legs were chair legs were St. Michael and all angels."[3])

> That humanity will ever be able to dispense with Artificial Paradises seems very unlikely. Most men and women lead lives at the worst so painful, at the best so monotonous, poor, and limited that the urge to escape, the longing to transcend themselves if only for a few moments, is and has always been one of the principal appetites of the soul. Art and religion, carnivals and saturnalia, dancing and listening to oratory—all these have served, in H.G. Wells's phrase, as Doors in the Wall.[4]

The phrase derives from Wells' 1911 short story, "The Door in the Wall," concerning a boy's discovery of just that, along with the revelation, when he opens it, of a magical garden of similar "supernaturally brilliant colours":

> There was something in the very air of it that exhilarated, that gave one a sense of lightness and good happening and well-being; there was something in the sight of it that made all its colour clean and perfect and subtly luminous. In the instant of coming into it one was exquisitely glad—as only in rare moments, and when one is young and joyful one can be glad in this world. And everything was beautiful there…[5]

If this reminds one of Ray Stevens' immensely popular 1970s anthem "Everything Is Beautiful," it only demonstrates how easily the mystical origins of 1960s counter-culture were hijacked by right-wing commercialism.

In 1956, Wells' story inspired Glenn H. Alvey's important experimental film which features an early score by James Bernard and a technique Alvey called the "Dynamic Frame," in which the frame of the film expands and contracts according to the dramatic and psychological contours of the story. (In a scene set in the magic garden, there is also an intriguing prediction of the iPad: The boy is shown a photograph album of moving pictures.) When the Dynamic Frame opens out to its full extent, suggesting the expanded consciousness of the boy as he enters the magic garden, Bernard's music foreshadows the even more magical score he composed for Robert Day's *She* in 1965.

Jung regarded Rider Haggard's *She* (1886–1887) as an archetype of the imaginative and spiritually enriching feminine aspect of the psyche, "the guide and mediator to the inner world," which he termed the "animus," and which was known to medieval thought as "Flos Campi"—the flower of the field:

> I am the flower of the field and the lily of the valleys. I am the mother of fair love and of fear and of knowledge and of holy hope.... I am the mediator of the elements, making one to agree with another; that which is warm I make cold and the reverse, and that which is hard I soften.... I am the law in the priest and the word in the prophet and the counsel in the wise. I will kill and I will make to live and there is none that can deliver out of my hand.[6]

In "The Door in the Wall," the garden is the equivalent of discovering the beautiful immortal woman Ayesha beyond the Mountains of the Moon in *She*. Ayesha first appears from behind a curtain, rather than a door:

> The curtain agitated itself a little, then suddenly between its folds there appeared a most beautiful white hand, white as snow, and with long tapering fingers, ending in the pinkest nails. The hand grasped the curtain, and drew it aside, and as it did so I heard a voice, I think the softest and yet most silvery voice I ever heard. It reminded me of the murmur of a brook.[7]

When the boy in "The Door in the Wall" grows up, he encounters the door at significant moments in his life, but on each occasion he fails to go through it: "Each time, you see," he explains to his friend, "my whole life would have been changed if I'd gone through that door. Each time, I took the way to ... success." Wordsworth had discussed a similar problem in his 1803 ode "Intimations of Immortality From Recollections of Early Childhood":

> Shades of the prison-house begin to close
> Upon the growing Boy,
> But He beholds the light, and whence it flows,
> He sees it in his joy;
> The Youth, who daily farther from the east

Must travel, still is Nature's Priest,
And by the vision splendid
Is on his way attended;
At length the Man perceives it die away,
And fade into the light of common day.[8]

The Door in the Wall was released only two years after Aldous Huxley's *The Doors of Perception*, the title of which later lent its name to Jim Morrison's "occult" rock group, The Doors. In 1960, an even more sensational pop eruption had taken place with the formation of the Beatles. The argument about the Beatles' involvement in occultism still rages, fueled by the inclusion of Aleister Crowley as one of the "people we like" on the cover of the Sgt. Pepper album, along with the supposed occult hand signals and "secret society" top hats on their album covers. All this rather depends on one's own point of view, but what is undeniable is the use of occult imagery in the Beatles' films. This is largely treated with a degree of satire, while simultaneously flirting with the undeniable appeal of mysticism. Such satire can also be found in other aspects of '60s popular culture, from the U.S. comedy series *Bewitched*, concerning the domestic arrangements of a suburban witch (Elizabeth Montgomery) who unsuccessfully attempts not to practice magic to please her suburban husband. In Britain, Hammer Films' rival, Amicus, also satirized the occult in the compendium horror film *From Beyond the Grave*. Somewhat in the manner of Madame Arcarti in Noël Coward's earlier *Blithe Spirit*, Margaret Leighton plays Madame Orloff, an eccentric psychic who exorcises an elemental from an unbelieving businessman played by Ian Carmichael. "He's a particularly nasty specimen," she insists. "A real stinker, and he's growing stronger every moment." After the elemental makes the businessman attack his wife, Madame Orloff is called in. "Well, stay put, and I'll belt down there. It is rather a nuisance because I have one table-tapping session and a voice from beyond on the books for tomorrow, but never mind. It can't be helped."

The elemental proves to be genuine, and it puts up an impressive fight. The tone of the piece is also reminiscent of the approach to the occult in the Beatles' film *Help!* (dir. Richard Lester, 1965). This opens with a scene in the orientalist manner of Hammer Films: Reflecting the Beatles' involvement in Indian mysticism, the action begins with the silhouette of a statue of the goddess Kali, accompanied with gong and sitar, which immediately plunges the audience into a ritualistic milieu. Leo McKern's obviously fake Indian accent soon assures the audience that none of this is to be taken seriously; but the shot of him wearing a bronze mask, his hands raised before Kali's similarly waving arms, curiously anticipates the kind of imagery we encounter in ritualistic opening sequences of Hammer's *The Plague of the*

Zombies and *The Reptile*, not to mention the specifically Hindu horror story *The Ghoul* (dir. Freddie Francis, 1975), starring Peter Cushing as a tormented cleric whose son, locked in his upstairs room, has been corrupted into a cannibal by an Indian cult. In *Help!*, the golden headdresses of McKern's temple maidens are also reminiscent of what adorns Ursula Andress in Hammer's *She* (1965), as is the ritual sacrifice that is about to take place. This, however, is prevented by another worshipper (Eleanor Bron), who points out that the victim, wrapped in Hammer-esque scarlet robes, is not wearing the appropriate sacrificial ring. It is possible that Alan Gibson had these opening shots in mind when directing Hammer's *The Satanic Rites of Dracula,* for he also shoots the ritual gathering of Satanists that opens the action from above.

The rest of *Help!* is a satire not only on the James Bond films but also of Wilkie Collins' *The Moonstone*, as the Indian cult members attempt to remove the missing ring from the appropriately named Ringo's finger. From today's perspective, the abundance of Indian stereotypes performed by established English actors severely undermines the supposed "cool" of the Beatles, and seems at odds with the group's later transcendentalist leanings. One scene, set in an Indian restaurant with pantomime Indian musicians, includes a waiter who is standing on his head in the cellar before rushing off to lie down on a bed of nails. Earlier, McKern's high priest shares a tea table with a Church of England bishop, and manages to send up mysticism, fox-hunting, censorship, Indians and the British establishment in one short speech:

> Sex is creeping in. It's being thrown at youth. They see it everywhere; in the bazaars, in the market places—in the temple even. No wonder they turn up their noses at a mystical impulse. We are taking up fox-hunting so that young people can be involved in their own sacrifice and will understand the full significance of blood worship. Of course, I don't expect you to see eye to eye with me, but I'm sure that we can agree to differ.

The cover for the *Help!* LP album shows the Beatles gesturing semaphore signs (NVUJ), which evangelical detractors like to suggest stands for "Envy You Jesus?" Some see the radiating lines of the scallop behind them not only as the corporate logo of Shell Petroleum, but also as a symbol of sun-worship; and Ringo's semaphore sign has been interpreted as a suggestion of the text, "As above, so below," from the Emerald Tablet of Hermes Trismegistus. But such interpretations perhaps say more about the preoccupations of those who make them than the beliefs of the Beatles.

The 1967 Summer of Love coincided with the release of Michael Reeves' *The Sorcerers,* which fused psychedelic imagery with magickal theories about willpower. It also exposed the violence that lay beneath the mystic flower-power of the period, which was later to be manifested in the infamous Manson murders. Karloff's Prof. Montserrat promises, "Intoxication with no hangover. Ecstasy with no consequence," but there *is* a particularly drastic consequence, as we have seen. Though this story of willpower and mind control is presented in a scientific rather than occult context, its effect is no different from any other magickal operation (which Crowley would have claimed as an aspect of science anyway). The means by which this is achieved employs psychedelic imagery distinctly of its time. The all-white laboratory where this takes place betrays the low-budget of the film, but Reeves more than compensates for these shortcomings by his use of colored lights and electronic sounds, which create a synesthetic display in a direct line of descent from the dreams of Scriabin. The laboratory becomes a light show, Ian Ogilvy's face being grotesquely distorted by means of projected slides of shifting, multi-colored shapes as though his skin has erupted in violent rashes, scars and contusions. Reeves' camera also loses focus and zooms in and out, further disorienting the viewer during this extended sequence, which is far more engaging than the frankly rather dull scenes set in a night club in which various pop acts entertain bored teenagers.

ALL IN THE MIND: **Poster for** *Yellow Submarine* **(dir. George Dunning, 1968).**

Psychedelia fused more overtly with mysticism in *Yellow Submarine* (dir. George Dunning, 1968). The basic philosophy of this film was recapitulated a few years later in Serge Danot's *Dougal and the Blue Cat* (1970), in which a similar color-war takes place. Both the Blue Meanies in the former and Buxton the Blue Cat in the latter intend to wipe out all other colors but blue. The message of both films is also love and peace, and both are responses to the hallucinogenic imagery of the time; but *Yellow Submarine* contains a great deal more esoteric symbolism than the Magic Roundabout film. How conscious Dunning and his animators were of these symbols remains open to question, but they are undoubtedly present. The Beatles themselves were hardly involved in the project beyond providing extra musical material, so whatever occult input the film might contain does not appear to have derived from them. Various esoteric interpretations have been put forward over the years, such as that theory that the Yellow Submarine itself is a symbol of balance between the male and female principles (what Jung called the *anima* and *animus* of the psyche). Yellow can also be interpreted as a symbol of the masculine sun, whereas a submarine, which operates beneath the water, can be seen as a symbol of the feminine. It is originally shown perched on top of a Mayan-style pyramid, reminiscent of Noah's Ark run aground on Mount Ararat, and also of the light-radiating eye-within-a-triangle atop the pyramid we find on the Seal of the United States of America. (This is another metaphor of psychic and sexual balance, if one regards the pyramid a mammary symbol.) However, the problem with such symbolism is its ambiguity; everything can become symbolic of anything given enough imagination and determination.

Even the name "The Beatles" has been claimed to signify more than merely a reference to the Beat movement out of which the group emerged. Advocates of this approach relate it to the ancient Egyptians' worship of the scarab beetle and its symbolism of rebirth. The Blue Meanies also wear Mickey Mouse ears, suggesting that they represent the evils of the corporate world, of which Disney has long been regarded by conspiracy theorists as being the epitome and dedicated to materialistic mind control. (That top hats turn into rainbows might also suggest the transcendence of these oppressions.) *Yellow Submarine* also contains hexagrams, the sign of the "Devil's Horn" (a supposed gesture of hypnotic influence, which many of the characters in the film perform). One may also watch out for hidden-hand and one-eyed masonic symbolism, the symbolic handshake of freemasonry, sphinxes, winged lions and apples, the latter suggestive of the Beatles' company, Apple computers and of the forbidden fruit itself. The Nowhere Man character, Jeremy Hillary Book, Ph.D., also ends up hanging by his ankles echoing the

Hanged Man Arcana of Tarot. Ringo is shown pierced with arrows like St. Sebastian, while twin pillars might even suggest Jachin and Boaz, the sacred columns of the temple of Solomon, another important symbol of Freemasonry. (A photograph of Jim Morrison and members of the Doors standing between two columns has also been given this Biblical interpretation.) The film's ultimate message of Love, combined with the appearance of Aleister Crowley on the record sleeve of the Sgt. Pepper album, suggests for many that the film it inspired is a response to Crowley's dictum: "Do What Thou Wilt Shall Be the Whole of the Law: Love is the Law. Love under Will."

Less ambiguous in its intent if not in its symbolism is Kenneth Anger's tribute to Crowleyan magic in *Lucifer Rising* (1974). Erupting volcanoes, a baby crocodile emerging from its egg, and bubbling mud suggest the imminent arrival of Lucifer, whom Anger, after Crowley's example, interprets as a herald of light and freedom. Isis appears on a rock and signals to Osiris. An initiate in a coat of many colors enters a temple, sits on an Egyptian throne, and is drenched in blood, which he washes off in a roll-top bath. Next, Lilith (Marianne Faithfull) rises from a stone sarcophagus. Magma from the volcanoes draws closer. Lilith poses significantly before the Sphinx at Giza. We move from Stonehenge to the famous Eksternsteine rock formations near the Teutoburg Forest in Germany, where hooded worshipers walk carrying flambeau. Crossing the iron bridge that connects the two stones, we enter the ancient pagan temple carved into the rock, which pre-historian Otto von Bennigsen suggests had once been a solar observatory. (The Externsteine are on approximately the same latitude as Stonehenge, hence their shared alignment with midsummer sunrise.)

The initiate now puts the title of Anger's film into practice, raising Lucifer by running around the rim of a magic circle. A translucent cone appears over the circle, surrounded by flashing lights, and Lucifer appears in a jacket emblazoned with his name. Crowley's photograph, framed in a black laurel wreath, is unveiled. One of Crowley's books is taken from its shelf and Jimmy Page of Led Zeppelin holds up the Stele of Revealing, an artifact of central importance to Crowley when founding his religion of Thelema. Such is the allusive style of this cinematic collage, which is really a procession of psychedelic occult imagery, designed to create a ritualistic mood (with the help of Billy Beausoleil's soundtrack score), rather than a distinct narrative.

Alexandro Jodorowsky's *The Holy Mountain* (1973), in part financed by John Lennon, is usefully viewed alongside *Yellow Submarine,* as both films brilliantly exploit psychedelic colors and surreal imagery to explore the nature of reality. *The Holy Mountain* is more alchemical in a Jungian sense than overtly occult, being less about the development of the will to effect change than its renunciation to attain spiritual enlightenment. Jung's analysis of alchemical symbolism makes clear the psychological value of what was once dismissed as a pseudo-science:

> The alchemical *opus* deals in the main not just with chemical experiments as such, but with something resembling psychic processes expressed in pseudo chemical language. ... On the one hand the alchemist declares that he is concealing the truth intentionally, so as to prevent wicked or stupid people from gaining possession of the gold and thus precipitating a catastrophe. But, on the other hand, the same author will assure us that the gold he is seeking is not—as the stupid suppose—the ordinary gold (*arum vulgi*), it is the philosophical gold or even the marvelous stone, the *lapis invisibilitatis* (the stone of invisibility), or the *lapis aethereus* (the ethereal stone), or finally the unimaginable hermaphroditic *rebus*, and he will end up by saying that all recipes whatsoever are to be despised. For psychological reasons, however, it is highly unlikely that the motive prompting the alchemist to secrecy and mystification was consideration for mankind. Whenever anything real is discovered it is usually announced with a flourish of trumpets. The fact is that the alchemists had little or nothing to divulge in the way of chemistry, least of all the secret of goldmaking.[9]

As was possibly the case with Mr. Nowhere Man, the protagonist of Jodorowsky's film is a personification of the Tarot card known as "The Fool." He is an Everyman who, along with other representatives of the world (all of whom represent materialist and negative human traits), makes his way towards the mountaintop of initiation, only to be informed by the Alchemist who initiated this quest (Jodorowsky) that ultimate reality (presumably God) can only be aspired to, which is not to diminish the value of such aspiration. The Alchemist has previously transformed the Fool's excrement into gold, providing a metaphor for the Fool's spiritual quest. The Fool wrestles with religion (represented by a statue of Christ, which we see him carry, like Christ on His way to Calvary, eat, as if taking Holy Communion, and then release into the heavens with the aid of balloons). He also casts aside the burden of his own doubts in the shape of an armless dwarf. He and his fellow pilgrims burn effigies of themselves, and cast all worldly wealth into purifying flames.

Though in part inspired by the sixteenth-century treatise *The Ascent of Mount Carmel* by St. John of the Cross, *The Holy Mountain* uses symbolism that had been long established by filmmakers such as Arnold Fanck and Leni Riefenstahl. However, these German examples were much more firmly rooted in the traditions of the sublime than Jodorowsky. Riefenstahl's first appearance was in a film also called *The Holy Mountain*. Directed by Fanck in 1926, its superficial love triangle story provides a somewhat flimsy structure for a series of sublime mountain tableaux derived from the pantheistic nineteenth-century example of Romantic artist Caspar David Friedrich. The way Fanck photographs the mountains invests them with an aura of spiritual significance beyond their mere sublimity. The final card of the film explains that the mountain is "a symbol of the greatest values humanity can embrace— Fidelity—Truth—Loyalty." Such symbolism extends beyond the confines of the love story that articulates the narrative action, and implies the kind of enlightenment for which Jodorowsky is searching.

This is even more the case in *Der blaue Licht* (*The Blue Light*, 1932), which Riefenstahl both directed and starred in. Here, the mountains become even more significant of spiritual yearning, the blue light that emerges from them being created by the kind of crystals so many New Age boutiques now like to sell at occult watering places such as Glastonbury. As in Fanck's *The Holy Mountain*, the cave in *Der blaue Licht* is presented as a kind of temple, and the search for and discovery of the blue crystals represents a kind of pantheistic Eucharist. The imagery in fact derives from Novalis' 1802 romance *Heinrich von Ofterdingen* in which the eponymous hero seeks a mystical blue flower. But Novalis also makes reference to a cave coated with a golden liquid "cool to the touch and which cast from the walls a weak blue light."[10]

In Riefenstahl's films, individuals are never as important as the landscape in which they move, their ultimate aim being to achieve her audience's *absorption* into the greater whole. This aspect of Romanticism, which Wordsworth described in "A slumber did my spirit seal" as being "Roll'd round in earth's diurnal course,/With rocks, and stones, and trees," became politically manipulated when the seductive esthetic of these mountain films was absorbed into the tawdry sublimity of the Nazi state. Hitler was fully aware of this:

> [S]ince true idealism is nothing but the subordination of the interests and life of the individual to the community, and this in turn is the precondition for the creation of organizational forms of all kinds, it corresponds in its innermost depths to the ultimate will of Nature. It alone leads men to voluntary recognition of the privilege of force and strength, and thus makes them into a dust particle of that order which shapes and forms the whole universe.[11]

This was obviously not the kind of enlightenment envisioned by Jodorowsky's *Holy Mountain*, and Hitler's words demonstrate all too clearly how ambivalent metaphors can be. (The swastika itself is an excellent example of how the originally positive connotations of a symbol can be completely reversed and polluted, perhaps forever.)

The attraction of rock musicians to the occult ultimately found expression in the Crowley-inspired *Chemical Wedding* (dir. Julian Doyle, 2008), in which Bruce Dickinson of the Heavy Metal group Iron Maiden paid tribute to his hero by writing the screenplay. He also put in a cameo appearance as Crowley's landlord at the beginning of the film. The movie is more Hammer-esque than psychedelic: Economic considerations ruled out a period approach, so Dickinson set everything but the prologue in present-day Cambridge and had Crowley reincarnated in the body of Simon Callow's Oliver Haddo by means of a virtual reality machine. Crowley intends to perform a ritual, last enacted by Abelard and Héloïse, which will elevate him into a god—hence the title of the film. A young student reporter (Lucy Cudden) will be his Heloise, with Crowley as Abelard, but the plot fails. Instead, time is reversed, Crowley is banished to another dimension and the Democrat Al Gore is elected president of the United States, rather than the dangerous Republican alternative, which would no doubt have been the case had Crowley succeeded. (No one suspected Donald Trump in those days.) There is rather more sex than psychedelia going on here, with orgies, love bites, masturbation and an appearance by the Whore of Babylon herself, not to mention Crowley-Haddo's sensational micturition over a group of students during a lecture on *Hamlet*. But Doyle also revels in all the esoteric paraphernalia and has fun exposing the absurdity of New Age marketing by having one of Crowley's ceremonies take place in an crystal-bedecked, dream-catcher–filled occult boutique. This being over-subscribed, one of the applicants is turned away: "But I've come all the way from Glastonbury," she complains. Dickinson further connected the antics to rock culture by including songs by Iron Maiden, exploiting the title track from their otherwise unrelated album *Chemical Wedding*.

Throughout the 1960s and '70s, psychedelic imagery was often used to suggest magical events. In Paul Wendkos' *The Mephisto Waltz*, the transference of Duncan Ely's soul into the body of journalist Miles Clarkson is photographed as though it were a drug-induced hallucination, which in many ways it is. The camera zooms in on Miles' eye and appears to penetrate it, delving into his unconscious—even his soul, which seems able to observe what happens next, even though his body has been rendered inert. We see Roxanne enter the room, the scarlet walls illuminated like blood-red gashes, the whole filmed through an obscured lens, as though it has been smeared with gelatin. Wendkos also uses a very moderate slow-motion technique to enhance the dream-like quality of the action. The psychedelic effect of the soul transference itself is created by the contrast between the scarlet walls in which the ritual takes place and the deep blue of the liquid in the bottle, which forms an important part of the ritual. A spot of the liquid is placed on Miles' forehead in the manner of an Indian bindi. The same liquid is then used to trace the inevitable pentagram on the floor. In the middle of the pentagram, a candle is placed. Wendkos now slants his camera to enhance the atmosphere of disorientation, and the whole is immeasurably enriched by the French prayer to the Devil, which the dying Ely whispers on his deathbed.

This, coupled with Jerry Goldsmith's equally disjointed score, completes the hallucinatory ingredients. A plaster mask of Miles is placed over Ely's features, curtains billow and the candle blows out (signifying the death of the pianist), while the pale blue light that illuminates all this suggests eerie inversion of Novalis.

The style of filming in this sequence directly relates to the earlier party scene set in Ely's home in which we encounter a dog unnervingly wearing the mask of a man, men and women wearing masks of animals and birds, a belly dancer, a statue pierced with arrows *à la* St. Sebastian, a man with a blue turban (the same shade as the later potion) and women (including the belly dancer) wearing the same shade of scarlet we later see on the ritual chamber walls. The color scheme is recapitulated by the red fez worn atop Miles' gorilla mask, and the dusky blue of a net curtain that hangs behind him. Wendkos also exploits similarly slanted camera angles. Though the musical entertainment is hardly rock or pop, someone is clearly smoking dope on the stairs as Miles' wife makes her escape.

Party scenes were a frequent happening in occult films of this period. *The Curse of the Crimson Altar* begins with one, this time with somewhat "hipper" music. Drugs are consumed, a woman's breasts are painted, another woman pours champagne over her own, scarlet light bathes the proceedings and a piggyback duel with paint brushes keeps the guests entertained. Hammer kicked off the occult proceedings in *Dracula A.D. 1972* with a real pop group (Stoneground) and an extended party scene with dancing, sexual fumbling under a table and more snogging than Hammer had ever countenanced before, while a dismayed elder generation watches the proceedings from the sidelines.

The Haunted House of Horror (dir. Michael Armstrong, 1969), which teases the audience into thinking it is an occult rather than a serial killer thriller, also has a party scene and pop music, but neither of these indulged in a dream sequence, unlike *Curse of the Crimson Altar* which, clumsy though it may be as a whole, does offer one of the 1960s' kinkiest occult hallucinations. It begins with kaleidoscopic flame (or billowing silk) effects swirling around the sleeping body of Robert Manning (Mark Eden). These intensify over his head, causing him to wake and "see" his missing brother, his face illuminated green against the red kaleidoscope effect. The kaleidoscope then becomes more exotic as we realize that the new patterns are fragmented aspects of the green-faced witch Lavinia (Barbara Steele) who is worshipped by her acolytes at the mansion in which Manning finds himself spending the night. The kaleidoscope next gives way to a medium shot of Steele, her torso painted green, wearing a headdress of golden ram's horns adorned with feathers. Her throne is flanked by two Gothic turrets and surmounted with red pinnacles, lending it a distinctly phallic connotation. Steele's lips are scarlet, and though this color is offset against a deep blue jewel hanging on her forehead, complementary red and green are the predominate colors here.

A trial is in progress, with a judge formally robed in red but bathed in green light. The jury members all wear animal heads similar to those in *The Mephisto Waltz* (not to mention Robin Hardy's *The Wicker Man* in 1973). An executioner, attired in leather briefs, studded leather armbands and chains, with a Herne-the-Hunter headdress, forces Manning to kneel before Lavinia and sign away his soul. He refuses. Lavinia stabs him. The kaleidoscope returns, multiplying the image of the phallic pinnacles of her throne, along with Lavinia's green face and her disturbingly crimson lips, now rather more pink than crimson. Later, Christopher Lee's character, revealed as one of Lavinia's disciples, uses a revolving lampshade of alternating red and green stripes to induce an occult mood. Its tasseled fringing is distinctly quaint, but the effect is suitably on trend.

In *Dracula A.D. 1972*, the traditional elements of the Black Mass are updated more by the aural psychedelia of the soundtrack than by the rather more conventional visual element. Mike Vickers' imaginatively improvised music for this scene, using acoustic instruments, is diegetic: The sounds are meant to emerge from the tape recorder being played during the ritual. But when the tape runs out, the disturbing electronic sounds of Delia Derbyshire's radiophonic "A Black Mass in Hell" are employed to suggest the manifestation of demonic forces. Later in the film, Stephanie Beacham's Jessica Van Helsing apparently dreams one of Dracula's attacks in the church where the Black Mass took place. Gibson cuts between shots of Jessica asleep and very rapid glimpses of Dracula, which almost stroboscopic alternation is indeed somewhat psychedelic in its effect, made even more unnerving by our realization that Jessica's "dream" is actually happening.

Psychedelic dream sequences became something of a trademark in Roger Corman's earlier Poe adaptations. In *The Masque of the Red Death*, Hazel Court's Juliana dedicates her soul to the Devil in a black room with windows that glow red. She then hallucinates a series of disturbing visions. After running on tiptoe in slow motion through billowing chiffon and dry ice, previous images from the film wavering as in a distorting mirror, Juliana finds herself lying on a kind of altar, where she is "sacrificed" several times, first by a Mayan dancer in another feathered headdress, who stabs her. Next, a Jewish magician wields a sickle over her, followed by an Egyptian priest with another dagger. Finally, an African dancer with even more feathers causes Juliana to scream and scream again.

Some of Corman's main title sequences also indulge in psychedelic imagery. His comedy *The Raven* (1963), concerning rival magicians (Vincent Price and Boris Karloff), nicely complements *Yellow Submarine* in its satirical use both of psychedelia and magickal imagery. It opens with Corman's characteristic effect of swirling colors—oil paints mixed with water as used in the marbling process. Over these, he superimposes the silhouette of a Raven, which returns for the end titles over a spinning emerald vortex, shot through with flashing circles of light.

Corman's *Pit and the Pendulum* (1961), though not an occult film, is also topped and tailed by this trademark marbling effect, to which Hammer seemed to be responding in the opening titles of *Dracula Has Risen From the Grave*, in which abstract networks of blood-red veins dissolve one into the other against a violently violet background. In the same year, 1968, the ultimate expression of such imagery was surely the "Ultimate Trip" enjoyed by so many hippies when they first experienced Stanley Kubrick's *2001—A Space Odyssey*. The self-indulgence of this extended light show, whose narrative function is to transport us into another time dimension, was fully in accordance with drug culture at the time, in which, to quote Wagner's *Parsifal*, "Time becomes Space" ("Zum Raum wird hier die Zeit"). The emotional impact in fact far outweighs the narrative function of the special effects here, which are designed to induce a magickal state of mind in which consciousness is expanded and critical faculties are suspended as in a kind of hypnosis. Though not technically a magickal film, the terrain Kubrick explores here is indeed magickal, in the sense that will is indeed seen to have effected change. The meaning of *2001* is an evolutionary one: The enigmatic black slab that appears at intervals throughout symbolizes significant milestones in humanity's development, from the moment apes learned how to use tools, through our exploration of space, to our ultimate destination as a form of pure spiritual energy, symbolized by the Cosmic Child that floats through space at the end of the film. In this respect, *2001* is a distinctly theosophical film, and a significant syntheses of magickal thinking and psychedelia.

Kubrick's ultimate trip was recapitulated in the 2016 superhero film *Doctor Strange* (Scott Derrickson). Here, Benedict Cumberbatch's arrogant New York surgeon Stephen Strange encounters Tilda Swinton's sorcerer, "The Ancient One," in a Nepalese monastery, which is what Harry Potter's Hogwarts would have been like if Madame Blavatsky and Ian Fleming's "Q" from the James Bond novels had been in charge. Here, the monks practice psi-martial arts, punching people into alternative dimensions of space and time; we are also shown shaven-headed novices conjuring fiery hoops out of pure willpower through which they can teleport themselves. At first skeptical of the Ancient One's claims that there are other dimensions, Strange is given conclusive proof of their existence by being thrust from the Earth into the astral plane, where everything and anything is possible. Floating around in time and space, he joins Kubrick's ultimate trip, which appears to have carried on long after the final frames of *2001* left the gate of the projector. He travels through a multi-colored vortex of light, into what is described to him as a "vast multiverse," "worlds without end." Various hallucinogenic visions affect him: His fingers, for instance, grow hands, the fingers of which grow more hands and eventually crawl all over him. The influence of mind-altering substances must surely have inspired the makers of this film. With over 32 million users of hallucinogenic drugs in the United States alone,[12] many people who have seen *Doctor Strange*, which had grossed $667 million in under a month, were no doubt able to relate to Dr. Strange's hallucinations from personal experience. "What is real?" asks the Ancient One. Well, under the influence of drugs, anything can seem real, even when it is an illusion, but the question is still a valid one, if we consider that our understanding of the world is entirely dependent upon what our brains tell us it is: Alter the brain and reality alters with it, at least for the person who is receiving the neurological impulses.

Doctor Strange's plot really does resemble the outer reaches of the Nazis' esoteric conspiracy theories. Instead of a Master Race, we have superheroes

STRANGE MAGIC: **Benedict Cumberbatch in the title role of** *Doctor Strange* **(dir. Scott Derrickson, 2016).**

with super powers. Instead of the Grail Knights of Hitler's SS, we have psychic warrior-monks. Instead of the Jews being the eternal enemies of mankind, we have the Dormammu of the Dark Dimension, who are trying to destroy the Earth by demolishing the three buildings (one in New York, one in London and one in Hong Kong) known as "Sanctums," which shield the planet from attacks by other dimensions. When one Sanctum is destroyed, the Dark Dimension gradually engulfs the earth. Buildings collapse in on themselves and "reality" begins to unravel. Using the mystical "Eye of Agamotto," Strange reverses time, saves the world, survives his own multiple deaths, returns to New York and joins up with the Norse gods Thor and Loki, who are searching for Odin on Earth. Himmler, who thought of himself as a reincarnation of the tenth-century King Henry the Fowler, could easily have written this screenplay and probably cast himself in the title role. Viewed from this perspective, *Doctor Strange* demonstrates the appalling comic-book foundations of Nazi Germany, which, as we shall see in the upcoming chapter on conspiracy theories, really did emerge out of half-baked Blavatskian barminess like this.

A word of warning, therefore, seems in order for a world that is increasingly enslaved by computer-generated imagery, fake news, alternative facts, conspiracy theories and ever-increasing xenophobia and political intolerance, and who better to provide it than that scourge of Nazi thinking, Kurt Vonnegut: "We are what we pretend to be," he wrote in his 1961 novel *Mother Night*, "so we must be careful about what we pretend to be."

Chapter Eleven

Conspiracy

Could it be that authors invent plots for their novels because real life does not have one? As T.S. Eliot once put it, "Human kind cannot bear very much reality." We abhor chaos and chance as much as nature abhors a vacuum. This is why Voltaire claimed that if God did not exist, it would be necessary for humanity to invent Him.

This need for explanation underlies the popularity of conspiracy theories. The 1997 death of Princess Diana surely cannot have been a mere accident, conspiracy theorists insist, unable to accept the implication that if even the rich and famous can die a meaningless death, what hope have the rest of us of finding meaning in our lives—or, more to the point, in our deaths? Such a view is of the opinion that death wipes out the possibility of a meaningful life. Those impatient with conspiracies would argue that death is the one thing that invests life with the urgency to live creatively, which would certainly be lacking if immortality were our fate. Conspiracy theorists therefore fear death far more than loving life, and would rather live a lie than develop the courage to face the truth and benefit from it.

The very word "occult" suggests its obsession with conspiracy. It means "hidden," and secrecy is one of the main attractions for those with a taste for it. Alchemists infamously disguised their "truths" in obscure, often impenetrable language, ostensibly to dissuade the casual dilettante from sullying their profound wisdom; but it was just as likely to have disguised delusional nonsense. Conspiracy was central to the appeal of Blavatsky's theosophy. Her introduction to *The Secret Doctrine* is a catalog of hints, rumor and secrecy:

> [T]here is a well-known fact, a very curious one, corroborated to the writer by a reverend gentleman attached for years to a Russian Embassy—namely, that there are several documents in the St. Petersburg Imperial Libraries to show that, even so late as during the days when Freemasonry, and Secret Societies of Mystics flourished unimpeded in Russia, i.e., at the end of the last and the beginning of the present century, more than one Russian Mystic travelled to Tibet via the Ural mountains in search of knowledge and initiation *in the unknown crypts of Central Asia.* And more than one

returned years later, with a rich store of such information as could never have been given him anywhere in Europe. Several cases could be cited, and well-known names brought forward, but for the fact that such publicity might annoy the surviving relatives of the said late Initiates. Let any one look over the Annals and History of Freemasonry in the archives of the Russian metropolis and he will assure himself of the fact stated.[1]

In the introduction to her 1897 book *The Ancient Wisdom,* Blavatsky's disciple Annie Besant, whose earlier socialism was overwhelmed by her wholesale conversion to theosophy, was entirely convinced of a giant conspiracy regarding the similarities of all the world's religions:

> The ... explanation of the common property in the religions of the world asserts the existence of an original teaching in the custody of a Brotherhood of great spiritual Teachers, who—Themselves the outcome of past cycles of evolution—acted as the instructors and guides of the child-humanity of our planet, imparting to its races and nations in turn the fundamental truths of religion in the form most adapted to the idiosyncrasies of the recipients. According to this view, the Founders of the great religions are members of the one Brotherhood, and were aided in Their mission by many other members, lower in degree than Themselves, Initiates and disciples of various grades, eminent in spiritual insight, in philosophical knowledge, or in purity of ethical wisdom. These guided the infant nations, gave them their polity, enacted their laws, ruled them as kings, taught them as philosophers, guided them as priests; all the nations of antiquity looked back to such mighty men, demigods and heroes, and they left their traces in literature, in architecture, in legislation.[2]

This is *Warlords of Atlantis,* in theosophical, *fin de siècle* form: an explanation for everything, peace at last from doubt and chaos, the unveiling of Isis and her mysteries for all time. The subtitles of so many chapters in Blavatsky's first work *Isis Unveiled* also relish conspiratorial sensations: "Paul a cabalist," "Occult arts practiced by the clergy," "Jesus considered an adept by some Pagan philosophers and early Christians," "Secret doctrine taught by Jesus," "Secret Masonic ciphers," "Schools of magic in Buddhist lamaseries" and "Were the ancient Egyptians of the Aryan race?" Greatly indebted to Blavatsky, the twentieth-century occultist Israel Regardie used Qabalistic magick as a means of discovering a universal theory: "The universe will then begin to appear as a synthetic homogeneous whole, and the student will discover that the sum total of his knowledge will become unified, and find himself able to transmute even on the intellectual plane the many into the one."[3]

Regardie first published these words in 1932, during the rise of Nazism in Germany. As we have seen, occult conspiracy combined with the conspiracy of anti–Semitism is not a recipe for world peace. From his earliest days in Vienna, Jewish "conspiracy" was undeniably Hitler's explanation for everything: "Wherever I went, I began to see Jews, and the more I saw, the more sharply they became distinguished in my eyes from the rest of humanity."[4]

Though Hitler expressed impatience with Himmler's mysticism, his disagreements, as we have seen, were more of degree than of kind, and it is undeniable that the borrowed "glamor" of ritual and occultism contributed immensely to the esthetic and psychological power of the Third Reich. As Eric Kurlander convincingly argues, occultism underpinned the entire disastrous adventure:

> The power of National Socialism was not in resuscitating "mythical-magical thinking," observes Wolfgang Emmerich, "and even less so the various contents of myths." Supernatural thinking was already prevalent in the Weimar Republic. Hitler's genius lay in "refunctionalizing the mythical in the sense of fascist rule." Interwar Germany, a place where "unrealistic perceptions and unsubtle modes of thought" found wide acceptance, where mentalities that were out of touch with reality were believed capable of changing reality, was the perfect place to carry out this project.[5]

British wartime propaganda films naturally enough stressed the political rather than occult intentions of the Nazis. Most British people at the time— and even now—would have found the considered irrationality of the Third Reich far too fantastic to take seriously. Consequently, the early British propaganda film *The Lion Has Wings* (dir. Michael Powell *et al.*, 1939) contrasts the regimentation, the marching, the uniforms and the territorial claims of the Nazis against peaceful images of cows in English fields and King George IV and Queen Elizabeth singing "Underneath the Spreading Chestnut Tree" in the midst of their cheery British subjects. Hollywood was at first reluctant to discuss Hitler for commercial reasons. Indeed, recent research suggests that Hollywood actively collaborated with Hitler[6]; but once America was in the war, Hitler was attacked in various ways. He was portrayed as a gangster by the astonishing Hitler lookalike Bobby Watson in *The Hitler Gang,* (dir. John Farrow, 1944), and lampooned by Donald Duck in Walt Disney's *Der Führer's Face* (1943). This latter starts off with the prelude to Wagner's *Die Meistersinger,* after which Donald is woken by both a swastika alarm clock and a Hitler cuckoo clock. Even the tree in his garden has been fashioned into a topiary swastika. Donald then finds himself on a production line, prodded by a Nazi bayonet, in a scene that echoes a comparable one in Chaplin's *Modern Times* (1936). Chaplin similarly used comedy to attack the mannerisms and megalomania of Hitler in *The Great Dictator* (1940).

It took rather longer for films to take up occult conspiracy theories about the Nazis, and even longer for academics to countenance the conclusions of Kurlander that occultism was not merely one of the roots of the Third Reich (which Goodrich-Clarke had argued in the 1980s) but was absolutely central to the deluded aims of Hitler and National Socialism as a whole. *The Devil's Rock* demonstrates how much film's approach to this subject has changed from the early days of anti–Nazi propaganda. Kurlander also cites *Captain*

America: The First Avenger (dir. Joe Johnston, 2011) as an example, containing "all the elements of Nazi supernaturalism in the popular mind: the connection to occult forces, mad scientists, fantastical weapons, a superhuman master race, a preoccupation with pagan religions, and magical relics supposed to grant the Nazis unlimited power."[7] *Captain America: The First Avenger* is really a superhero story concerning a serum that transforms ordinary soldiers into unstoppable, muscle-bound death machines, in the mold of the male nudes of the Third Reich's state sculptor, Arno Breker; but it also concerns an occult society called Hydra, which is presented as the motivating force and ideological structure behind the Nazi project. *Captain America*'s Nazis also want an ancient relic of illimitable powers, much as they want the Ark of the Covenant in Steven Spielberg's *Raiders of the Lost Ark* (1981) and the Holy Grail in *Indiana Jones and the Last Crusade* (1989).

Kurlander also mentions that the Nazi explorers Otto Rahn and Ernst Schäfer have been seen as models for Indiana Jones. Rahn did indeed set out on a search for the Holy Grail, while Schäfer—good-looking and intrepid—led the Tibet Expedition in search of Aryan heritage set up by Himmler in 1938.[8] Another Indiana candidate, however, is Lt.-Col. Percy Fawcett, the British explorer who famously disappeared in the Amazon Jungle in 1925. Fawcett, also a theosophist, used psychometry to discover the identity of a mysterious stone idol given to him by H. Rider Haggard, experienced a haunting Santa Cruz and a ghost-laying ceremony (*tapi*) in a Maxubi village. A recent theory suggests that he actually planned to disappear to found a theosophical community in the jungle.[9]

Himmler's advocacy of SS research into the mind-reading and magical abilities Kurlander describes found its cinematic equivalent in *The Men Who Stare at Goats* (dir. Grant Heslov, 2009), which takes a satirical view of Jon Ronson's non-fiction book of the same name concerning the U.S. Army's "New Earth Army" of self-styled psi-warriors.

In the realm of pulp fiction, as Phil Baker remarks, "Nazi occultism has become part of twentieth-century mythology and spawned a heap of trashy—almost *definitively* trashy books, symptoms of a public appetite for morbid kitsch and Nazi trivia, as well as the overlap between the esoteric and ultra-right sensibilities."[10] One of the trashiest, Jon Ruddy's novel *The Bargain* (1990), even pits the Führer against Count Dracula: Eva Braun has been bitten and Dracula now "wants to punish her husband for making a vassal state of his homeland."

"Trust me," Dracula tells her. "It is in his nature to take pleasure from your teeth as he took pleasure from the pricking needles of the quack Morell [Hitler's doctor]."[11] The idea of Hitler as a vampire would no doubt have appealed to Karl Marx, who, as we shall see, happily used vampiric imagery to personify the evils of capitalism. Hitler preferred to think of the Jews as vampires—quite literally suckers of pure Aryan blood. As he wrote in *Mein Kampf,* after an 18-page anti–Semitic *crescendo*, Jews are a "parasite upon the nation. After the death of his victim, the vampire sooner or later dies too."[12] Continuing his imagery of blood, Hitler regards Jewish blood as a kind of supernatural AIDS virus: "It seemed as though a continuous stream of poison was being driven into the outermost blood-vessels of this once heroic body by a mysterious power, and was inducing progressively greater paralysis of sound reason and the simple instinct of self-preservation."[13] Kurlander draws our attention to the fact that Murnau's *Nosferatu* was regarded by some significant supporters of Hitler's views as an anti–Semitic allegory, and concludes: "Without the supernatural figuring of the monstrous Jew, the highly technical process of genocide could never have been applied as widely or vociferously as it was."[14]

The Boys from Brazil (dir. Franklin J. Schaffner, 1978), somewhat in the manner of *The Frozen Dead,* posits the cryogenic survival of Nazi top brass. Whereas Nazis are kept on ice in *Frozen Dead*, *Boys* has 95 Hitler clones (created by Gregory Peck's Dr. Mengele) who are then subjected to childhoods identical to that experienced by the original Hitler, and groomed to create a Fourth Reich in the near future. (Bruno Ganz, later to play the great dictator in Oliver Hirschbiegel's *Downfall* [2005], appears here as Dr. Bruckner, who explains the process of cloning to Laurence Olivier's Nazi hunter, Lieberman.) Like the swastika flags that drape a spectacular party scene at the movie's midpoint, this premise has an aura of occult pseudo-science and even alchemy about it, suggesting the legend of the doppelgänger and even the ghost of the old *Homunculus* serial with its artificially created tyrant.

Peck's portrayal of Mengele as a crazed esthete in a white three-piece suit is a compelling portrait of a fanaticism fully commensurate with Hitler's own mystical racism. The hysterical absurdity of Mengele's views might tempt us to regard the story (and that of *The Frozen Dead*) as mere movie schlock. The uncomfortable truth, however, is that a great deal of what the Third Reich put into practice was movie schlock made horribly real. Fortunately, no B-movie has ever plumbed the actual depths of Nazi racial experimentation. We will hopefully never see a horror film that matches the true horror of the films made by Himmler, which recorded the effects of decompression on concentration camp victims, let alone the attempts to revive the dead by having female prisoners "warm" corpses back to life, which, as Kurlander rightly suggests, created scenes "more reminiscent of a Roman orgy than a scientific experiment."[15] Given their irrational commitment to magickal "sci-

DR. SWASTIKA: Gregory Peck as Dr. Josef Mengele in *The Boys from Brazil* (dir. Franklin J. Schaffner, 1978).

ence," it is not beyond the bounds of belief that the Nazis might have contemplated the cloning of the Führer, who himself believed that scientific limitations could indeed be overcome by the power of the will alone. "Jewish" science was the enemy in this respect, because it "stubbornly refused to endorse scientific conclusions without empirical evidence."[16] That cloning has now been demonstrated as quite possible makes the proposition even more credible.

Unfortunately, one of Mengele's clones in *The Boys from Brazil* takes exception to having his foster parents disposed of by the evil doctor and takes his revenge. "You freaked-out maniac!" he shouts, before setting his dogs on him. For all the film's absurdity, it is nowhere near as crazy as the esoteric racial theories of Lanz von Liebenfels, which ultimately resulted in the unspeakable horrors of Auschwitz.

Peck's performance as Mengele is a kind of reverse negative image of the role he played in *The Omen*. Though Senator Thorn in *The Omen* is on the side of the angels, a similar dynamic between him and the infant monsters for whom he is responsible drives the film forward. The various Hitler clones played by Jeremy Black in *Boys from Brazil* are skinnier than the cherubic features of Harvey Spencer Stevens' Damien, but he is similarly pale, dark-featured and, particularly in his incarnation as an English boy, arrogant and insufferable. ("Don't you understand English, you arse? We are not at home," is his way of turning away visitors.) The young Hitler clones could easily audition as Antichrists. Though viewers of *The Omen* soon come to realize that Damien is responsible for the deaths of those who stand in his way, the conspiracy in Schaffner's film is only revealed gradually. In essence, *The Omen* is no different from Robert Hamer's *Kind Hearts and Coronets* (1949), being a series of bizarre murders committed to attain a position of power. Damien's atrocities are really only magnified playground tantrums; but the film's theological context and, as we have seen, the extraordinary impact of Jerry Goldsmith's demonic music, impose a monumentality upon it that is in a direct line of descent from Milton's descriptions of Satan in *Paradise Lost*.

> So farewell hope, and with hope farewell fear,
> Farewell remorse: all good to me is lost;
> Evil, be thou my good; by thee at least
> Divided empire with heaven's King I hold,
> By thee, and more than half perhaps will reign;
> As Man ere long and this new world shall know.[17]

It is the growing sense of conspiracy that drives films like *The Witches* and *Rosemary's Baby*. Conspiracy stories are at their most compelling when they are set in an everyday environment, which emphasizes the contrasting shock of the plot's eventual revelations. *The Witches* takes place in an idyllic English village setting, where all seems normal but is not. The school's new headmistress, Miss Mayfield (Joan Fontaine), arrives to find her grace-and-favor cottage with roses round the door and helpful staff, who nonetheless appear to be concealing something. That something is that nearly all the villagers are members of a coven ruled by Stephanie Bax (Kay Walsh), the apparently benign writer who lives in the old manor house. The evocation of rural tranquility, normal village life and picturesque vernacular architecture are the most important things about this film, for they signal the exact opposite of what is really going on. A witchcraft film such as *The City of the Dead* (dir. John Moxey, 1960) makes it quite clear what we are to expect with its decaying, Lovecraftian town of Whitewood, Massachusetts, filled with swirling mist and sinister inhabitants; but there is an element of conspiracy working here too: Christopher Lee's seemingly respectable academic Prof. Driscoll is eventually revealed to be one of the witches at work in Whitewood, and it is exactly this kind of Satanic double-life that Lee reprised in his role as Morley in *The Curse of the Crimson Altar*.

Properly, however, these are mystery plots. Conspiracy requires a much greater subversion of perceived reality, and this finds its most eloquent expression with Polanski's *Rosemary's Baby*, in which the occult element is only hinted at, but the film's conspiratorial crescendo develops like Ravel's *Bolero*,

URBAN NIGHTMARE: **Rosemary Woodhouse (Mia Farrow) is dwarfed by the city and forces beyond her control in** *Rosemary's Baby* **(dir. Roman Polanski, 1968).**

until the shattering chords of the dénouement. Even then, Polanski sensibly resists the temptation to reveal the infant Satan in his cradle. This degree of ambiguity made the whole affair more believable, as he explains in his memoir:

> The book [by Ira Levin] was an outstandingly well-constructed thriller, and I admired it as such. Being an agnostic, however, I no more believed in Satan as evil incarnate than I believed in a personal God—the whole idea conflicted with my rational view

of the world. For credibility's sake, I decided that there would have to be a loophole—the possibility that Rosemary's supernatural experiences were figments of her imagination. The entire story, as seen through her eyes, could have been a chain of only superficially sinister coincidences, a product of her feverish fancies. The machinations of her next-door neighbours, the witches' Sabbath at which the Devil possesses her in her husband's presence, even the final scene around the baby's cradle, had to have some rational explanation. That is why a thread of deliberate ambiguity runs throughout the film. The witches' Sabbath and Rosemary's possession by the Devil *could* have been a nightmare, Guy *might* have scratched her while making love, the series of accidents *could* have been merely coincidences.[18]

To create a greater sense of reality, Polanski set the action in '60s New York:

> I decided to include glimpses on TV of Pope Paul VI's New York visit, which was fresh enough in people's minds to ring the right bell, together with a shot of the "God Is Dead" issue of *Time* magazine. I also put in another highly topical allusion. "Don't tell me you *paid* for this?" says Guy, when Rosemary comes home with her hair bobbed. "It's Vidal Sassoon," she retorts, "and it's very in."[19]

The film itself led to conspiracy theories in the aftermath of the events that became known as "The Curse of *Rosemary's Baby*." These included the coincidence that the film's producer William Castle became paranoid after receiving hate mail from people accusing him of unleashing evil on the world. He suffered from excruciatingly painful kidney stones and was treated for them in the same hospital where the film's composer, Christopher Komeda, had been treated for a cerebral hemorrhage—a condition that eventually led to his death. Polanski's wife Sharon Tate was then murdered on the orders of Charles Manson, and Polanski was even rumored to have sold his own soul to the Devil to attain success. Even more bizarre were the supposed connections with John Lennon, another friend of Polanski, who lived with Yoko Ono in the building that had been chosen for the location of Rosemary's apartment. Outside this same building, Lennon was later shot by the devil-worshipping Mark David Chapman.

The "conspiracy" of the film—that Rosemary has been impregnated by the Devil—is presented in such a realistic manner that Polanski is able to use the story as a vehicle for much less far-fetched and far more important issues. These include the subservient role of women in a patriarchal society (Rosemary is dominated, constrained and used by her ambitious husband). Whether her baby is the spawn of Devil or a perfectly human child, the fact remains that Rosemary has no control over what happens to her. She longs for her own baby but is deeply troubled by the idea of sexual intercourse. As we have already seen, when discussing *The Midwich Cuckoos*, Mary Shelley had articulated the potentially horrific reality of reproduction and gestation in *Frankenstein*, describing it as "the filthy workshop of creation," which might well result in monsters for any of us. Rosemary's Catholic upbringing rules out the option of having an abortion, and she defers to the male authority of the devil-worshipping doctor who treats her. She is also discouraged from reading books and further attacked for taking control of her own appearance (her husband hates the Vidal Sassoon hair style she at least has the initiative to arrange for herself). Polanski also articulates the paranoia of living in a modern city—its continual invasion of private space, represented by Rosemary's intrusive, devil-worshipping neighbors, not to mention the oppressive crowds, noise, pollution and anonymity of New York itself. A conspiratorial plot is the perfect means by which to explore these sexual and social issues, as the reason for all conspiracies is that they articulate our perceptions of powerlessness. Conspiracy theories are reassuring because they suggest that life's thousand natural shocks, injustices and existential horrors have some reason, no matter how corrupt. More important, they furnish life's victims with someone to blame, and the Devil has always been a very popular scapegoat.

In this sense, *Rosemary's Baby* has more in common with the typical Hitchcock product than one might expect. *North by Northwest* (1959) could just as easily be about devil worshippers as the spy drama it is. Hitchcock's theory of the "MacGuffin" applies to both genres. The MacGuffin is what the spies (or the devil worshippers) want, and that is what drives the plot. From a purely narrative point of view, the nature of the MacGuffin is immaterial. What matters are the consequences. Devil worshippers usually want to sacrifice a girl; spies want the microfilm with the state secrets. In *North by Northwest*, the hapless main character (Cary Grant's Roger Thornhill) finds himself alone and vulnerable in a hostile world in which no one is as they appear to be. Eva Marie Saint's Eve Kendall, who befriends Thornhill, turns out to be working for the enemy, and, of course, Thornhill himself is all the while suffering from the consequences of mistaken identity. Neither *Rosemary's Baby* nor *North by Northwest* are mystery films, as the solving of the mystery is nowhere near as significant as the sense of mounting paranoia.

Based on another Ira Levin novel, Bryan Forbes' *The Stepford Wives* (1974) is the science fiction equivalent of *Rosemary's Baby*. Though less imaginatively handled, it similarly attacks a patriarchy that strips women of their independence, creativity and identity, all of which have been brainwashed out of them at the club organized by their husbands. This process makes them all frighteningly subservient to their husbands' wishes, just as Rosemary is apparently groomed by her husband and his devil-worshipping friends. Wes Craven updated this idea in 1984 in the TV movie *Invitation to Hell*, in which the "Steaming Springs" corporate health spa proves to be Hell on earth, quite literally. The woman who runs it (Susan Lucci) is the embodiment of 1980s power-dressing, big hair and ruthless materialism. Here, the Faust legend receives a Marxist critique of corporate conformity. Significantly, Marx used Gothic imagery in *Das Kapital*:

> Capital is dead labour, that, vampire-like, only lives by sucking living labour, and lives the more, the more labour it sucks. The time during which the laborer works, is the time during which the capitalist consumes the labour-power he has purchased of him. If the laborer consumes his disposable time for himself, he robs the capitalist.[20]

The astonishing success of Dan Brown's novel *The Da Vinci Code* and its film adaptation (dir. Ron Howard, 2006) demonstrates the continuing popularity of occult conspiracy. This fictionalized version of a theory that had been presented as fact in an earlier bestseller, *The Holy Blood and the Holy Grail*, is an attempt to undermine the entire structure of Western civilization, or at least that significant part of it that has been based on Christianity. When *The Holy Blood and the Holy Grail* was published in 1982, it was favorably reviewed in the *Observer* newspaper by Anthony Burgess, who presciently suggested that it was a marvelous theme for a novel, to which form it should perhaps have been confined. The idea that Christ married Mary Magdalene, initiated the Blood Line of the House of David, which apparently continues to the present day, and whose womb is the real identity of the Holy Grail, is certainly a sensational theme, and far more suited to the realm of fiction than history, though Michael Baigent, Richard Leigh and Henry Lincoln, the authors of *Holy Blood*, insist that their findings are more than mere speculation. In turn, Dan Brown, perhaps in an attempt to increase the lucrative controversy the subject courts, insists that what he describes in his novel is also based on the truth. Had Burgess attempted a novel based on this theory, he would no doubt have sensibly avoided such a claim.

Again, the desire to find an answer to everything, one that addresses the needs of a post–Darwinian, post–Nietzschean age in which God is dead but kept on life support by evangelicals and fundamentalists, is still desired by many. One might say that religion itself is a vast conspiracy theory, in which God supposedly pulls the strings of humanity. Madame Blavatsky translated this into pseudo-scientific terms in *The Secret Doctrine*, while *The Holy Blood and the Holy Grail* adopts a form of pseudo-history to explain the whole thing in purely human terms. *The Da Vinci Code* is an uncompromising attack on the Christian establishment. ("The greatest cover-up in human history," "'The Greatest Story Ever Told' is actually a lie.") "For 2000 years," says Ian McKellen's Grail-quester Sir Leigh Teabing in the film version, "the Church has rained oppression and atrocity upon mankind, crushed passion and idea alike, all in the name of their walking God. Proof of Jesus' mortality can bring an end to all that suffering, drive this church of lies to its knees. The living heir must be revealed. Jesus must be shown for what he was—not miraculous, simply man."

Printed fiction at least has to be constructed by the reader, the page forming some kind of barrier between fantasy and reality, but the film industry has now become such a dominant force in modern culture that it has actually enabled "post-truth" to thrive. Movies now set the agenda, articulating conspiracy theories with a verisimilitude that more than adequately occupies the space previously filled by faith. Despite the rigorous deconstruction of Brown's interpretations, the taste for conspiracy remains undiminished in a world where traditional structures and assumptions are fragmenting fast. The fantasies promoted by film have now re-entered the political sphere. The "alternative truths" of today's politicians are not so far removed from the bogus theories of the Third Reich and the Spanish Inquisition.

Chapter Twelve

Faust

At the end of F.W. Murnau's *Faust* (1926), as in Goethe's version of the famous story, Mephistopheles is defeated by Love—or "Liebe," the letters of which are shown to radiate with beneficent light. Murnau also approximates Goethe's Prologue in Heaven, though cuts down the cast of characters to one archangel and Mephisto himself, who argue about good and evil. "If you can win Faust's soul," the Angel insists, "the earth is yours." But the Angel is confident that love is stronger than evil. Even Mephistopheles agrees, explaining himself to Faust as "part of that Power which would/Do evil constantly, and constantly does good."[1] His opinion of Creation, and particularly of humanity, would be contemptuous if it were not so sardonic:

> The little earth-god still persists in his old ways,
> Ridiculous as ever, as in his first days.
> He'd have improved if you'd not given
> Him a mere glimmer of the light of heaven;
> He calls it Reason, and it only has increased
> His power to be beastlier than a beast.[2]

Disillusioned and weary with the world himself, theology and faith are no longer enough for Faust, who is now devoted to magick. Goethe's lines for Faust explain exactly the desires that inspired so many *fin de siècle* and twentieth-century occultists. He begins with his despair:

> For here you sit, surrounded not
> By living Nature, not as when
> God made us but by reek and rot
> And mouldering bones of beasts and men.[3]

He then reads a book by Nostradamus, and exalts at the prospect of understanding of Nature's powers. "Am I a god?" he asks, as so many occultists have asked before and since.

> That sage's words at last I understand
> 'The spirit-world is open wide,
> Only your heart has closed and died....'[4]

He begins to understand the inter-connectedness of the macrocosm and the microcosm—the "as above, so below" of the Emerald Tablet of Hermes Trismegistus:

> How it all lives and moves and weaves
> Into a whole! Each part gives and receives,
> Angelic powers ascend and redescend
> And each to each their golden vessels lend.[5]

But when he succeeds in raising the Spirit of the Earth, he is disappointed. The spirit explains that it works at Time's whirring wheel, weaving the living cloak of God, but then vanishes, expressing scorn for Faust's presumption: "You are like the spirits you can comprehend: not me."[6]

These early attempts and failures at magic cause Faust to contemplate suicide, but the sound of Easter bells, reminding him of his youth, prevents this. Inspired to attempt a translation of the Bible, he considers ways in which to render the opening line of "Genesis." He rejects "In the beginning was the Word," in favor of "In the beginning was the Mind," before finally deciding

GOETHE HELL: Gösta Ekmann in the title role of *Faust* (dir. F.W. Murnau, 1926).

on "In the beginning was Action." These three alternatives nicely sum up the intent of all magicians: to use language as the servants of the will in order to achieve change.

At this point, Mephistopheles makes his tumultuous entrance in human form as a medieval wandering student. "How very comical," Faust remarks.[7] (Murnau's Mephisto is much more melodramatic, with bald head, horns, immense black wings, glowing eyes and huge eyebrows, not unlike those worn by Max Schreck's vampire in Murnau's *Nosferatu*.) He brushes himself down in the costume of a wandering student, and the pact is eventually signed: Mephisto can have Faust's soul if Faust ever experiences absolute contentment in the moment—a condition the habitually discontented Faust despairs of ever achieving.

Murnau had necessarily to condense all this. His Faust (played by Gösta Ekmann) at first resembles a chiaroscuro portrait by Rembrandt, and Murnau's visual shorthand for Faust's mystical quest employs alchemical imagery: a transparent sphere, which Faust heats and peers into while it flashes with light from within. This image is also a response to the creation of the Homunculus in Part Two of Goethe's poem, where, in the second act, we are taken to a laboratory built "in the fashion of the Middle Ages [with] cumbrous, heavy apparatus for fantastic purposes." In other words, the kind of alchemical laboratory we find in Joseph Wright of Derby's painting *The Alchemist* (1771). Faust's assistant Wagner describes how the homunculus he has created grows inside the glass "phial:"

> The glass rings low, the charming power that lives
> Within it makes the music that it gives.
> It dims! it brightens it will shape itself.
> And see!—a graceful dazzling little elf.[8]

Quite what Murnau's Faust is hoping to achieve with his glass sphere is not explained, but that is hardly the point. What matters is its magickal symbolism. Murnau now departs from Goethe, having Mephisto cause a plague, which Faust is beseeched by the population to help cure. In despair at his impotence to achieve this, Faust burns his books, even his Bible; but at the last minute, he saves one grimoire from the flames, and this offers the possibility of raising the Devil. "Go to a crossroads and call Him three times," he reads, before enacting an occult ritual much emulated in subsequent movies. Amid a blasted tree and gibbous moon, wreathed in mist, Faust arrives at a lonely crossroads, which is depicted in the manner of Caspar David Friedrich. Faust raises the book above his head, like Moses with the Ten Commandments, and then uses it to trace a circle around himself. Holding the book aloft once more, he bows down at each of the four points of the compass, and after commanding the spirit to appear, a burning ring arises around his feet. This multiplies into concentric circles, which envelop him as similar rings would animate the robot of Fritz Lang's *Metropolis* the following year. Lightning and fireballs then announce the arrival of Mephisto, who sits quietly on a stone, waiting patiently in distinct contrast to all the commotion. (The first words of Goethe's Mephisto are, "Why all the fuss? How can I serve you, sir?"[9])

The signing of the pact follows, Mephisto insisting on cutting Faust's wrists to extract the necessary drop of blood with which to seal the contract. ("Blood is a juice with curious properties,"[10] he says in Goethe's play, a line that Murnau borrows for his intertitle here.) Faust's wound is used as a kind of demonic inkwell; the pen is charged and the signature is written. Unfortunately, the people turn against Faust when they realize he is in league with the Devil, and once more in despair, he decides to drink poison. Mephisto intervenes, and in the reflection of the poison in Faust's dish, he causes an image of Faust as a young man to appear. "Is that Death?" Faust asks. "No," Mephisto replies. "It is life. Why do you seek death? You have not lived enough yet," on which observation he promptly restores Faust's youth to him. Thus begin the rejuvenated Faust's adventures and his doomed love affair with Gretchen, the magickal part of the story now being largely told. What remains is a morality tale.

Richard Burton's distinctly stodgy interpretation of Marlowe's *Doctor Faustus*, which he and the scholar Neville Coghill directed in 1967, has none of Murnau's visual magic, and, this being Marlowe's version, Faust is damned at the end. Andreas Tauber's interesting Mephistopheles sports a shaven head, similar to Jannings', but is otherwise quite different, being soft-spoken, melancholy and generally understated, which makes him all the more convincing. Burton should have excelled as Faust, having sold his own soul, figuratively speaking, for Hollywood wealth and fame. It was there that he made the kind of films that the *Doctor Faustus* project was no doubt intended to counterbalance as "art," but he failed to rise to the challenge, while the appearance of Elizabeth Taylor, with whom Burton had for so long been ensnared, makes one think all too readily of their roles in Joseph Mankiewicz's 1963 *Cleopatra*.

Much more enjoyable is Peter Cushing's carefully judged performance as a sinister antiques dealer in *From Beyond the Grave*. Though the Faustian element in this is really only used as a framing device to link four individual stories, Cushing's segments are by far the film's most compelling moments. With a dry Yorkshire accent and a pipe clenched between his teeth, Cushing

OFFERS YOU CAN'T REFUSE: Peter Cushing as the proprietor of Temptations Limited in *From Beyond the Grave* (dir. Kevin Connor, 1974).

presides over Temptations, an antiques emporium with "offers you cannot refuse." Each of the customers who enter do something they shouldn't—such as stealing or cheating. "Naughty," Cushing mutters under his breath, fully aware of what they are up to. His understated performance befits a Devil from the north of England, but he is quite able to withstand two shots in the chest from a pair of dueling pistols when he is attacked by an unfortunate robber at the end. "Come in," he concludes, facing the camera. "I'm sure I have the very thing to tempt you. Lots of bargains. All tastes catered for—and a big novelty surprise comes with every purchase."

The same idea forms the basis of *Needful Things* (dir. Fraser C. Heston, 1993), based on Stephen King's same-name novel. Max von Sydow plays Leland Gaunt, the rather more suave but no less demonic antique dealer of the shop that gives the film its title. Having tempted the town's inhabitants with their particular "needful things," he sets them against one another, but one of his victims takes his revenge at the end. All Peter Cushing had to put up with was to be shot at twice, but here, von Sydow survives the spectacular explosion of his shop, emerging from the wreckage as untroubled and immaculately dressed as usual:

> Ah, you know, there are days when I really hate this job. This is not my best work. Not by a long shot. Ah, sure: a few murders and a couple of rather lovely explosions. I would hardly call it a rousing success; but, what the hell, I'll be back.

As he walks away to his smart but slightly old-fashioned limousine, composer Patrick Doyle sets the text of the "Dies Irae" to music, which then turns into a pastiche of Jerry Goldsmith's music for *The Omen*. The car vanishes into thin air and the end titles roll. King's novel is rather more melodramatic, the car turning into a medicine-show wagon "which might have criss-crossed the country a hundred years ago." With the words *Caveat Emptor* written on the side, it is pulled by a black horse "with eyes as red as Mr. Gaunt's, ... and when the smoke cleared, Leland Gaunt and his hell wagon were gone."[11]

In fact, the urbane humor of the film version of King's story is more in accordance with Goethe's witty and ironical approach to Mephistopheles:

> I am the spirit of perpetual negation.
> And rightly so, for all things that exist
> Deserve to perish, and would not be missed—
> Much better it would be if nothing were
> Brought into being. Thus, what you men call
> Destruction, sin, evil in short, is all
> My there, the element I most prefer.[12]

Goethe's drama also informs Jan Svankmajer's *Faust* (1994), which blends live action, puppetry and stop-motion animation to both grotesque and comic effect. Here, mid–European anxiety, filtered through the pessimism of an intellectual who has experienced communist Czechoslovakia, forms the untidy, grimy, sometimes rather disgusting vision of the Hell on Earth, which Marlowe's Mephistopheles describes:

> Hell hath no limits, nor is circumscrib'd
> In one self place, but where we are is hell,
> And where hell is, there must we ever be.
> And to be short, when all the world dissolves
> And every creature shall be purified,
> All places shall be hell that is not heaven.[13]

Svankmajer quotes from Marlowe's play, along with other Faust sources, to create an overview of and commentary on the Faust legend, rather than a conventional performance. By setting the action in late twentieth-century urban settings, he is able to emphasize the continuing relevance of the story and make Faust an Everyman figure. The eruption of magickal forces out of this context also undermines materialism's complacent attitude to "reality," which we cannot know, and which is far less predictable than we think. Later in the film, Mephisto is sent back and forth in a comic scene involving Faust's foolish assistant, Wagner, who summons and exorcises the demon until it is exhausted. Mephisto leaves the "magickal" building disguised in hat and cloak like the Invisible Man, and walks the modern streets, encountering ordinary passersby, before a sinister red car picks him up and drives him away. Similarly, when Faust walks into a café, two "students" are discovered nearby. One of them plays an accordion, the other, dressed as a waiter, presents Faust with an empty glass and encourages him to pull a cork out of the middle of his table, from which a fountain of wine plumes up, magickally controlled by the student waiter, whom we see turning a faucet.

One key decision links Svankmajer's approach to the Faustian elements in Robert Louis Stevenson's *The Strange Case of Dr. Jekyll and Mr. Hyde:* The same actor (Petr Cepek) performs both Faust and Mephisto, suggesting that Mephisto, like Mr. Hyde, dwells within each one of us. In Dr. Jekyll's case, the pact with the Devil is presented as the potion that transforms him into Mr. Hyde. Hyde, like Mephisto, attempts to kill his alter ego but, like Faust in Goethe's version, Jekyll is redeemed at the end, his identity restored to him in death.

Svankmajer's vision is a surreal one, transforming everyday reality into magickal spaces and vice versa. On his way home from work, Faust, wearing a raincoat and carrying an attaché case, is handed a curious map. (The two men who distribute these leaflets are later identified as the scholars in Marlowe's play and, in other versions of the story, the students from Prague. Indeed, Prague provides the film's location.) When Faust enters his untidy apartment, pale and hungry, he discovers that a bird has broken in and dropped excrement all over his carpet. He clears this up before eating an unappetizing meal, Svankmajer dwelling on the ungainly process of mastication, which we all try to disguise with manners and cutlery. (He returns to this necessary but potentially nauseating process on several occasions in the film.)

Faust later discovers that the map is of a decaying part of the city, which he visits, entering the derelict building indicated. In the hallway, a man rushes violently past him, seemingly desperate to escape. Faust will do exactly the same after his adventure at the end of the film, when another Faust, map in hand, arrives to take his place—again emphasizing the Everyman approach to the story. Inside the building, Faust finds a medieval costume complete with lace ruff and academic headgear. He puts them on, applies makeup to his face and discovers that he seems to be expected to play the role of the legendary Faustus on the stage of a theater. Unwilling to do this, he strips off the costume and wipes away the greasepaint he has smeared over his face; but we are all on the stage of life, and we are all offered our pact with the Devil, so this is not the end of the affair.

Back in the dressing room–laboratory, Faust sets about creating his homunculus, in one of Svankmajer's most disturbing animations: A lifelike fetus grows in a glass sphere, which develops into a baby. Faust brings this to life by inserting a piece of paper with magical symbols written on it into the baby's mouth, echoing the technique used to bring the legendary Golem to life. The baby grows into a boy, then into adult and is finally to a skull, in such a graphic demonstration of mortality that Faust destroys it. The squashed clay scurries away like curious polyps, each with its own blinking eye, before scuttling into the undergrowth.

Presented with a kind of Mephisto-summoning kit by the two students, whom he next encounters in a restaurant, Faust sets about the magical ritual of raising the demon. He unfolds a square of material with a magic circle inscribed upon it. Donning a white robe, he whips the circle while declaiming the appropriate Latin. Once the magical sign he first saw on the map is whipped away, a group of brooms advance towards him raising a cloud of dust—an obvious reference to Goethe's "Sorcerer's Apprentice."

Faust now finds himself in a wood beneath the moon. Drums are beaten by disembodied hands, while back in the corridor in which he began, crossbows appear like the hands that clutch the candelabra in Cocteau's *La Belle et la Bête* (1946). The arrows they fire cannot penetrate the magic circle, but embed themselves around it. We then move to a curious rock formation, reminiscent of the Exsternsteine. Faust finds himself perched on top of one of these stone pillars, continuing his incantation before being transported to a snowbound waste. He is then drenched in water, and a blazing wagon rolls towards him. (Fiery wheels also form part of the magical display in the famous Wolf's Glen scene in Weber's *Der Freischütz*.) At last, Mephisto emerges from a lump of clay, which then becomes a demon's head before turning into Faust's own features, peering up through the split boards of the floor.

Although Mephisto is presented as an aspect of Faust himself, Svankmajer suggests his demonic nature by animating Cepek's up-lit face, creating a disjoined series of movements while retaining a perfectly naturalistic image. But the pact is made using puppet versions of the two characters. Puppets interact with living actors throughout the film, and the combination of these different media contributes immensely to the magickal mood. Stop-motion demon puppets appear from the head of the Mephisto puppet, which rolls along a moss-covered woodland path into the theater where the action takes place. Similarly, cherubs appear from the head of the angel's head, which rolls in from a less sinister place. The demons provide the quill pen, which the cherubs break in two before being overcome by the forces of evil.

In the end, Faust is run down by the red car that had earlier whisked Mephisto away (rather like Leland Gaunt's black limousine the end of *Needful Things*). His body is stowed inside and he is taken ... where? To Hell? To

Heaven? To Oblivion? Svankmajer leaves the audience to decide, though after such a series of unexpected reality-defying occurrences it is hard to be certain of anything. It is Svankmajer's hybrid *style* that creates the unnerving impression of the magical aspect of everyday life in which nothing is as it seems, and forces beyond our control affect our destiny.

CHAPTER THIRTEEN

Animagick

Animated films are perhaps the most obvious place in which to find magickal thinking, to realize alternative reality, to distort, to amplify, to metamorphose, to defy gravity, to dematerialize and empower.

Having explored some aspects of occult conspiracy, we now turn our attention to the astonishing conspiracies around that prince of animators Walt Disney, whose name has also been unreliably associated with Nazi ideology, occultism and even pedophilia. The known facts are that he was a member of the Masonic Order of DeMolay, named after Jacques DeMolay, one of the medieval Knights Templar. He was also a member of the Rosicrucian Ancient Mystical Order Rosae Crucis, while the involvement of ex-Nazi Wernher von Braun in Disneyland's Tomorrowland project further clouds the picture, but nowhere near as much as some recent biographies have claimed. These are interesting not so much for what they say about Disney as for what they say about the theories and theorists themselves.

The Walt Disney controversy is really a tributary of occult and Nazi conspiracy theory. It has been claimed that Disney has been cryogenically frozen, or at least to have been interested in cryogenics; and because cryogenics were supposedly one of the techniques experimented with at Auschwitz, he is therefore supposed to be tainted by association. Disney is also been accused of anti–Semitism and to have worked as a spy for the FBI. His films are allegedly filled with pornographic imagery: Peter Pan's shadow has a penis, "Sex" is spelled out by twigs and drifting smoke, female anatomy is disguised in other shapes and even the loops of Disney's hallmark signature are seen to contain three sixes: 666, the number of the Beast.

Along with the attractions of conspiracy theories discussed earlier, other reasons for these accusations should be added here. Disney's wholesome image as a family entertainer makes him an obvious target at a time when conspiracy drives politics and the Internet, and a sense of powerlessness among the disillusioned encourages a belief that everything is corrupt. Disney appears to be too good to be entirely true, especially when linked with his hardheaded approach to business matters. Professing to expose a conspiracy, right-wing evangelicals have in fact created a conspiracy of their own. A prurient fascination with the perceived sexual imagery in Disney's films is matched by a hysterical reaction against magical and "occult" imagery, which are, after all, merely a part of the folk tales the Disney studio so often took as its inspiration. Even the Donald Duck anti–Nazi cartoon, discussed earlier, has been singled out as evidence of Disney's alleged Nazi sympathies. Such theorists point to the great many Nazi swastikas it contains, while ignoring the obviously satirical context.

Occult imagery in Disney is interesting for other, more legitimate reasons. That *Snow White and the Seven Dwarfs* (dir. David Hand *et al.*, 1937) was one of Hitler's favorite films should come as no surprise, given that the story is a German folk tale and deals with many of the mythical tropes that feature in Wagner's music-dramas, also Hitler favorites (a wicked witch like Ortrud in *Lohengrin*, dwarves like the Nibelungen, and the sleeping beauty, awoken like Brünnhilde from a magical sleep). Whereas Disney was inspired

MUMMY DUST, BLACK OF NIGHT, OLD HAG'S CACKLE AND A SCREAM OF FRIGHT: The Wicked Queen in Walt Disney's *Snow White and the Seven Dwarfs* (dir. William Cottrell *et al.*, 1937).

Thirteen. Animagick 181

"The Monster of the Id" in *Forbidden Planet* (dir. Fred M. Wilcox, 1956).

by what the Germans call "Märchen," but which the English language misleadingly translates as fairy tales (fairies rarely feature in them), Universal based its horror films on folklore and nineteenth-century Gothic novels. There are no vampires or werewolves in Disney, but there are plenty of magickal occurrences, and the witch's kitchen in *Snow White* in fact recapitulates many of Universal's clichés for a family audience. Its chunky masonry echoes the laboratories in James Whale's two *Frankenstein* films. The allusions to alchemical equipment and the queen's library of books on astrology, the black arts, alchemy, black magic and witchcraft echo Rex Ingram's *The Magician*. The skull and chained skeleton not only place the queen in a strongly Gothic context but also remind us of the settings in Tod Browning's *Dracula*. A quaint pair of scales supported by a crowned skeleton also suggests Murnau's *Nosferatu*, with its grotesque *memento mori* clock. Most intriguing of all are the parallels with Rouben Mamoullian's *Dr. Jekyll and Mr. Hyde* (1931). The witch's transformation from an icy beauty into an old hag is effected by a potion that resembles Dr. Jekyll's. It is colored green, as it probably would have been for Mamoullian had his film had been made in color. A change in color is effected by a thunderbolt, that ubiquitous instrument of magick and transformation. The queen drinks the potion just as Fredric March's Jekyll drinks his and, like him, she grips her throat with both hands as the drug begins to take effect. A vortex of multi-colored lights swirls around the screen, an effect Mamoullian also pioneered in black-and-white. The queen's hands are the first part of her anatomy to change: Four years later, Lon Chaney's hairy feet would be the first signs that he was turning into a wolf man.

Disney's *Snow White* is perhaps even more frightening than Universal's horror films, and if played out as live action the film would probably have been deemed inappropriate viewing for children. The queen's magic mirror speaks through the features of a grim guardian resembling Paul Wegener's Golem, with echoes of the spectral features of the Green Face in Gustav Meyrinck's 1916 novel of that name. There is also more than an echo of Bela Lugosi's Dracula when preparing to bite in the expression of this malevolent creature with green cheeks, blue forehead and purple lips. But from a purely occult point of view, the queen's circular convex magic mirror is no less than a scrying glass. It is also exactly the kind of thing Wagner had in mind for Klingsor's magic mirror in Act II of *Parsifal,* and we see an impressive prototype of it in Sidney Meteyard's late-Victorian painting *I Am Half-Sick of Shadows*, based on Tennyson's "The Lady of Shalott," in which a deep blue circular mirror hangs behind the Lady, who has fallen asleep at her tapestry.

Disney became positively Wagnerian in his later adaptation *Sleeping Beauty* (dir. Clyde Geronimi *et al.,* 1959). Indeed, many of the turrets and rocky settings with vertiginous pathways in Chuck Jones' slightly earlier homage to Wagner, the 1957 Bugs Bunny film *What's Opera, Doc?*, were recapitulated in Disney's vision. The thunderbolts that Elmer Fudd hurls at Bugs also foreshadow Queen Maleficent's meteorological assault on the prince in *Sleeping Beauty.* Last but not least, the castle itself, Disney's most iconic image, is often said to have been inspired by Neuschwanstein, the fantasy castle of Wagner's patron King Ludwig II of Bavaria.

Queen Maleficent casts her magic spells by means of a wand. She eventually feels the need to transform herself into a giant fire-breathing dragon, like Fafner in Wagner's *Siegfried.* Disney's prince, like Siegfried, plunges his magic sword into the breast of the evil dragon to save the day, and as he looks over the shattered precipice to the valley below, all that remains of Maleficent is a dark shadow. Freddie Francis may well have had this scene in mind when staging the death of Dracula in *Dracula Has Risen from the Grave,* where a crucifix takes the place of the sword. The settings are remarkably similar.

The use of Tchaikovsky's ballet music in *Sleeping Beauty* further emphasizes the European origin and aspirations of Disney's fairy tale animations, which yearned for the status of Old World culture while simultaneously recasting the stories for modern American audiences. Universal horror films had also provided what David J. Skal perceptively regards as "a geographically indeterminate 'Europe,' anxiously blurring together elements of America, England and the Continent, rather as the Great War had done literally, and the new war was in the process of doing all over again. The Europe of American horror movies was a nearly surreal pastiche of accents, architecture and costumes, like the scrambled impressions of a soldier/tourist on a whirlwind tour of duty."[1]

Disney's embrace of European classical music reached its peak in *Fantasia* (1940), which also gave the studio several opportunities to explore occult and magical imagery, most famously in the segment starring Mickey Mouse as the Sorcerer's Apprentice using the music by Paul Dukas. Dukas was a sober, intellectual and hugely self-critical artist, deeply influenced by Wagner in his approach to orchestration and leitmotif, so it is ironic that he is most famous for what is really a comic work. A blend of the scherzo style of Henri Litolff's *Concerto symphonique No. 4*, Liszt's *Mephisto Waltz No. 1* and Wagnerian orchestration derived from moments such as the scene in Act I of *Siegfried*, when the dwarf Mime is terrified by flashing lights in the forest, *L'Apprentie sorcière* (1898) uses a theme and variation form to suggest the action of Goethe's poem "Der Zauberlehrling," (1797) in which the apprentice misuses his master's spells to animate a broomstick to help him clean the laboratory. Comic it may be, but there is a definite sense of threat in the music, to which Disney responds in a disturbing manner as the enchanted brooms get out of control. In a different context, with a real child rather than Mickey Mouse as the apprentice, this situation could easily venture into nightmare territory.

To begin with, the silhouette of the conductor, Leopold Stokowski, slowly raises his arms in the manner of a magician himself, which is arguably what a conductor is anyway, but here, the gesture is deliberately "magickal" and prepares us for the first shot of the segment in which the sorcerer, in traditional pointed hat adorned with moon and stars, gestures over a mysterious glowing light. From the smoke that rises from this light, a huge butterfly is suggested, as though conjured from multi-colored ectoplasm. Meanwhile, we see Mickey struggling with two heavy pails of water. The sorcerer claps his hands, the butterfly disintegrates, and Mickey casts a giant "horror film" shadow over the wall as he follows the sorcerer towards the steps that lead outside. Mickey places a hat over his trademark ears and begins to enchant the broomstick with the kind of gestures we see Martin Landau's Bela Lugosi use when watching a television screening of one of his old films in *Ed Wood*.

Like the wicked queen in *Snow White* who asks, "Spieglen, spieglein an der Wand/Wer ist die schönste im ganzen Land?" (Mirror, mirror on the wall/Who is the fairest of them all?), Goethe's apprentice enchants the broom with a comparable "magick" meter:

> Walle! walle!
> Manche Strecke,
> Daß, zum Zwecke,
> Wasser fließe
> Und mit reichem, vollem Schwalle
> Zu dem Bade sich ergieße.
> (Water, flow in rich, full draughts to fill the bath.)

This all forms the introduction of Dukas' piece, which now proceeds as the broom is transformed into a water carrier with two arms. The accompaniments to each variation grow increasingly chromatic and denser in orchestration, so what began as quietly mysterious, with muted strings and harps, becomes much more troubling. Disney responds in kind, emphasizing Goethe's moral. Whereas Mickey dreams at first of playing with the universe, he wakes up to find a real disaster on his hands. Just as industrialization has caused global warming, playing with magick initiates a flood.

For all this, Disney fairy tale world of magic is less an affair of the will than of techniques, and "The Sorcerer's Apprentice" is more akin to Harry Potter and Mary Poppins than the more truly magickal concerns of Michael Reeves' similarly titled *The Sorcerers*. However, *Fantasia* has another occult affiliation in its association of music with color. This is nowhere near as schematic as it is in the mystical application of synesthesia in the later music of Alexander Scriabin; but it nonetheless points in that direction. Scriabin's aim to flood the concert hall with colored light during the performance of his last symphony *Prometheus, the Poem of Fire* (1910) derived from his own synesthetic impressions in which every musical tone had its corresponding hue. As the theosophical program of *Prometheus* unfolds in the orchestra, a "keyboard of light" (he wrote "music" for this instrument in the score, even though it did not exist at the time) would affect the psychic state of the audience by reinforcing the message of the music. This was nothing less than the evolution of humanity from primeval chaos, through the arrival of divine will and sexual activity, to the New Man, who sings the vowel sounds of a newborn baby, the whole erupting into violet light on the final F-sharp major chord, expressing "Creativity."

Disney's use of color is certainly vivid, but purely sensual. It plays no philosophical or esoteric role, though some attempt is made to use color to express the character of different orchestral timbres: During the prologue, in which the orchestra members arrive and tune up, colored lights illuminate the different instruments. We open with a blue background (Scriabin interestingly associated blue with "contemplation"). A red light then glows on the side of double bass, pink highlights a bass tuba, and pink light blossoms out of the blue background behind Stokowski, with the opening bars of Bach's Toccata and Fugue in D minor. Bassoons are then picked out with blue light, clarinets with green, first violins in red, second violins in orange, cellos taking over the orange with blue for the second desk. Midnight blue for the harps is alternated with pink for the orchestral tutti with which it is contrasted. Timpani rolls are provided with red light glowing on the sides of the drums, and so forth. This is only the briefest hint of the possibilities of a synesthetic presentation in the way Scriabin envisioned it, but does go some way to achieving what he had in mind.

The succeeding visualization of the Bach Fugue continues, in its abstract manner, to experiment with color combinations in conjunction with abstract suggestions of the instruments themselves: violin bows, violin strings, discs suggestive of the keys of a flute, then Gothic shapes implying a cathedral, bursting stars and a tottering stone to imitate the ponderous double-bass line towards the end. Rays of light pierce through the gloom to correspond to ethereal strings, before the final chords are bathed in deep red for the return of Stokowski's silhouette.

The Disney Studio was later asked to visualize the truly psychic force of the Id in *Forbidden Planet* (dir. Fred M. Wilcox, 1956). This creature, modeled on MGM's Leo the Lion mascot, represents the unconscious of Walter Pidgeon's Prof. Morbius. Having harnessed the mind-expanding technology of the now extinct former inhabitants of the planet Altair IV, the Krell, Morbius has also unwittingly unleashed "the monsters of the Id"—his own destructive subconscious force. Jealous of the starship captain who falls in love with his daughter, Morbius' Id threatens to destroy everything.

Here, Disney expressed the will far more powerfully than the fairy tale magic of *Snow White*. Visualized as the vicious scarlet outline of a roaring beast, with narrowed eyes and enormous fangs, Morbius' Id can easily destroy people, and in its raging fury it aptly expresses what Freud wrote about the subconscious mind in *The Ego and the Id*:

> Eros and the death instinct struggle within it; we have seen with what weapons the one group of instincts defends itself against the other. It would be possible to picture the id as under the domination of the mute but powerful death instincts, which desire to be at peace and (prompted by the pleasure principle) to put Eros, the mischief-maker, to rest; but perhaps that might be to undervalue the part played by Eros.[2]

Morbius' Id is exactly that unconscious force which Nietzsche, before Freud, termed "Das Es"—"The It." Nietzsche argued that consciousness only developed out of the need to communicate. Humanity, "like every living creature, is constantly thinking but does not know it; the thinking which becomes *conscious* is only the smallest part of it. ... At bottom, all our actions are incomparably and utterly personal, unique and boundlessly individual, there is no doubt; but as soon as we translate them into consciousness, *they no longer seem to be*...."[3]

Nietzsche argued that becoming conscious "involves a vast and thorough corruption, falsification superficialization and generalization."[4] In other words, consciousness is in most respects a lie, for it denies (or at least restrains) what Nietzsche calls "the instincts of freedom, [which] caused all the instincts of the wild, free, nomadic man to turn backwards *against man himself*. Hostility, cruelty, pleasure in persecution, in assault, in change, in destruction."[5]

Almost as though he had been reading Nietzsche, Leslie Nielsen's Commander Adams points out that this is why we have laws and religion; and when the Id goes on the rampage, Morbius at last realizes that it is "my evil self." But there is also a magical aspect to the *Forbidden Planet* Id. Adams explains that the Krell machine is operated by the "electro-magnetic impulses of individual Krell brains. In return, that machine would instantaneously project solid matter to any part of the planet in any shape or color they might imagine. For *any* purpose, Morbius. Creation by mere thought," and this is a fascinating expression of Crowley's definition of magick: the science of effecting change by means of the will.

Forbidden Planet thus reveals itself to be far more occult than psychological or scientific, which even more firmly connects it to its well-known basis in Shakespeare's *The Tempest,* where magic is again a driving force of the play: A distant island inhabited by a father (Morbius) and his daughter, a robot servant, a magic machine, a visiting spaceship...

These elements all reflect the structure of Shakespeare's play. Morbius is the magician Prospero, his daughter is Miranda, Robby the Robot is Caliban, and the Krell machine is the science fiction equivalent of Prospero's magic power—a vehicle by which to amplify the power of the will, which is in effect no different from any other kind of magical practice. Shakespeare's language for Prospero is filled with magical imagery:

> Ye elves of hills, brooks, standing lakes and groves,
> And ye that on the sands with printless foot
> Do chase the ebbing Neptune and do fly him
> When he comes back; you demi-puppets that
> By moonshine do the green sour ringlets make,
> Whereof the ewe not bites, and you whose pastime

> Is to make midnight mushrooms, that rejoice
> To hear the solemn curfew; by whose aid,
> Weak masters though ye be, I have bedimm'd
> The noontide sun, call'd forth the mutinous winds,
> And 'twixt the green sea and the azured vault
> Set roaring war: to the dread rattling thunder
> Have I given fire and rifted Jove's stout oak
> With his own bolt; the strong-based promontory
> Have I made shake and by the spurs pluck'd up
> The pine and cedar: graves at my command
> Have waked their sleepers, oped, and let 'em forth
> By my so potent art. But this rough magic
> I here abjure, and, when I have required
> Some heavenly music, which even now I do,
> To work mine end upon their senses that
> This airy charm is for, I'll break my staff,
> Bury it certain fathoms in the earth,
> And deeper than did ever plummet sound
> I'll drown my books.

In 2010, Helen Mirren gave Prospero a sex change as Prospera, intoning these lines herself from within a circle of fire, drawn by her wand in Julie Taylor's film adaptation. Against the backdrop of the Jurassic landscape of Hawaii, which is strange and terrifying enough, computer-generated animation aids the invocation, swirling "reality" around her as the flames reach higher. Ariel, Prospera's fairy slave, is shown as he once was, imprisoned in a tree trunk, before Prospera released him. CGI creates fire-breathing dogs and transforms Ariel into a terrifying harpy: "I have made you mad," he leers at Proserpa's enemies, shipwrecked on the island too.

In 1991, Stanislav Sokolov created a much more conventional and radically condensed children's version of the play, using stop-motion techniques for the Soyuzmultifilm series of animated Shakespeare films. But CGI is now the obvious choice for this most "magickal" play. Peter Greenaway exploited digital image manipulation as early as 1991 in *Prospero's Books*: Its approach was based on his imagining of the 24 books Prospero took with him into his insular exile, and which form the basis of his magick. Each book is described both on the soundtrack and visually by means of electronic animation: books of water, mirrors, mythologies, *Primer of the Small Stars*, an atlas belonging to Orpheus, geometry, colors, music, anatomy and so forth. Greenaway's approach is to provide a commentary on the magickal background of the play, rather than a performance of it, somewhat in the manner of Syberberg's 1982 film of Wagner's *Parsifal*, which is both a performance *and* a commentary. The last book is one of 36 plays, with 19 pages left blank for the last one to be written on. This is to be called *The Tempest,* and the initials on the cover of the book are "W.S."

The ultimate magician is therefore revealed to be Shakespeare himself, and if one wishes to find a definition of magick that does not defy the known laws of cause and effect, Shakespeare's plays, Mozart's music, Michelangelo's statues—all of Art, indeed, and film in particular—are undeniable examples of the power of the will to effect change. As Lotte H. Eisner wrote in her study of *The Haunted Screen*, "Mind, Spirit, Vision and Ghosts seem to gush forth, exterior facts are continually being transformed into interior elements and psychic events are exteriorized. Is this not precisely the atmosphere we find in the classic films of the German cinema?"[6] But it is not only the atmosphere of the German cinema, as we have seen, but the whole world of Movie Magick.

Chapter Notes

Introduction

1. Sigmund Freud (trans. James Strachey), *The Origins of Religion,* The Penguin Freud Library, vol. 13 (London: Penguin, 1999), 149 ("Totem and Taboo").
2. Sir James Frazer, *The Golden Bough,* abridged edition (London: Macmillan, 1950), 51.
3. Aleister Crowley (ed. Hymenaeus Beta), *Magick Liber Aba: Book Four, Parts I–IV* (San Francisco: Red Wheel/Weiser, 1994), 139 ("Magick in Theory and Practice").
4. *Ibid.*, 267 ("Magick in Theory and Practice").
5. *Ibid.*, 269 ("Magick in Theory and Practice").
6. *Ibid.*, 126 ("Magick in Theory and Practice").
7. Israel Regardie (ed. Chic Cicero & Sandra Tabatha Cicero) *A Garden of Pomegranates: Skrying on the Tree of Life* (St. Paul: Llewellyn, 2004), 172.
8. Eric Kurlander, *Hitler's Monsters: A Supernatural History of The Third Reich* (New Haven and London: Yale University Press, 2017), 73.
9. Friedrich Nietzsche (trans. Josefine Nauckhoff), *The Gay Science* (Cambridge: Cambridge University Press, 2001), 120.
10. Sigmund Freud (trans. James Strachey), *The Interpretation of Dreams,* The Penguin Freud Library, vol. 4 (Harmondsworth: Penguin, 1983), 61.
11. C. G. Jung (trans. R. F. C. Hull), *Psychology and the Occult* (London: Routledge and Kegan Paul, 1982), 139 ("Psychology and Spiritualism").

Chapter One

1. Philip Hoare, *Wilde's Last Stand: Decadence, Conspiracy & The First World War* (London: Duckworth, 1997), 84.
2. J.-K. Huysmans, *Là Bas [Lower Depths]* (Sawtry: Dedalus, 1986), 9–10.
3. *Ibid.*, 138.
4. Richard Gilman, *Decadence: The Strange Life of an Epithet* (New York: Farrar, Straus and Giroux, 1979), 12.
5. Robert W. Gutman, *Richard Wagner: The Man, His Mind, and His Music,* Time-Life Records Special Edition (New York: Time Incorporated, 1972), 468.
6. Charles Baudelaire (trans. P. E. Charvet), *Selected Writings on Art and Artists,* (Cambridge: Cambridge University Press, 1981), 101 ("The Salon of 1846").
7. H. P. Blavatsky, *Isis Unveiled: A Master-Key to the Mysteries of Ancient and Modern Science and Theology* (Pasadena: Theosophical University Press, 1998), ix.
8. Friedrich Nietzsche (trans. R. J. Hollingdale), *Ecce Homo* (Harmondsworth: Penguin, 1982), 40.
9. Friedrich Nietzsche (trans. Walter Kaufmann), *The Birth of Tragedy and The Case of Wagner* (New York: Vintage, 1967), 165 ("The Case of Wagner").
10. Henri Dorra (ed.), *Symbolist Art Theories: A Critical Anthology* (Berkeley: University of California Press, 1994), 33.
11. Oscar Wilde, *Complete Works of Oscar Wilde* (London: Collins, 1977), 101 ("The Picture of Dorian Gray").
12. Jane Desmarais & Chris Baldick (eds.), *Decadence: An Annotated Anthology* (Manchester: Manchester University Press, 2012), 132 (Arthur Symons, "Lilian I: Proem").
13. Geraldine Beare (ed.), *Adventure Stories from the "Strand* (London: Folio Society, 1995), 55 (Fred M. White, "The Purple Terror").
14. Sarah Bernhardt, *My Double Life: The Memoirs of Sarah Bernhardt,* (London: Peter Owen, 1977), 258.
15. Jean Lorrain (trans. Francis Amery),

Monsieur de Phocas (Sawtry: Dedalus, 1994), 60.
16. *Ibid.*, 184.
17. *Ibid.*, 254.
18. Jimmy Sangster, *Inside Hammer* (London: Reynolds & Hearn, 2001), 32.
19. Bram Stoker, *Dracula* (London: Constable, 1904), 17.
20. Villiers de l'Isle Adam, *Axël* (London: Soho Book Company, 1986), 41.
21. Oscar Wilde, *Complete Works of Oscar Wilde,* 27 ("The Picture of Dorian Gray").
22. *Ibid.*, 91 ("The Picture of Dorian Gray").
23. *Ibid.*, 32 ("The Picture of Dorian Gray").
24. Peter Haining (ed.), *The Frankenstein Omnibus* (London: Orion, 1994), 106 (Villiers de l'Isle Adam, "The Future Eve").
25. Jane Desmarais and Chris Baldick (eds.), *Decadence: An Annotated Anthology,* 189–190 (Jean Moréas, "La Faënza").
26. M. P. Shiel, *Prince Zaleski* (Kansas City: Valancourt Books, 2010), 6.
27. *Ibid.*
28. Jean Lorrain (trans. Francis Amery), *Monsieur de Phocas,* 134.
29. Jane Desmarais & Chris Baldick (eds.), *Decadence: An Annotated Anthology,* 137 (Arthur Symons, "Andante of Snakes").
30. Jean Lorrain (trans. Francis Amery), *Monsieur de Phocas,* 187.
31. Charles Baudelaire, *Art in Paris 1845–62. Salons and Other Exhibitions.* (London: Phaidon Press, 1965), 119.
32. F. W. J. Hemmings, *Baudelaire the Damned* (London: Hamish Hamilton 1982), 76.
33. Charles Baudelaire (trans. Jonathan Mayne), *The Painter of Modern Life and Other Essays* (New York: Da Capo Press, 1964), 7 ("The Painter in Modern Life").
34. Prince Felix Youssoupoff (trans. Ann Green and Nicholas Katkoff), *Lost Splendour* (London: Folio Society, 1996), 125.
35. Richard Gilman, *Decadence: The Strange Life of an Epithet,* 24.

Chapter Two

1. Henri Dorra (ed.), *Symbolist Art Theories: A Critical Anthology* (Berkeley: University of California Press, 1994), 131 (Paul Bourget "Baudelaire and the Decadent Movement").
2. Edmund Wilson, *Axel's Castle: A Study in the Imaginative Literature of 1870–1930,* (New York: Collier Books/Macmillan, 1991), 266.
3. Sir Arthur Conan Doyle, *The Sign of Four* (London: Leopard, 1996), 40.
4. *Ibid.*, 31.
5. Villiers de L'Isle Adam (trans. Robert Baldick), *Cruel Tales* (Oxford: Oxford University Press, 1985), viii (introduction by A. W. Raitt).
6. Edmund Wilson, *Axel's Castle: A Study in the Imaginative Literature of 1870–1930,* 259.
7. Villiers de l'Isle-Adam, *Axël* (London: Soho Book Company, 1986), 143.
8. Henri Dorra (ed.), *Symbolist Art Theories: A Critical Anthology,* 269 (Joséphin Péledan, "In Search of the Holy Grail").
9. *Ibid.*, 127.
10. *Ibid.*, 137.
11. Thomas Mann (trans. H. T. Lowe-Porter), *Buddenbrooks* (London: Secker & Warburg, 1956), 562.
12. Villiers de l'Isle-Adam, *Axël,* 171.
13. Ted Honderich (ed.), *The Oxford Companion to Philosophy* (Oxford: Oxford University Press, 1995), 342 (Peter Singer's entry on Hegel).
14. Villiers de L'Isle Adam (trans. Robert Baldick), *Cruel Tales*), 20 ("Véra").
15. *Ibid.*, x (A. W. Raitt's introduction).
16. Villiers de L'Isle Adam (trans. Robert Baldick), *Cruel Tales,* 29 ('Two Augurs").
17. *Ibid.*, 105 ("The Very Image").
18. *Ibid.*, 102 ("The Very Image").
19. *Ibid.*, 141 ("The Desire to be a Man").
20. *Ibid.*, 146 ("The Desire to be a Man").
21. *Ibid.*, 64 ("The Duke of Portland").
22. *Ibid.*, 71 ("The Duke of Portland").
23. *Ibid.*, 67 ("The Duke of Portland").
24. Peter Haining (ed.) *The Frankenstein Omnibus* (London: Orion, 1994), 106 (Villiers de l'Isle Adam [trans. Florence Crewe-Jones], "The Future Eve").
25. *Ibid.*, 134–135 ("The Future Eve").
26. *Ibid.*, 121 ("The Future Eve").
27. *Ibid.*, 89 ("The Future Eve")
28. *Ibid.*, 83 ("The Future Eve").
29. Villiers de l'Isle Adam (trans. Brian Stableford), *The Vampire Soul,* Encino: Black Coat Press, 2004, 48.
30. *Ibid.*, 134.
31. Villiers de L'Isle Adam (trans. Robert Baldick), *Cruel Tales,* 234 ("Occult Memories").

Chapter Three

1. Christopher Marlowe (ed. E. D. Pendry), *Complete Plays and Poems* (London: Dent, 1983), 277 ("Doctor Faustus").
2. *Ibid.*, 281 ("Doctor Faustus").
3. *Ibid.*, 286 ("Doctor Faustus").
4. *Ibid.*, 324 ("Doctor Faustus").

5. Matthew Lewis, *The Monk* (London: Folio Society, 1984), 311.
6. Sir Walter Scott, *Letters on Demonology and Witchcraft* (Ware: Wordsworth, 2001), 232.
7. Johann Wolfgang von Goethe (trans. David Luke), *Faust: Part One* (Oxford: Oxford University Press,1987), 41.
8. *Ibid.*, 73.
9. W. Somerset Maugham, *The Magician/The Gentleman in the Parlour,* London: Heron Books, 1968, 124 ("The Magician").
10. J.-K. Huysmans, *Là-bas (Lower Depths)*, Sawtry: Dedalus, 1986, 227.
11. Dennis Wheatley, *The Devil Rides Out*, London: Heron 1972, 8.
12. *Ibid.*, 165.
13. Richard Wagner (trans. Andrew Porter), *Parsifal* (Opera Guide), London: John Calder, 1986, 91
14. *Ibid.*, 102.
15. Charles Williams, *War in Heaven* (Dennis Wheatley Library of the Occult), London: Sphere, 1976, 116.
16. Richard Wagner (trans. Andrew Porter), *Parsifal* (Opera Guide), p. 101.
17. *Ibid.*, 103.
18. *Ibid.*, 101.
19. *Ibid.*, 102.
20. Eero Tarasti, *Myth and Music* (Helsinki: Suomen Musiikkitieteellinen Seura, 1978), 111.
21. Dennis Wheatley, *The Devil Rides Out*, 166.
22. Robert L. Delevoy (trans. Barbara Bray, Elizabeth Wrightson and Bernard C. Swift), *Symbolists and Symbolism* (London: Macmillan, 1982), 18.
23. *Ibid.*, 47.
24. Charles Baudelaire (trans. Joanna Richardson), *Selected Poems* (London: Penguin, 1986), 83 ("Possessed").
25. *Ibid.*, 89 ("Entire").
26. *Ibid.*, 189 ("Destruction").
27. *Ibid.*, 57 ("Hymne à la beauté").
28. *Ibid.*, 107 ("L'Irréparable").
29. *Ibid.*, 197 ("Les Litanies de Satan").
30. Friedrich Nietzsche (trans. Walter Kaufmann), *The Birth of Tragedy and The Case of Wagner* (New York: Vintage, 1967), 164 ("The Case of Wagner").
31. *Ibid.*, 184 ("The Wagner Case").
32. J.-K. Husymans (trans. P. G. Lloyd), *À Rebours* (London: The Fortune Press, 1946), 185–186.
33. J. K. Huysmans, *Là-bas*, 245–246.
34. *Ibid.*, 80.
35. Henry Cornelius Agrippa (trans. Robert Turner), *Fourth Book of Occult Philosophy of Geomancy, Magical Elements of Peter de Abano, Astronomical Geomancy, the Nature of Spirits, Arbatel of Magick,* http://quod.lib.umich.edu/e/eebo/A26562.0001.001/1:12.7?rgn=div2;view=fulltext, 65–66.
36. Francis Barrett, *The Magus, or Celestial Intelligencer; being a complete system of Occult Philosophy, Book II* (London: Lackington, Allen & Co., 1801), 105–106.
37. Richard Wagner (trans. William Ashton Ellis), *Religion and Art* (Lincoln: University of Nebraska Press, 1994), 213 ("Religion and Art").
38. J.-K. Huysmans, *Là-bas*, 11.
39. August Strindberg (trans. Mary Sandbach), *Inferno and From an Occult Diary* (Harmondsworth: Penguin, 19790, 211 ("Inferno").
40. *Ibid.*, 219 ("Inferno").
41. *Ibid.*, 221 ("Inferno").
42. *Ibid.*, 144 ("Inferno").

Chapter Four

1. Peter Haining (ed.), *The Ghouls* (London: Chancellor Press, 1994), 18 (Francis Oscar Mann: "The Devil in a Convent").
2. Gustav Meyrinck (trans. Mike Mitchell), *The White Dominican* (Sawtry: Dedalus, 1994), 38.
3. Oscar Wilde, *Complete Works of Oscar Wilde* (London: Collins, 1977), 789 ("The Harlot's House").
4. Éliphas Lévi (trans. Arthur Edward Waite), *Transcendental Magic: Its Doctrine & Ritual* (Twickenham: Senate,1995), 86.
5. Aleister Crowley, *Magick Liber Aba: Book Four* (San Francisco: Weiser, 1997), 51.
6. Bram Stoker, *Dracula* (London: Constable, 1904), 377.
7. Marie Corelli, *The Sorrows of Satan* (London: Methuen, 1918), 18.
8. Siegfried Kracauer, *From Caligari to Hitler: A Psychological History of the German Film,* Princeton: Princeton University Press, 1970, 81.
9. *Ibid.*, 82.
10. *Ibid.*, 83.
11. C. G. Jung, *Collected Works*, vol. 7 (London: Routledge, 2015), 2740 ("On The Psychology of the Unconscious").
12. W. Somerset Maugham, *The Magician/Gentlemen in the Parlour,* (London: Heron, 1968), 6 ("The Magician").
13. *Ibid.*, 9.
14. *Ibid.*, 8,
15. Aleister Crowley, *The Confessions of Aleister Crowley,* ed. John Symonds and Kenneth Grant (London: Arcana/Penguin, 1989), 571.

16. Robin Maugham, *Conversations with Willie: Recollections of W. Somerset Maugham* (New York: Simon and Schuster, 1978), 179.
17. W. Somerset Maugham, *The Magician/Gentlemen in the Parlour*, 6 ("The Magician") (Note 12).
18. Dennis Wheatley, *To the Devil: A Daughter* (London: Heron, 1972), 238.
19. W. Somerset Maugham, *The Magician/Gentlemen in the Parlour,*, 92 (Note 12).
20. *Ibid.*, 123 ("The Magician").
21. *Ibid.*, 106 ("The Magician").
22. *Ibid.*, 104 ("The Magician").
23. *Ibid.*, 107 ("The Magician").
24. *Ibid.*, 111 ("The Magician").
25. Benvenuto Cellini, *The Autobiography of Benvenuto Cellini* (London: Folio, 1967), 307.

Chapter Five

1. E. T. A. Hoffmann (ed. Christopher Lazare), *Tales of Hoffmann* (New York: A. A. Wyn, 1946), 104 ("Don Juan").
2. *Ibid.*, 109 ("Don Juan").
3. Dennis Wheatley, *The Devil Rides Out* (London: Heron, 1972), 200.
4. Aleister Crowley, *Magick Liber Aba: Book Four,* San Francisco: Weiser, 1997, 106.
5. Dennis Wheatley, *The Devil Rides Out,* 201.
6. Gerard Encausse, *How to Fight Hexes,* http://martinismo.com/Papus/Como Combatir los Maleficios.pdf, 24.
7. Dennis Wheatley, *The Devil Rides Out,* 201.
8. *Ibid.*, 20.
9. Christopher Lee, *Tall, Dark and Gruesome: An Autobiography* (London: Victor Gollancz, 1997), 235.
10. Grillot de Givry (trans. J. Courtenay Locke), *Witchcraft, Magic and Alchemy* New York: Dover, 1972), 113.
11. Dennis Wheatley, *The Devil Rides Out,* 126.
12. *Ibid.*, 110.
13. Phil Baker, *The Devil is a Gentleman* (Sawtry: Dedalus, 2009), 312.
14. J.-K. Huysmans, *Là-bas [Lower Depths]* (Sawtry: Dedalus, 1986_), 242.
15. Dennis Wheatley, *The Devil Rides Out,* 300.
16. *Ibid.*, 303.
17. *Ibid.*, 304.
18. J.-K. Huysmans, *Là-bas [Lower Depths],* 249.
19. Aleister Crowley, *Magick Liber Aba: Book Four,* 276.
20. *Ibid.*, 277.
21. Aleister Crowley, *The Confessions of Aleister Crowley,* ed. John Symonds and Kenneth Grant (London: Arcana/Penguin, 1989), 623.
22. Peter Sykes interviewed for the documentary "To the Devil ... the Death of Hammer" (dir. David Gregory, 2002).
23. *Ibid.* (Gerald Vaughan Hughes interviewed).
24. Renée Haynes, *The Society for Psychical Research, 1882–1982: A History* (London: Macdonald & Co., 1982), 144.
25. *Ibid.*, 145.
26. Aleister Crowley, *Magick Liber Aba: Book Four,* 243.
27. *Ibid.*, 51.
28. Adolf Hitler (trans. Ralph Manheim), *Mein Kampf* (London: Hutchinson, 1980), 452.
29. Eric Kurlander, *Hitler's Monsters: A Supernatural History of the Third Reich* (New Haven and London: Yale University Press, 2017), 57.
30. Albert Speer (trans. Richard and Clara Winston) *Inside the Third Reich* (London: Macmillan, 1970), 112.

Chapter Six

1. Aleister Crowley, *Magick Liber Aba: Book Four* (San Francisco: Weiser, 1997), 126.
2. Phil Baker, *The Devil is a Gentleman* (Sawtry: Dedalus, 2009), 539.
3. Dennis Wheatley, *They Used Dark Forces* (London: Heron, 1973), 481.
4. Siegfried Kracauer, *From Caligari to Hitler: A Psychological History of the German Film* (Princeton: Princeton University Press, 1970), 77.
5. *Ibid.*, 79.
6. *Ibid.*, 81.
7. *Ibid.*, 302–303.
8. *Ibid.*, 303.
9. Robert W. Gutman, *Richard Wagner: The Man, His Mind, and His Music,* Time-Life Records Special Edition (New York: Time Incorporated, 1972), 467.
10. Claude Debussy, *Monsieur Croche et autres écrits* (Paris: Gallimard, 1987), 243–244.
11. Aleister Crowley, *Magick Liber Aba: Book Four,* 279.
12. Thorold Dickinson interview in *Film Dope,* 1977, reproduced in the DVD booklet for Dickinson's *The Queen of Spades,* Optimum Releasing, 2010, 3.
13. Don Sharp interviewed in *Hammer: The Studio That Dripped Blood* (dir. David Thompson, 1987).

14. Christopher Lee, *Tall, Dark and Gruesome: An Autobiography* (London: Victor Gollancz, 1997), 32.
15. *Ibid.*, 231.
16. Edvard Radzinsky (trans. Judson Rosengrant), *Rasputin: The Last Word* (London: Weidenfeld & Nicolson, 2000), 303.
17. *Ibid.*, 436.
18. Maria Rasputin with Patte Barham, *Rasputin* (London: Arrow, 1979), 87.
19. George Du Maurier, *Novels of George Du Maurier* (London: Pilot Press & Peter Davis, 1947), 248 ("Trilby").
20. Aleister Crowley, *Magick Liber Aba: Book Four*, 144.
21. *Ibid.*, 134.
22. Aleister Crowley, *Moonchild*, Dennis Wheatley Library of the Occult (London: Sphere, 1974), 134.
23. Lotte H. Eisner (trans. Roger Greaves), *The Haunted Screen* (London: Thames and Hudson, 1973), 110.
24. Siegfried Kracauer, *From Caligari to Hitler* (Princeton: Princeton University Press, 1970), 32–33.
25. Friedrich Nietzsche (trans. R. J. Hollingdale), *Twilight of the Idols/The Anti-Christ* (Harmondsworth: Penguin, 1981), 115 ("The Anti-Christ").
26. Aleister Crowley, p. 292
27. Eric Kurlander, *Hitler's Monsters: A Supernatural History of The Third Reich,* (New Haven and London: Yale University Press, 2017), 251.
28. Fred Mustard Stewart, *The Mephisto Waltz* (London: Michael Joseph, 1969), 78.
29. *Ibid.*, 109.
30. Aleister Crowley, *Magick Liber Aba: Book Four*, 126.

Chapter Seven

1. Richard Cavendish, *The Tarot* (London: Chancellor Press, 1986), 67.
2. *Ibid.*, 68.
3. *Ibid.*, 70.
4. Aleister Crowley, *Magick Liber Aba: Book Four* (San Francisco: Weiser Books, 1994), 127.
5. Sir Arthur Conan Doyle, *The Memoirs of Sherlock Holmes* (London: Leopard, 1996), 223–224 ("The Naval Treaty").
6. John Fowles, *The Magus* (London: Jonathan Cape, 1966), 459.
7. *Ibid.*, 73.
8. *Ibid.*, 118.
9. *Ibid.*, 130.
10. *Ibid.*, 138.

11. *Ibid.*, 375.
12. *Ibid.*, 458.
13. *Ibid.*, 459–460.
14. Albert Speer (trans. Richard and Clara Winston), *Inside the Third Reich* (London: Macmillan, 1970), 20–21.
15. Hans-Jürgen Syberberg (trans. Joachim Neugroschel), *Hitler: A Film from Germany* (Manchester: Carcanet, 1982), 127.
16. *Ibid.*, 242.

Chapter Eight

1. Mark Gatiss, *A History of Horror* (dir. John Das), BBC, 2010 ("The American Scream").
2. *The Exorcist, 25th Anniversary Edition* DVD, Z1 16176 ("The Fear of God Documentary").
3. William Peter Blatty, *The Exorcist* (London: Folio Society, 2017), 175–176.
4. *Ibid.*, 295.
5. *Ibid.*, 272.
6. *Ibid.*, 288.
7. *Ibid.*, 256.
8. *Ibid.*, 295.
9. *Ibid.*, 254.
10. Mark Gatiss, *A History of Horror.*
11. *Ibid.*
12. Zoé Oldenbourg, *Massacre at Montségur: A History of the Albigensian Crusade* (London: Phoenix Press, 2001), 37.
13. Richard Cavendish, *The Black Arts* (New York: Perigee, 1983), 7.
14. Aleister Crowley, *Magick Liber Aba: Book Four* (San Francisco: Weiser, 1997), 163–164.
15. Robert Barry, "Sound on Film: Penderecki and the sound of radical evil" www.soundandmusic.org/features/sound-film/penderecki-and-sound-radicalmusic:
16. Salka Viertel, *The Kindness of Strangers* (New York: Holt, 1969), 207–8.
17. *The Exorcist:25th Anniversary Edition* DVD.
18. *The Omen, 30th Anniversary Edition*, DVD F1-OGB 3448001001 (commentary).
19. *Ibid.* (Jerry Goldsmith on *The Omen* score).

Chapter Nine

1. Francis Hodgson Burnett, *The Secret Garden* (London: Folio Society, 2006), 214.
2. *Ibid.*, 215.
3. *Ibid.*, 217–218.
4. Nicholas Goodrick-Clarke, *The Occult Roots of Nazism* (Wellingborough: Aquarian Press, 1985), 100.

5. *Ibid.*, 101.
6. *Ibid.*
7. *Ibid.*, 102.
8. A. P. Sinnett, *Esoteric Buddhism* (London: Theosophical Publishing House, 1972), 54.
9. H. P. Blavatsky, *The Secret Doctrine,* vol. 2. (Los Angeles: The Theosophy Company, 1982), 6.
10. *Ibid.*, vol. 2, 7.
11. *Ibid.*, vol. 2, 152.
12. Nicholas Goodrick-Clarke, *The Occult Roots of Nazism*, 95.
13. *Ibid.*, 130.
14. Edward Bulwer-Luytton, *The Coming Race* (London: Hesperus Press, 2007), 129.
15. Hans-Jürgen Syberberg (trans. Joachim Neugroschel) *Hitler: A Film from Germany* (Manchester: Carcanet, 1982), 131.
16. *Ibid.*, 136.
17. *Ibid.*, 246.
18. John Wyndham, *The Day of the Triffids* (London: Book Club Associates, 1981), 787 ("The Midwich Cuckoos").
19. *Ibid.*, 822 ("The Midwich Cuckoos").
20. *Ibid.*, 837 ("The Midwich Cuckoos").
21. H. P. Blavatsky, *The Secret Doctrine,* vol. 2., 222.
22. Dez Skinn (ed.) *House of Hammer Magazine*, No. 21, June 1978 (London: Top Sellers, 1978), 34–35 (Catherine O'Brien & Tony Crawley, "Warlords of the Deep").
23. Eric Kurlander, *Hitler's Monsters: A Supernatural History of The Third Reich* (New Haven and London: Yale University Press, 2017), 243.
24. Adolf Hitler (trans. Ralph Manheim), *Mein Kampf* (London: Hutchinson, 1980), 268.
25. Dez Skinn (ed.) *House of Hammer Magazine*, No. 21, June 1978, 36 (Catherine O'Brien & Tony Crawley, "Warlords of the Deep").
26. Friedrich Nietzsche (trans. Walter Kaufmann), *The Birth of Tragedy and The Case of Wagner* (New York: Vintage, 1967), 157 ("The Case of Wagner").
27. H. P. Blavatsky, *The Secret Doctrine,* vol. 2, 222.
28. H. P. Lovecraft, *The Fiction* (New York: Barnes and Noble, 2008), 355 ("The Call of Cthulhu").
29. *Ibid.*, 367 ("The Call of Cthulhu").
30. *Ibid.*, 613–614 ("The Colour out of Space").

Chapter Ten

1. Aldous Huxley, *The Doors of Perception* (Harmondsworth: Penguin, 1959), 25.

2. *Ibid.*, 51.
3. *Ibid.*, 25.
4. *Ibid.*, 51–52.
5. H. G. Wells, *Selected Short Stories* (Harmondsworth: Penguin, 1958), 109 ("The Door in the Wall").
6. C. G. Jung (ed.) *Man and His Symbols* (London: Aldus Books, 1979), 186 (M.-L. von Franz, "The process of individuation").
7. H. Rider Haggard, *She* (London: Collins, 1974), 151.
8. William Wordsworth (ed. Thomas Hutchinson), *The Poetical Works of Wordsworth* (London: Oxford University Press, 1965), 460–461 ("Ode—Intimations of Immortality from Recollections of Early Childhood").
9. C. G. Jung (trans. R. F. C. Hull), *Psychology and Alchemy* (London: Routledge & Kegan Paul, 1980), 243.
10. Novalis (Friedrich von Hardenberg), *Henry of Ofterdingen* (New York: Dover, 2015), 4.
11. Adolf Hitler (trans. Ralph Manheim), *Mein Kampf* (London: Hutchinson, 1980), 271.
12. https://www.ncbi.nlm.nih.gov/pmc/articles/PMC3917651/

Chapter Eleven

1. H. P. Blavatsky, *The Secret Doctrine* (Los Angeles: The Theosophy Company, 1982), xxxvi.
2. Annie Besant, *The Ancient Wisdom* (London: Theosophical Publishing Society, 1897), 3–4.
3. Israel Regardie (ed. Chic Cicero & Sandra Tabatha Cicero), *A Garden of Pomegranates: Skrying on the Tree of Life* (St. Paul, Minnesota: Llewellyn Publications, 2004), 33.
4. Adolf Hitler (trans. Ralph Manheim), *Mein Kampf* (London: Hutchinson, 1980), 52.
5. Eric Kurlander, *Hitler's Monsters: A Supernatural History of The Third Reich* (New Haven and London: Yale University Press, 2017), 95.
6. Ben Urwand, *The Collaboration: Hollywood's Pact with Hitler* (Cambridge MA: Harvard University Press, 2015).
7. Eric Kurlander, *Hitler's Monsters: A Supernatural History of The Third Reich,* p. x.
8. *Ibid.*, 187.
9. Lt.-Col. P. H. Fawcett, *Exploration Fawcett* (London: Heron, 1969), 12, 185, 204. The theory that Fawcett planned to set up a theosophical community in the Amazon jungle was put forward by Misha Williams in 2004. https://www.theguardian.com/uk/2004/mar/21/research.brazil.

10. Phil Baker, *The Devil is a Gentleman* (Sawtry: Dedalus, 2009), 540.
11. Jon Ruddy, *The Bargain* (New York: Knightsbridge, 1990), 290–291.
12. Adolf Hitler (trans. Ralph Manheim), *Mein Kampf,* 296.
13. *Ibid.*, 141.
14. Eric Kurlander, *Hitler's Monsters: A Supernatural History of The Third Reich,* 252.
15. *Ibid.*, 248.
16. *Ibid.*, 245.
17. John Milton, *The Poetical Works of John Milton* (London: Frederick Warne, 1896, 179 ("Paradise Lost").
18. Roman Polanski, *Roman* (London: Heinemann, 1984), 228.
19. *Ibid.*, 230,
20. Karl Marx, *Capital* (Oxford: Oxford University Press, 1995), 149.

Chapter Twelve

1. Johann Wolfgang von Goethe (trans. David Luke), *Faust: Part One* (Oxford: Oxford University Press, 1987), 42.
2. *Ibid.*, 10.
3. *Ibid.*, 16.
4. *Ibid.*, 17.
5. *Ibid.*
6. *Ibid.*, 19.
7. *Ibid.*, 41.
8. Johann Wolfgang von Goethe (trans. John Anster), *Faustus* (London: Routledge, 1883), 91.
9. Johann Wolfgang von Goethe (trans. David Luke), *Faust: Part One,* 41.
10. *Ibid.*, 53.
11. Stephen King, *Needful Things* (London: BCA, 1991), 691.
12. *Ibid.*, 42.
13. Christopher Marlowe (ed. E. D. Pendry), *Complete Plays and Poems* (London: Dent, 1995), 287.

Chapter Thirteen

1. David J. Skal, *The Monster Show: A Cultural History of Horror* (London: Plexus, 1993), 214–215.
2. Sigmund Freud (trans. James Strachey), *On Metapsychology,* The Penguin Freud Library, vol. 11 (London: Penguin, 1991), 401 ("The Ego and the Id")
3. Friedrich Nietzsche (trans. Josefine Nauckhoff), *The Gay Science* (Cambridge: Cambridge University Press, 2001), 213.
4. *Ibid.* 213–214.
5. Friedrich Nietzsche (trans. Douglas Smith), *On the Genealogy of Morals* (Oxford: Oxford University Press, 1996), 65.
6. Lotte H. Eisner (trans. Roger Greaves), *The Haunted Screen* (London: Thames and Hudson, 1973), 15.

Bibliography

Agrippa, Henry Cornelius (trans. Robert Turner). *Fourth Book of Occult Philosophy of Geomancy, Magical Elements of Peter de Abano, Astronomical Geomancy, the Nature of Spirits, Arbatel of Magick.* http://quod.lib.umich.edu/e/eebo/A26562.0001.001/1:12.7?rgn=div2;view=fulltext

Baker, Phil. *The Devil is a Gentleman.* Sawtry: Dedalus, 2009.

Barrett, Francis. *The Magus, or Celestial Intelligence: Being a Complete System of Occult Philosophy, Book II.* London: Lackington, Allen & Co., 1801.

Barry, Robert. "Sound on Film: Penderecki and the Sound of Radical Evil." www.soundandmusic.org/features/sound-film/penderecki-and-sound-radicalmusic:

Baudelaire, Charles. *Art in Paris 1845–62: Salons and Other Exhibitions.* London: Phaidon Press, 1965.

Baudelaire, Charles. (trans. Jonathan Mayne). *The Painter of Modern Life and Other Essays.* New York: Da Capo Press, 1964.

Baudelaire, Charles. (trans. Joanna Richardson). *Selected Poems.* London: Penguin,1986.

Baudelaire, Charles. (trans. P. E. Charvet). *Selected Writings on Art and Artists.* Cambridge: Cambridge University Press, 1981.

Beare, Geraldine (ed.). *Adventure Stories from the "Strand."* London: Folio Society,1995.

Bernhardt, Sarah. *My Double Life—The Memoirs of Sarah Bernhardt.* London: Peter Owen, 1977.

Besant, Annie. *The Ancient Wisdom.* London: Theosophical Publishing Society,1897.

Blavatsky, H. P. *Isis Unveiled: A Master-Key to the Mysteries of Ancient and Modern Science and Theology.* Pasadena: Theosophical University Press, 1998.

Blavatsky, H. P. *The Secret Doctrine.* Los Angeles: The Theosophy Company, 1982.

Bulwer-Luytton, Edward. *The Coming Race.* London: Hesperus Press, 2007.

Burnett, Francis Hodgson. *The Secret Garden.* London: Folio Society, 2006.

Cavendish, Richard. *The Black Arts.* New York: Perigee, 1983.

Cavendish, Richard. *The Tarot.* London: Chancellor Press, 1986.

Cellini, Benvenuto. *The Autobiography of Benvenuto Cellini.* London: Folio, 1967.

Conan Doyle, Sir Arthur. *The Memoirs of Sherlock Holmes.* London: Leopard, 1996.

Conan Doyle, Sir Arthur. *The Sign of Four.* London: Leopard, 1996.

Crowley, Aleister. *The Confessions of Aleister Crowley* (ed. John Symonds and Kenneth Grant), London: Arcana/Penguin, 1989.

Crowley, Aleister (ed. Hymenaeus Beta). *Magick Liber Aba: Book Four, Parts I-IV.* San Francisco: Red Wheel/Weiser, 1994.

Crowley, Aleister. *Moonchild.* (Dennis Wheatley Library of the Occult), London: Sphere,1974.

Debussy, Claude. *Monsieur Croche et autres écrits.* Paris: Gallimard, 1987.

Delevoy, Robert L. (trans. Barbara Bray, Elizabeth Wrightson and Bernard C. Swift). *Symbolists and Symbolism.* London: Macmillan, 1982.

Desmarais, Jane, and Baldick, Chris (eds.). *Decadence: An annotated anthology.* Manchester: Manchester University Press, 2012.

Dorra, Henri (ed.). *Symbolist Art Theories: A Critical Anthology.* Berkeley & Los Angeles: University of California Press, 1994.

Du Maurier, George. *Novels of George Du Maurier.* London: Pilot Press & Peter Davis,1947.

Eisner, Lotte H. (trans. Roger Greaves). *The Haunted Screen.* London: Thames and Hudson, 1973.

Encausse, Gerard. *How to Fight Hexes.* http://martinismo.com/Papus/Como Combatir los Maleficios.pdf.

Fawcett, Lt.-Col. P. H. *Exploration Fawcett.* London: Heron, 1969.

Bibliography

Fowles, John. *The Magus*. London: Jonathan Cape, 1966.
Frazer, Sir James. *The Golden Bough* (abridged edition), London: Macmillan, 1950.
Freud, Sigmund (trans. James Strachey). *The Interpretation of Dreams* (The Penguin Freud Library, vol. 4). Harmondsworth: Penguin, 1983.
Freud, Sigmund (trans. James Strachey). *On Metapsychology* (The Penguin Freud Library, vol. 11). London: Penguin, 1991.
Freud, Sigmund (trans. James Strachey). *The Origins of Religion* (The Penguin Freud Library, vol. 13). London: Penguin, 1999.
Gilman, Richard. *Decadence—The Strange Life of an Epithet*. New York: Farrar, Strausand Giroux, 1979.
Givry, Grillot de (trans. J. Courtenay Locke). *Witchcraft, Magic and Alchemy*. Boston: Houghton Mifflin, 1931 (Dover reprint, New York, 1972).
Goethe, Johann Wolfgang von (trans. David Luke). *Faust—Part One*. Oxford: Oxford University Press, 1987.
Goethe, Johann Wolfgang von (trans. John Anster). *Faustus*. London: Routledge, 1883.
Goodrick-Clarke, Nicholas. *The Occult Roots of Nazism*. Wellingborough: Aquarian Press, 1985.
Gutman, Robert W. *Richard Wagner—The Man, His Mind, and His Music* (Time-Life Records Special Edition). New York: Time Incorporated, 1972.
Haggard, H. Rider. *She*. London: Collins, 1974.
Haining, Peter (ed.). *The Frankenstein Omnibus*. London: Orion, 1994.
Haining, Peter (ed.). *The Ghouls*. London: Chancellor Press, 1994.
Haynes, Renée. *The Society for Psychical Research, 1882–1982—A History*. London: Macdonald & Co., 1982.
Hemmings, F. W. J. *Baudelaire the Damned*. London: Hamish Hamilton 1982.
Hitler, Adolf (trans. Ralph Manheim). *Mein Kampf*. London: Hutchinson, 1980.
Hoare, Philip. *Wilde's Last Stand: Decadence, Conspiracy & The First World War*. London: Duckworth, 1997.
Hoffmann, E. T. A. (ed. Christopher Lazare). *Tales of Hoffmann*. New York: A. A. Wyn, 1946.
Honderich, Ted (ed.). *The Oxford Companion to Philosophy*. Oxford: Oxford University Press, 1995.
Huxley, Aldous. *The Doors of Perception*. Harmondsworth: Penguin, 1959.
Huysmans, J.-K. (trans. P. G. Lloyd). *À Rebours*. London: The Fortune Press, 1946.
Huysmans, J.-K. *Là-bas (Lower Depths)*. Sawtry: Dedalus, 1986.
Jung, C. G. *Collected Works*. vol. 7, London: Routledge, 2015.
Jung, C. G. (ed.). *Man and His Symbols*. London: Aldus Books, 1979.
Jung, C. G. (trans. R. F. C. Hull). *Psychology and Alchemy*. London: Routledge & Kegan Paul, 1980.
Jung, C. G. (trans. R. F. C. Hull). *Psychology and the Occult*. London: Routledge and Kegan Paul, 1982.
Kracauer, Siegfried. *From Calgary to Hitler: A Psychological History of the German Film*. Princeton: Princeton University Press, 1970.
Kurlander, Eric. *Hitler's Monsters: A Supernatural History of The Third Reich*. New Haven and London: Yale University Press, 2017.
Lee, Christopher. *Tall, Dark and Gruesome: An Autobiography*. London: Victor Gollancz, 1997.
Lévi, Éliphas (trans. Arthur Edward Waite). *Transcendental Magic: Its Doctrine & Ritual*. Twickenham: Senate, 1995.
Lorrain, Jean (trans. Francis Amery). *Monsieur de Phocas*. Sawtry: Dedalus, 1994.
Lovecraft, H. P. *The Fiction*. New York: Barnes and Noble, 2008.
Mann, Thomas (trans. H. T. Lowe-Porter). *Buddenbrooks*. London: Secker & Warburg, 1956.
Marlowe, Christopher (ed. E. D. Pendry). *Complete Plays and Poems* (London: Dent, 1983.
Marx, Karl. *Capital*. Oxford: Oxford University Press, 1995.
Maugham, Robin. *Conversations with Willie: Recollections of W. Somerset Maugham*. New York: Simon & Schuster, 1978.
Maugham, W. Somerset. *The Magician/The Gentleman in the Parlour*. London: Heron Books, 1968.
Meyrinck, Gustav (trans. Mike Mitchell). *The White Dominican*. Sawtry: Dedalus, 1994.
Milton, John. *The Poetical Works of John Milton*. London: Frederick Warne, 1896.
Nietzsche, Friedrich (trans. Walter Kaufmann). *The Birth of Tragedy and The Case of Wagner*. New York: Vintage, 1967.
Nietzsche, Friedrich (trans. R. J. Hollingdale). *Ecce Homo*. Harmondsworth: Penguin, 1982.
Nietzsche, Friedrich (trans. Josefine Nauckhoff). *The Gay Science*. Cambridge: Cambridge University Press, 2001.
Nietzsche, Friedrich (trans. Douglas Smith). *On the Genealogy of Morals*. Oxford: Oxford University Press, 1996.
Nietzsche, Friedrich (trans. R. J. Hollingdale). *Twilight of the Idols/The Anti-Christ*. Harmondsworth: Penguin, 1981.

Novalis (Friedrich von Hardenberg). *Henry of Ofterdingen*. New York: Dover, 2015.

Oldenbourg, Zoé. *Massacre at Montségur: A History of the Albigensian Crusade*. London: Phoenix Press, 2001.

Polanski, Roman. *Roman*. London: Heinemann, 1984.

Radzinsky, Edvard (trans. Judson Rosengrant). *Rasputin: The Last Word*. London: Weidenfeld & Nicolson, 2000.

Rasputin, Maria, with Patte Barham. *Rasputin*. London: Arrow, 1979.

Regardie, Israel (ed. Chic Cicero & Sandra Tabatha Cicero). *A Garden of Pomegranates: Skrying on the Tree of Life*. St. Paul, Minnesota: Llewellyn Publications, 2004.

Ruddy, Jon. *The Bargain*. New York: Knightsbridge, 1990.

Sangster, Jimmy. *Inside Hammer*. London: Reynolds & Hearn, 2001.

Sinnett, A. P. *Esoteric Buddhism*. London: Theosophical Publishing House, 1972.

Skal, David J. *The Monster Show: A Cultural History of Horror*. London: Plexus, 1993.

Skinn, Dez (ed.). *House of Hammer* magazine, No. 21, June 1978, London: Top Sellers, 1978.

Speer, Albert (trans. Richard and Clara Winston). *Inside the Third Reich*. London: Macmillan, 1970.

Stewart, Fred Mustard. *The Mephisto Waltz*. London: Michael Joseph, 1969.

Stoker, Bram. *Dracula*. London: Constable, 1904.

Strindberg, August (trans. Mary Sandbach). *Inferno and From an Occult Diary*. Harmondsworth: Penguin, 1979.

Syberberg, Hans-Jürgen (trans. Joachim Neugroschel). *Hitler: A Film from Germany*. Manchester: Carcanet, 1982.

Tarasti, Eero. *Myth and Music*. Helsinki: Suomen Musiikkitieteellinen Seura, 1978.

Urwand, Ben. *The Collaboration: Hollywood's Pact with Hitler*. Cambridge MA: Harvard University Press, 2015.

Viertel, Salka. *The Kindness of Strangers*. New York: Holt, 1969.

Villiers de l'Isle Adam, Auguste. *Axël*. London: Soho Book Company, 1986.

Villiers de L'Isle Adam, Auguste (trans. Robert Baldick). *Cruel Tales*. Oxford: Oxford University Press, 1985.

Villiers de l'Isle Adam, Auguste (trans. Brian Stableford). *The Vampire Soul*. Encino: Black Coat Press, 2004.

Wagner, Richard (trans. Andrew Porter). *Parsifal* (Opera Guide), London: John Calder, 1986.

Wagner, Richard (trans. William Ashton Ellis). *Religion and Art*. Lincoln and London: University of Nebraska Press, 1994.

Wells, H. G. *Selected Short Stories*. Harmondsworth: Penguin, 1958.

Wheatley, Dennis. *The Devil Rides Out*. London: Heron 1972.

Wheatley, Dennis. *They Used Dark Forces*. London: Heron, 1973.

Wheatley, Dennis. *To the Devil: A Daughter*. London: Heron, 1972.

Wilde, Oscar. *Complete Works of Oscar Wilde*. London: Collins, 1977.

Williams, Charles. *War in Heaven* (Dennis Wheatley Library of the Occult). London: Sphere, 1976.

Wilson, Edmund. *Axel's Castle: A Study in the Imaginative Literature of 1870–1930*, New York: Collier Books/Macmillan, 1991.

Wordsworth, William (ed. Thomas Hutchinson). *The Poetical Words of Wordsworth*. London: Oxford University Press, 1965.

Wyndham, John. *The Day of the Triffids, et al.* London: Book Club Associates, 1981.

Youssoupoff, Prince Felix (trans. Ann Green and Nicholas Katkoff). *Lost Splendour*. London: Folio Society, 1996.

Index

Numbers in **_bold italics_** indicate pages with illustrations

À Rebours (J.K. Huysmans) 11, 14, 17, 18, 45
Adams, Ansel 79
Adams, Tom 112
Addams, Dawn 21
The Adventures of Sherlock Holmes (TV series) 105
Agrippa, Cornelius 47
Ahmed, Rollo 66
Alda, Alan 98
Alien (dir. Ridley Scott) 8, 73, 95
Allen, Maud 11
Alther, Lisa 32
Alvey, Glenn H. 144
Ancient Mystical Order Rosa Crucis 179
The Ancient Wisdom (Annie Besant) 159
And God Created Woman (dir. Roger Vadim) 37
"Andante of Snakes" (Arthur Symons) 22
Anderson, Gerry 104
Andress, Ursula 146
Andrews, Dana 75, 134
Anger, Kenneth 149
The Antichrist (Friedrich Nietzsche) 96–97
L'Anticristo (dir. Alberto De Martino) 125
L'Apprentie sorcière (Paul Dukas) 183–184
Arabian Adventure (dir. Kevin Connor) 76
Arlen, Richard **_104_**
Armadel 70
Armstrong, Michael 153
Artenfels, Rainer von 135
Ascent of Mount Carmel (St. John of the Cross) 150
Asher, Jack 21
Atlantis: The Antediluvian World (Ignatius Donnelly) 131
Atlantis, the Lost Continent (dir. George Pal){en}137
Attenborough, Richard 74
Axël (Villiers de l'Isle Adam) 19–20, 29, 30–32, 37
Axël's Castle (Edmund Wilson) 29

Bach, Johann Sebastian 16, 185
Badel, Alan 137
Baigent, Michael 168
Baker, Graham 118
Baker, Phil 71, 83, 161
Baker, Roy Ward 8, 34, 35, 115, 137
Baker, Tom 8, 34, 87, **_87_**, 89, 103
The Bargain (Jon Ruddy) 161
Barrett, Francis 46–47
Barry, John 74
Barrymore, John 8, 86, 89–91, **_90_**
Bates, Ralph 20, 66
Baudelaire, Charles 7, 12, 15, 17, 23, 25, 29, 38, 44, 45
Beacham, Stephanie 154
The Beatles 8, 145, 148
Beaudine, William 79
Beausoleil, Bobby 149
Beethoven, Ludwig van 61
La Belle et la Bête (dir. Jean Cocteau) 177
Bennett, Richard Rodney 72
Bennigsen, Otto von 149
Benson, Martin 119
Bergen, Candice 106
Bergman, Ingmar 6, 76
Berlioz, Hector 67, 99, 127
Bernard, James 61, 65, 67, 70, 71, 78–79, 124, 144
Bernhardt, Sarah 14, 15
Berova, Olinka 77
Besant, Annie 131, 159
Bewitched (TV series) 145
The Bible 106, 171, 172
Binder, Maurice 74
Black, Jeremy 163
The Black Cat (dir. Edgar G. Ulmer) 7, 15–17, **_16_**
Blair, Linda 48, 66
Blatty, William Peter 116–117, 125
Der blaue Licht (dir. Leni Riefenstahl) 151
Blavatsky, Helena Petrovna 3, 4, 8, 9, 12, 48, 129, 131, 132, 133, 137, 139, 155, 157, 158–159, 168
Blithe Spirit (Noël Coward) 145
Blood from the Mummy's Tomb (dir. Seth Holt and Michael Carreras) 100, 115
Bolero (Maurice Ravel) 164
Book Four (Aleister Crowley) 103
Booth, Harry 115

Borgnine, Ernest 79
Boulting, Ingrid 98
Bourget, Paul 28
The Boys from Brazil (dir. Franklin J. Shaffner) 9, 162–164, **163**
Brahm, John 34, **34**,
Bram Stoker's Dracula (dir. Francis Ford Coppola) 26–27, 54
Braun, Eva 161
Breck, Kathleen **134**
Breker, Arno 161
Brett, Jeremy 29, 105
Bride of Frankenstein (dir. James Whale) 36
The Brides of Dracula (dir. Terence Fisher) 20
Brommage, Bernard 66
Bron, Eleanor 146
Bronson, Katrina Holden 78
Brown, Dan 168–169
Browning, Tod 15, 25, 82, 181
Bryan, Dora 74
Buck, Pearl S. 124
Buddenbrooks (Thomas Mann) 32
Bulwer-Lytton, Edward (Lord Lytton) 52, 61, 133, 134
Buñuel, Luis 5
Burgess, Anthony 168
Burke, Kathleen **104**
Burnett, Francis Hodgson 129
Burstyn, Ellen 122, 123
Burton, Richard 101, 173
Burton, Tim 15
Busoni, Ferruccio 42

The Cabinet of Dr. Caligari (dir. Robert Wiene) 7, 82–84
Caine, Michael 106, 110
"The Call of Cthulhu" (H.P. Lovecraft) 140
Callow, Simon 59, 100, 152
Cammell, Donald 8, 95
Campion, Paul 7, 80, **81**
Captain America: The First Avenger (dir. Joe Johnston) 160–161
Carlson, Veronica 33, 37
Carmichael, Ian 145
Carpenter, John 119, 120
Carradine, John 61, 79
Carreras, Michael 8
Carson, John 73, 78
Casares, María 77
"Casting the Runes" (M.R. James) 75
Castle, William 166
Cat People (dir. Jacques Tourneur) 122
Cavendish, Richard 102, 106, 120
Cayce, Edgar 138
Cellini, Benvenuto 63
Cepek, Petr 176, 177
Chaney, Lon 33
Chaney, Lon, Jr. 182
Chaplin, Charles 160
Chapman, Mark David 166
Charisse, Cyd 139

Chemical Wedding (dir. Julian Doyle) 59, 96, 100, 151–152
Un chien Andalou (dir. Luis Buñuel) 5
Children of the Damned (dir. Anton Leader) 137
Chopin, Frédéric 61
Choronzon 72–73, 74
Christensen, Benjamin 7, 52–53
Churchill, Sir Winston 95
Cicero, Chic 2
Cicero, Sandra 2
Citizen Kane (dir. Orson Welles) 111
City of the Dead (dir. John Moxey) 164
City Under the Sea (dir. Jacques Tourneur) 8, 140
Claire Lenoir (Villiers de l'Isle Adam) 38–39
Clavicule of Solomon 59
Clemens, Brian 117
Cleopatra (dir. Joseph Mankiewicz) 173
Cocteau, Jean 77, 100, 177
Collins, Wilkie 146
"The Colour Out of Space" (H.P. Lovecraft) 141
The Coming Race (Edward Bulwer-Lytton) 133–134
Conan Doyle, Sir Arthur 28–29, 30, 75, 105
Connor, Kevin 8, 9, 76, 77, 137, **174**
Coppola, Francis Ford 26, 54
Corelli, Marie 54
Corman, Roger 7, 33, 97, 111, 141, 154, 155
Cortez, Ricardo 54
Cottrell, William **180**
Coulouris, George 125
Count Dracula (dir. Philip Saville) 54
Count Yorga, Vampire (dir. Bob Kelljan) 23–24
Countess Dracula (dir. Peter Sasdy) 115
Court, Hazel 75, 154
Coward, Noël 145
Craven, Wes 167
Crawford, Broderick 88
Cregar, Laird 34, **34**
Crichton, Charles 104
Crowley Aleister 1–2, **2**, 3, 4, 7, 17, 31, 43, 51, 54, 58–60, 61, 66, 68, 72–73, 76–77, 78, 82, 85, 88, 94–95, 97, 100, 102, 103, 105, 106, 109, 112, 120, 145, 147, 149, 151, 152, 186
Cruel Tales (Villiers de l'Isle Adam) 30, 33–35, 39
Cudden, Lucy 152
Cumberbatch, Benedict 155, **156**
The Curse of Frankenstein (dir. Terence Fisher) 18, 115
The Curse of the Crimson Altar (dir. Vernon Sewell) 76, 153–154, 164
Cushing, Peter 9, 18, 20, 30, 33, 37, 38, 39, 66, 67, 80, 97, 103, 105, 115, 134, 146, 173, 174, **174**

Dagover, Lil 83
Dall, John 137
Damien: Omen II (dir. Don Taylor & Mike Hodges) 89, 126, 127

Danger Man (TV series) 112
Daniel, Jennifer 61
Danot, Serge 148
Dante Alighieri 80, 114
Da Ponte, Lorenzo 65
Darwin, Sir Charles 4, 168
Dashwood, Sir Francis 73
Davies, Rupert 66
da Vinci ... (i.e., Leonardo da Vinci) 103
The Da Vinci Code (dir. Ron Howard) 9, 168–169
Davis, Bette 117
Day, Robert 144
Dead of Night (dir. Robert Hamer, et al.) 77
Death in Venice (dir. Luchino Visconti) 110
Debussy, Claude 61, 85
de Chirico, Giorgio 6
Dee, John 52
De Martino, Alberto 125
Demolay, Jacques 179
Demon Seed (dir. Donald Cammell) 8, 95
Denberg, Susan 90
Denham, Maurice 75
de Rais, Gilles 11, 46
Derrickson, Scott 8, 155, **156**
Derbyshire, Delia 154
de Sade, Marquis 97
"The Desire to Be a Man" (Villiers de l'Isle Adam) 35
The Devil in a Convent (dir. Georges Méliès) 50
The Devil Rides Out (Dennis Wheatley) 5, 7, 40, 42, 44, 49, 59–60, 62, 68–71, 77, 81, 82, 84
The Devil Rides Out (dir. Terence Fisher) 5, 40, 53, 59, 68–72, **68**, 73, 118, 124
The Devils (dir. Ken Russell) 50, 118
The Devils of Loudon (Krzysztof Penderecki) 120
The Devil's Rain (dir. Robert Fuest) 79
The Devil's Rock (dir. Paul Campion) 7, 80–81, **81**, 133, 160
Dickinson, Bruce 151–152
Dickinson, Thorold 85
Dido and Aeneas (Henry Purcell) 64
Dietrich, Marlene 12
Dietrich, Robert A. 56
Diffring, Anton 21
Disney, Walt 160, 179–184
Doctor Faustus (dir. Richard Burton & Neville Coghill) 173
Doctor Faustus (Marlowe) 7, 40–41, 42, 173, 175
Dr. Jekyll and Mr. Hyde (dir. Rouben Mamoulian) 181–182
Dr. Jekyll and Mr. Hyde (Robert Louis Stevenson) 57
Dr. Jekyll and Sister Hyde (dir. Roy Ward Baker) 115
Dr. Mabuse, der Spieler (dir. Fritz Lang) 7, 54–55, **55**, 84, 96

Dr. Phibes (films) 34, 35, 79
Doctor Strange (dir. Scott Derrickson) 8, 155–157, **156**
Dr. Who (TV series) 102
Dodington, George Bubb (Lord Melcombe Regis) 73
Dogma et Rituel de la Haute Magie (Éliphas Lévi) 42, 59, 68
Don Giovanni (Wolfgang Amadeus Mozart) 64, 65
"Don Juan" (E.T.A. Hoffmann) 64–65
Donnelly, Ignatius 131
Donner, Richard 8, 115, **119**, 125, 127, 128
The Door in the Wall (dir. Glenn H. Alvey) 144
"The Door in the Wall" (H.G. Wells) 130, 143
The Doors 145, 149
The Doors of Perception (Aldous Huxley) 143, 145
Doré, Gustave 80, 114
Dors, Diana 117
Dougal and the Blue Cat (dir. Serge Dannot) 148
Downfall (dir. Oliver Hirschbiegel) 162
Doyle, Julian 59, 96, 151
Doyle, Patrick 175
Dracula (Bram Stoker) 19, 23, 54, 65
Dracula (dir. Terence Fisher) 18, 20
Dracula (dir. Tod Browning) 14, 25, 82, 89, 181, 182
Dracula A.D. 1972 (dir. Alan Gibson) 66, 115, 153, 154
Dracula Has Risen from the Grave (dir. Freddie Francis) 66, 67, 88, 155, 182
Dracula: Prince of Darkness (dir. Terence Fisher) 62, 65, 66, 86
Dreams That Money Can Buy (dir. Hans Richter) 5
Dreyer, Carl 7, 52
Duffell, Peter 78
Dujardin, Édouard{en}45
Dukas, Paul 183, 184
"The Duke of Portland" (Villiers de l'Isle Adam) 35–36
du Maurier, George 89, 91
Dunning, George **147**, 148
The Dunwich Horror (dir. Daniel Haller) 8, 141–142
Dürer, Albrecht 135

The Earth Dies Screaming (dir. Terence Fisher) 90
Ed Wood (dir. Tim Burton) 15, 183
Eddington, Paul **68**
Eden, Mark 153
Edwards, Mark 100
The Ego and the Id (Sigmund Freud) 185
Eisenstein, Sergei 91
Eisner, Lotte H. 96, 188
Ekman, Gösta **171**, 172
Eliot, T.S. 110, 158

Elliott, Denholm 73, 118
Emmerich, Wolfgang 160
"The Empire of Lights" (René Magritte) 124
Encausse, Gérard Anaclet Vincent 69
Eraserhead (dir. David Lynch) 8, 95
Ernst, Max 5-6
Esoteric Buddhism (A.P. Sinnett) 131
Evans, Clifford 65
Ewers, Hanns Heinz 57
The Exorcist (dir. William Friedkin) 8, 48, 53, 59, 66, 98, 115-116, 118, 120-125, *121*, 126
The Exorcist (William Peter Blatty) 116-117

"La Faënza" (Jean Moréas) 22
Fairchild, Edgar 61
Faithfull, Marianne 149
"The Fall of the House of Usher" (Edgar Allan Poe) 17
"Fall Out" (dir. Patrick McGoohan) 111
Fanck, Arnold 150, 151
Fantasia (dir. Samuel Armstrong et al.) 183-185
Fantasia for Strings (Hans Werner Henze) 124
Farrow, John 159
Farrow, Mia *165*
Faust (dir. F.W. Murnau) 7, 9, 53, 170, *171*, 172-173
Faust (dir. Jan Svankmajer) 9, 175-178
Faust (Goethe) 7, 41-43, 116, 170-173, 175
Fawcett, Lt. Col. Percy 161
"Feathertop" (Nathaniel Hawthorne) 57
Feuchwanger, Leon 92
Ffrangcon-Davies, Gwen 71
Fidus (aka Hugo Höppener) 109
Finch, Nigel 67
Fisher, Terence 5, 7, 18, 20, 21, 33, 36, 37, 62, *68*, 90, 105
Fleming, Ian 95, 155
Les Fleurs du Mal (Charles Baudelaire) 45
Fontaine, Joan 98, 164
Forbes, Bryan 74, 167
Forbidden Planet (dir. Fred M. Wilcox) *181*, 185-186
Four Quartets (T.S. Eliot) 110
Fowles, John 8, 105, 106, 108-112
Francis, Freddie 66, 97,146, 182
Franju, Georges 5, *5*, 6
Frankel, Cyril 72
Frankenstein (dir. James Whale) 61, 181
Frankenstein (Mary Shelley) 136, 166
Frankenstein Created Woman (dir. Terence Fisher) 37-38, 103
Frankenstein Must Be Destroyed (dir. Terence Fisher) 33-34
Franks, Chloe 78
Frazer, Sir James 1, 118
Der Freischütz (Carl Maria von Weber) 67, 177
Freud, Sigmund 1, 5, 185
Freund, Karl 82, *83*, 100
Friedkin, William 8, 115-116, 120-125, *121*, 127
Friedrich, Caspar David 58, 150, 172

Fritsch, Theodor 133
From Beyond the Grave (dir. Kevin Connor) 9, 77, 145, 173, *174*
From Caligari to Hitler (Siegfried Kracauer) 83-84
The Frozen Dead (dir. Herbert J. Leder) 7, 134, *134*, 162
Frye, Dwight 61
Fuest, Robert 79
Der Führer's Face (dir. Jack Kinney, 1943) 160, 180
Fuller, Loïe 22
Furneaux, Yvonne 21
The Future Eve (Villiers de l'Isle Adam) 21, 36-38

Galeen, Henrick 7, 58
Gallu, Sam 109
Gandy, Joseph 17, 26
Ganz, Bruno 172
Gaster, Moses 66
Gatiss, Mark 115
Gavira, Gonzalo 124
George IV, King 160
Germanenorden 80, 133
Geronimi, Clyde 182
The Ghoul (dir. Freddie Francis) 146
Gibbons, Cedric 17
Gibson, Alan 51, 66, 146, 154
Gilbert, W.S. 76
Gilling, John 29, 78, 90
Gilman, Richard 12, 27
Gilmore, Peter 138
Glanvill, Joseph 97, 99
Godfrey, Derek 77
Goebbels, Joseph 92
Goethe, Johann Wolfgang von 7, 9, 41-43, 53, 62, 116, 170, 172, 173, 175, 177, 183, 184
Gold, Jack 101
The Golden Bough (Sir James Frazer) 1
The Golden Voyage of Sinbad (dir. Gordon Hessler) 103
Goldoni, Lelia 109
Goldsmith, Jerry 98-99, 101, 124-127, 153, 164, 175
The Golem (dir. Henrik Galeen) 7, 12, 56-57
The Golem (Gustav Meyrinck) 56
The Good Earth (Pearl S. Buck) 124
Goodrick-Clarke, Nicholas 131, 133, 160
Gore, Al 152
Göring, Hermann 89
Gounod, Charles 41
Grant, Cary 167
Grau, Albin 50-52, *51*
Gravina, Carla 125
Gray, Charles 44
The Great Dictator (dir. Charles Chaplin) 160
Green, Guy 8, 106, *107*, 110, 112, 114
The Green Face (Gustav Meyrinck) 182
Greenaway, Peter 187
Griffith, D.W. 54

Griffiths, Kenneth 111
Grimoire ou la Cabale (Armadel) 70
Grint, Alan 105
"Guardian of the Abyss" (dir. Don Sharp) 73
Guinness, Sir Alec 103
Gutman, Robert W. 12, 84

Hadfield, Hurd 21, 61
Haggard, H. Rider 144, 161
Hall, Charles D. 19, 36
Hall, Craig 80–81, *81*
Haller, Daniel 8, 141, 142
Halperin, Victor 78
Hamer, Robert 77, 164
Hamlet (William Shakespeare) 152
Hammer House of Horror (TV series) 73
Hand, David 180
Hands of the Ripper (dir. Peter Sasdy) 74–75, 115
Hangover Square (dir. John Brahm) 34, *34*
Hardwicke, Edward 75
Hardy, Robin 153
Harlan, Veit 92
Harlequin (dir. Simon Wincer) 8, 88–89
"The Harlot's House" (Oscar Wilde) 52
Harry Potter (films) 2, 155, 184
Harun-al-Rashid 84
Haugland, Aage 44
The Haunted House of Horror (dir. Michael Armstrong) 153
The Haunted Screen (Lotte H. Eisner) 188
Hawthorne, Nathaniel 57
Häxen (dir. Benjamin Christensen) 7, 52–53
Haxton, Gerald 59
Hayles, Brian 137, 138, 139
Haynes, Renée 75
Hegel, Georg Wilhelm Friedrich 33
Heidegger, Martin 95
Heinrich von Ofterdingen (Novalis) 151
Help! (dir. Richard Lester) 145–146
Hemmings, David 88
Henson, Nicky 76
Henze, Hans Werner 120, 124
Hermes Trismegistus 146, 171
Héroux, Denis 78
Herrmann, Bernard 24, 120
Heslov, Grant 161
Hessler, Gordon 103
Heston, Fraser Clarke 9, 174
Hickox, Douglas 35
Hiller, Arthur 126
Himmler, Heinrich 80, 97, 138, 139, 157, 159, 161, 162
Hirschbiegel, Oliver 162
Hitchcock, Alfred 24, 97, 120, 167
Hitler, Adolf 3, 8, 54, 55, 56, 79–80, 81, 83, 84, 85, 92, 93, 94, 95, 96, 97, 113–114, 131, 133, 134, 135, 136, 138, 151, 157, 159–160, 161–162, 164, 180
Hitler, ein Film aus Deutschland (dir. Hans-Jürgen Syberberg) 114, 135

The Hitler Gang (dir. John Farrow) 159
Hitler Speaks (Hermann Rauschning) 134
Hoare, Philip 11
Hodges, Mike 89
Hoffmann, E.T.A. 58, 64–65
Holland, Agnieska 130
Holt, Seth 90, 117
The Holy Blood and the Holy Grail (Michael Baigent, Richard Leigh & Henry Lincoln) 168
The Holy Mountain (dir. Alejandro Jodorowski) 8, 149–150, 151
The Holy Mountain (dir. Arnold Fanck) 150–151
Home, D.D. 88
Homunculus (dir. Otto Rippert) 8, 96, 162
Hooper, Tobe 89
Höppener, Hugo *see* Fidus
Hörbiger, Hanns 138
Hordern, Michael 101
Horror Express (dir. Gene Martin) 38–39
L'hôtel des Invalides (dir. Georges Franju) 5
Hough, John 67
The Hound of the Baskervilles (dir. Terence Fisher) 105
House of Dracula (dir. Erle C. Kenton) 61
The House That Dripped Blood (dir Peter Duffell) 78
Howard, Ron 9, 168
Howlett, Noel 118
Hull, Henry *13*, 14
Huxley, Aldous 143, 145
Huysmans, Joris-Karl 7, 11, 13, 17, 18, 22, 28, 42, 45, 46, *46*, 47–48, 58, 60, 71, 72

I Don't Want to Be Born (dir. Peter Sasdy) 8, 95
Indiana Jones (films) 8, 81
Indiana Jones and the Last Crusade (dir. Steven Spielberg) 161
Inferno (August Strindberg) 7, 48
Inferno (Dante Alighieri) 80
Ingram, Rex 7, 44, 61–63, 181
Inside the Third Reich (Albert Speer) 114
"Intimations of Immortality from Recollections of Early Childhood" (William Wordsworth), 144–145
Invitation to Hell (dir. Wes Craven) 167–168
Iron Maiden 151
Isis Unveiled (Helena Petrovna Blavatsky) 12, 139, 159
The Island of Dr. Moreau (H.G. Wells) 104
The Island of Lost Souls (dir. Erle C. Kenton) 8, 104–105, *104*
Ivan the Terrible, Tsar 84, 91

Jack the Ripper 84
James, M.R. 75
James Bond (films) 111, 146
Jannings, Emil 12, 53, 173
Jaws (dir. Steven Spielberg) 126

204 Index

Jesus Christ 159, 168, 169
Jesus of Nazareth (dir. Franco Zeffirelli) 89
Jew Süss (dir. Veit Harlan) 92
The Jewel of Seven Stars (Bram Stoker) 100
Jodorowski, Alejandro 8, 149, 150, 151
Johnson, Fred 90
Johnston, Joe 160–161
Jones, Chuck 182
Jostenoode, Harald Grävel von 131
Joyce, James 45
Judex (dir. Georges Franju) 5, *5*, 6
Jung, Carl Gustav 3, 4, 6, 144, 148, 149–150
Jurgens, Curt 98

Kandinsky, Wassily 129
Kanner, Alexis 112
Kanon for Orchestra and Tape (Krzystof Penderecki) 120
Kant, Immanuel 33
Das Kapital (Karl Marx) 168
Karina, Anna 106
Karloff, Boris 15–16, *16*, 32, 82, *83*, 100, 132, 147, 155
Kelljan, Bob 23–25
Kelly, Edward 52
Kelly, Gerald 59
Kenton, Erle C. 8, 61, *104*
The Key to the Tarot (A.E. Waite) 106
Khnopff, Fernand 91
Kind Hearts and Coronets (dir. Robert Hamer) 164
Kinflicks (Lisa Alther) 32
King, Stephen 9, 174, 175
Kinski, Nastassja 73
The Kiss of the Vampire (dir. Don Sharp) *19*, 20, 34, 61, 65–66, 118
Klein-Rogge, Rudolf 54
Klimt, Gustav 27
Klingsor, Tristan 60
Kneale, Nigel 56
"Know Thyself" (Richard Wagner) 85
Komeda, Christopher 166
Kracauer, Siegfried 55, 56, 83–84, 96
Krauss, Werner 58, 83
Kubrick, Stanley 8, 127, 155, 156
Kupka, František 26
Kurlander, Eric 3, 80, 160, 161, 162

Là-Bas (J.K. Huysmans) 7, 11, 17, 42, 45, *46*, 58, 71, 72
Lacey, Catherine 32
"The Lady of Shalott" (Alfred, Lord Tennyson) 182
Lai, Francis 126
Landau, Martin 15, 183
Landers, Lew 7
Landor, Rosalyn 73
Lang, Fritz 7, 53, 54–55, *55*, 84, 96, 173
Lang, Judith 25
Lanz von Liebenfels, Jörg 131, 132–133, 163
Last Year at Marienbad (dir. Alain Resnais) 79

Latham, Philip 65
Laughton, Charles 104, *104*
LaVey, Anton 79
Lawson, Sarah *68*
Leader, Anton 137
Led Zeppelin 149
Leder, Herbert J. 8, 134, *134*, 137
Lee, Christopher 7, 20, 30, 38, 39, 65, 68, *68*, 69–70, 71, 73, 76, 78, 80, 82, 86, 87, 88, 90, 109, 118, 154, 164
Leigh, Richard 168
Leighton Margaret 145
Lenau, Nikolaus 99
Leni, Paul 84
Lennon, John 149, 166
Leon, Valerie 100
Leonardo da Vinci 103
Lester, Richard 145
Letters on Witchcraft and Demonology (Sir Walter Scott) 41
Lévi, Éliphas 41, 53, 60, 68
Levin, Ira 165, 167
Lewin, Albert 7, 17, 61
Lewis, Matthew 41
Lewis, Michael J. 101
Lewton, Val 122
"Ligeia" (Edgar Allan Poe) 17, 97, 99, 100
Lincoln, Abraham 90
Lincoln, Henry 168
The Lion Has Wings (dir. Michael Powell, et al.) 160
Liszt, Franz 41, 98, 99, 183
Litolff, Henri 183
Lodge, Sir Oliver 75
Lohengrin (Richard Wagner) 32, 133, 135, 180
Lom, Herbert 33, 36
Lonnen, Roy 73
Lorrain, Jean 13, 17–18, 22, 28, 60
The Lost Continent (dir. Michael Carreras) 8
Love Story (dir. Arthur Hiller) 126
Lovecraft, H.P. 140, 141, 142, 164
Lucas, George 8
Lucci, Susan 168
Lucifer Rising (dir. Kenneth Anger) 149
Ludwig II of Bavaria, King 36, 182
Lugosi, Bela 14, 15, 79, 82, 89, 90, 91, 182, 183
Lühr, Peter 135
Lutosławski, Witold 98
Lutyens, Elisabeth 98
Lynch, David 8, 95

MacGinnis, Niall 88
MacGraw, Ali 126
Macready, George 24
The Magic Roundabout (TV series), *148*
The Magician (dir. Ingmar Bergman) 6
The Magician (dir. Rex Ingram) 7, 44, 181
The Magician (W. Somerset Maugham) 7, 42, 44, 58–60
Magick in Theory and Practice (Aleister Crowley) 1–2, 82, 94–95

Magritte, René 6, 124
The Magus (dir. Guy Green) 8, 106–113, *107*
The Magus (Francis Barrett) 46–47
The Magus (John Fowles) 8, 105, 108–113
Magus, Simon 104
Mallarmé, Stéphane 29
Malleus Maleficarum 52, 53
Mamoullian, Rouben 181, 182
The Man Who Could Cheat Death (dir. Terence Fisher) 21
Mankiewicz, Joseph 173
Mann, Francis Oscar 50
Mann, Thomas 32, 110
Manners, David 15
Manson, Charles 147, 166
Marais, Jean 100
March, Frederic 182
Marien, Ferdinand 92
Marlowe, Christopher 7, 9, 40–42, 173, 175
Marschner, Heinrich 67
Martin, Gene 38
Marx, Harpo 24
Marx, Karl 162, 168
Marx, William 24–25
Masonic Order of DeMolay 179
The Masque of the Red Death (dir. Alan Birkinshaw) 36
The Masque of the Red Death (dir. Roger Corman) 33, 75–76, 111, 154
Massey, Anna 35
Massey, Daniel 35, 139
Massie, Paul 21
Matheson, Richard 40
Maugham, Robin 59
Maugham, W. Somerset 7, 42, 44, 58–62, 100
Mayo, Archie 8, 89, *90*
McCambridge, Mercedes 124
McClure, Doug 139
McGoohan, Patrick 111, 112
McKellen, Sir Ian 168
McKern, Leo 145, 146
The Medusa Touch (dir. Jack Gold) 101
Mein Kampf (Adolf Hitler) 79–80, 97, 138–139, 162
Meineke, Eva-Maria 74
Die Meistersinger von Nürnberg (Richard Wagner) 160
Méliès, Georges 7, 50
The Men Who Stare at Goats (dir. Grant Heslov) 161
The Men Who Stare at Goats (Jon Ronson) 161
Mengele, Dr. Josef 162, 163, *163*
Menjou, Adolphe 54
The Mephisto Waltz (dir. Paul Wendkos) 98–99, 115, 124, 152–153, 154
The Mephisto Waltz (Franz Liszt) 98, 99, 183
The Mephisto Waltz (Fred Mustard Stewart) 99–100
Merlin 104
The Merry Frolics of Satan (dir. Georges Méliès) 50

Meteyard, Sidney 182
Metropolis (dir. Fritz Lang) 7, 53, 173
Meyerbeer, Giacomo 64
Meyrinck, Gustav 52, 56, 182
Michael, Ralph 77
Michelangelo Buonarotti 188
The Midwich Cuckoos (John Wyndham) 136, 166
Miller, Jason 122
Milton, John 55, 164
Mirbeau, Octave 17
Mirren, Helen 187
Modern Times (dir Charles Chaplin) 160
Mondrian, Piet 129
The Monk (Matthew Lewis) 41
Monsieur de Phocas (Jean Lorrain) 17–18, 22–23
Montgomery, Elizabeth 145
Moonchild (Aleister Crowley) 95–96
The Moonstone (Wilkie Collins) 146
Moréas, Jean 13, 22
Moreau, Gustave 22, 44, 60
Morell, André 77
Morricone, Ennio 125
Morrison, Jim 145, 149
Mother Night (Kurt Vonnegut) 157
Mower, Patrick *68*
Moxey, John 164
Mozart, Wolfgang Amadeus 64, 65, 126, 188
Mucha, Alphonse 27
The Mummy (dir. Karl Freund) 82, *83*
The Mummy (dir. Terence Fisher) 20–21, 36, 70
Murnau, F.W. 7, 9, 50, *51*, 53, 57, 84, 162, *171*, 172, 181
Musset, Alfred de 57

The Nanny (dir. Seth Holt) 117
Napoleon Bonaparte 30
"The Naval Treaty" (dir. Alan Grint) 105
"The Naval Treaty" (Sir Arthur Conan Doyle) 105
Neame Christopher 66
Needful Things (dir. Fraser Clarke Heston) 9, 174–175
Needful Things (Stephen King) 174, 177
Neuburg, Victor 72
"New Adam and Eve" (dir. Charles Crichton) 104, 109
Nicholas and Alexandra (dir. Franklin J. Schaffner) 87–88, *87*, 103
Nielsen, Leslie 186
Nietzsche, Friedrich 4, 12, 45, 60, 96–97, 109, 139, 140, 168, 185–186
Night of the Demon (dir. Jacques Tourneur) 75, 88–89
Norman, Monty 22
North by Northwest (dir. Alfred Hitchcock) 167
Nosferatu, Eine Symphonie des Grauens (dir. F W. Murnau) 7, 50–52, *51*, 53, 56, 84, 162, 172, 181

Nostradamus 104, 119, 170
Novalis 151, 153
"Nurse Will Make It Better" (dir. Shaun O'Riordan) 117–118

Occult Diary (Strindberg) 7, 48
"Occult Memories" (Villiers de l'Isle Adam) 39
O'Driscoll, Martha 61
Ogilvy, Ian 32, 147
Oland, Werner **13**, 14
Oldenbourg, Zoé 118
Oldfield, Mike 122
Oldman, Gary 27
Olivier, Sir Laurence 162
The Omen (dir. Richard Donner) 8, 59, 88, 96, 97, 98, 101, 115, 117, 118, 119, **119**, 125–128, 163, 164, 175
Omen III: The Final Conflict (dir. Graham Baker) 118
On the Buses (dir. Harry Booth) 115
O'Neill, Ryan 126
Ono, Yoko 166
The Order of the Golden Dawn 4, 59
O'Riordan, Shaun 117
Orphée (dir. Jean Cocteau) 77, 100
Ostara magazine 131
Owen, Cliff 77

Page, Jimmy 149
Pal, George 137
Palk, Anna **134**
Papus *see* Encausse, Gerard
Paradise Lost (John Milton) 164
Parsifal (dir. Hans-Jürgen Syberberg) 44, 85, 187
Parsifal (Richard Wagner) 7, 12, 41–44, **43**, 57, 76, 82–83, 84–85, 130, 155, 182
Pastell, George 21
Pater, Walter 21, 60
Paul VI, Pope 166
Peck, Gregory 117, **119**, 125, 126, 162, 163, **163**
Peel, David 20
Péladan, Joséphin 31
Penderecki, Krzysztof 98, 120, 122, 123, 126
Périer, François 77
Peters, Hans 17
Photographing Fairies (dir. Nick Willing) 75
The Picture of Dorian Gray (dir. Albert Lewin) 7, 17, 21, 61
The Picture of Dorian Gray (Oscar Wilde) 20–21, 61
Pidgeon, Walter 185
Pit and the Pendulum (dir. Roger Corman) 7, 18, 155
Pitt, Ingrid 115
The Plague of the Zombies (dir. John Gilling) 78–79, 90, 146
Plato 131, 135
Pleasence, Donald 119
Poe, Edgar Allan 15, 17, 28, 30, 36, 57, 76, 90, 97, 99, 140

Poelzig, Hans 12
Pohl, Hermann 133
Polanski, Roman 8, 95, 164, 165–167, **165**
Polidori, John 67
Pollock, Channing **5**
Poltergeist (dir. Tobe Hooper) 89
Polymorphia (Krzystof Penderecki) 120, 124
Porter, Eric 75
Potthast, Hedwig 97
Powell, Michael 160
Powell, Robert 8, 88, 89
Price, Dennis 67
Price, Vincent 18, 33, 34, 75–76, 140, 155
Prince of Darkness (dir. John Carpenter) 119–120
Princess Diana, HRH 158
The Prisoner (TV series) 111, 112
Prometheus, the Poem of Fire (Alexander Scriabin) 184
Prospero's Books (dir. Peter Greenaway) 187–188
Psycho (dir. Alfred Hitchcock) 120
Psychomania (dir. Don Sharp) 26, 76, 125
Purcell, Henry 64
Puritan Passions (dir. Frank Tuttle) 57

Quarry, Robert 23–24
Quatermass and the Pit (dir. Roy Ward Baker) 8, 56, 137
Quinn, Anthony 8, 106, 111

Rachmaninoff, Sergei 98
Radcliffe, Ann 41
Rahn, Otto 161
Raiders of the Lost Ark (dir. Steven Spielberg) 161
Rains, Claude 33
Rait, A.W. 30, 33
Rasputin, Gregory 26, 86–87, 88, 89, 91
Rasputin and the Empress (dir. Richard Boleslawski & Charles Brabin) 86
Rasputin, Dämon der Frauen (dir. Adolf Trotz) 86
Rasputin: The Mad Monk (dir. Don Sharp) 62, 87
Rauschning, Hermann 134, 136
Ravel, Maurice 60, 164
The Raven (dir. Lew Landers) 7, 15
The Raven (dir. Roger Corman) 155
Ravenscroft, Trevor 81
Rebecca (dir. Alfred Hitchcock) 97
Redon, Odilon 6
Rees, Angharad 74
Reeves, Michael 32, 33, 146, 147, 184
Regardie, Israel 159
Reid, Beryl 26, 76
"Religion and Art" (Richard Wagner) 47
Rembrandt van Rijn *see* van Rijn, Rembrandt
Remick, Lee 101, 126, 127
The Renaissance (Walter Pater) 21
The Reptile (dir. John Gilling) 29, 146
Requiem (Giuseppe Verdi) 64

Requiem (Wolfgang Amadeus Mozart) 126
Resnais, Alain 79
The Return of Count Yorga (dir. Bob Kelljan) 24–26
The Revenge of Frankenstein (dir. Terence Fisher) 33
Revue Wagneriènne 45
Richardson, John 77
Richter, Hans 5
Riefenstahl, Leni 3, 7, 79, 84, 92, 93, 94, 95, 150–152
Rienzi (Richard Wagner) 114
Riller, Wolf 8
Der Ring des Nibelungen (Richard Wagner) 102, 108, 139
Rippert, Otto 8, 96
The Rite of Spring (Igor Stravinsky) 127
Robert le diable (Giacomo Meyerbeer) 64
Robinson, Bernard 18–19, 29
Robinson, Harry 67
Rohmer, Sax 60
Rolfe, Guy 104
Ronson, Jon 161
Rosemary's Baby (dir. Roman Polanski) 8, 95, 164–167, **165**
Ruddy, Jon 161
Ruskin, John 91
Russell, Ken 50, 118
Rye, Stellan 7

Saint, Eva Marie 167
St. John of the Cross 150
Salomé (Oscar Wilde) 11, 60
Sanders, George 26
Sangster, Jimmy 18, 40
Sasdy, Peter 8, 20, 51, 74, 95, 115
Sassoon, Vidal 166, 167
The Satanic Rites of Dracula (dir. Alan Gibson) 51, 62, 66–67, 115, 146
Savory, Gerald 54
Schaeffer, Pierre 124
Schäfer, Ernst 161
Schaffner, Franklin J. 9, 87, **87**, 162, **163**, 164
Scheler, Max 96
Schifrin, Lalo 120
Schild, Theodor **43**
Schoenberg, Arnold 24, 123–124
Schopenhauer, Arthur 3–4
Schreck, Max 50, **51**, 172
Scott, Ridley 8, 73, 95
Scott, Sir Walter 41
Scriabin, Alexander 61, 129, 147, 184–185
Séance on a Wet Afternoon (dir. Bryan Forbes) 74, 77
Sebottendorf, Rudolf von 131
The Secret Doctrine (Helena Petrovna Blavatsky) 132, 139, 158–159, 168
The Secret Garden (dir. Agnieska Holland) 130–131
The Secret Garden (Francis Hodgson Burnett) 129–130

Seltzer, David 117, 118, 119
Une semaine de bonté (Max Ernst) 5–6
The Seventh Seal (dir. Ingmar Bergman) 76
Sewell, Vernon 76
Shakespeare, William 106, 186–188
Sharp, Don **19**, 20, 26, 62, 73, 86
Shatner, William 79
She (dir. Robert Day) 144 146
She (H. Rider Haggard) 144
Shéhérazade (Maurice Ravel/Tristan Klingsor) 60
Shelley, Mary 57, 136, 166
Shelley, Percy Bysshe 3
Shiel, M.P. 22
The Shining (dir. Stanley Kubrick) 127
Shock Waves (dir. Ken Wiederhorn) 134–135
Siegfried (Richard Wagner) 182, 183
"The Sign of Four" (dir. Peter Hammond) 29
"The Sign of Four" (Sir Arthur Conan Doyle) 28–29, 30
Singer, Peter 33
Sinnett, A.P. 131–132, 139
Skal, David J. 183
Skeggs, Roy 74
The Skull (dir. Freddie Francis) 97–98
Sleeping Beauty (dir. Clyde Geronimi) 182
The Sleeping Beauty (Pyotr Illych Tchiakovsky) 182
Snow White and the Seven Dwarfs (dir. David Hand, *et al.*) 180–182, **180**, 184, 185
Society for Psychical Research 75
Sokolov, Stanislav 187
"Song of Solomon," 106
The Sorcerers (dir. Michael Reeves) 32, 33, 146–147, 184
"The Sorcerer's Apprentice" (Johann Wolfgang von Goethe) *see* "Der Zauberlehrling"
The Sorrows of Satan (dir. D.W. Griffith) 54, 58
The Sorrows of Satan (Marie Corelli) 54
Space: 1999 (TV series) 104, 109
The Spear of Destiny (Trevor Ravenscroft) 81
Speer, Albert 80, 114
"The Sphinx" (Oscar Wilde) 21
Spielberg, Steven 126, 161
Stableford, Brian 38
Stanley, Kim 75
Star Wars (dir. George Lucas) 8, 89, 103, 104
Starr, Ringo 146
Steele, Barbara 18, 153–154
Steiner, Max 124
Steiner, Rudolf 4, 131
The Stepford Wives (dir. Bryan Forbes) 167
Stephens, Harvey Spencer 126, 163
Stevens, Ray 143
Stevens, Toby 75
Stevenson, Robert Louis 176
Stewart, Fred Mustard 99
Stockwell, Dean 141
Stoker, Bram 19, 23, 51, 54, 58, 65, 100, 115
Stokowski, Leopold 183, 185

Stoneground 153
Stowitz 62
The Strange Case of Dr. Jekyll and Mr. Hyde (Robert Louis Stevenson) 176
A Strange Story (Edward Bulwer-Lytton) 61
Stravinsky, Igor 127
Strindberg, August 7, 48-49
Stuck, Franz von 22
The Student of Prague (dir. Stellan Rye) 7, 57
Summers, Montague 59, 71
Sunderland, Matthew 80-81, *81*, 133
Suzman, Janet 89
Svankmejer, Jan 9, 175-178
Svengali (dir. Archie Mayo) 8, 89-92, *90*
Swedenborg, Emanuel 48
Swinton, Tilda 155
Syberberg, Hans Jürgen 44, 85, 114, 135, 187
Sykes, Peter 57, 73, 141
Symons, Arthur 14, 22, 38
Symphonie fantastique (Hector Berlioz) 67, 99, 127

Tannhäuser (Richard Wagner) 44, 133
Tarasti, Eero 44
Taste of Fear (dir. Seth Holt) 90
Taste the Blood of Dracula (dir. Peter Sasdy) 20, 51, 66
Tate, Sharon 166
Tauber, Andreas 173
Taylor, Don 89
Taylor, Elizabeth 173
Taylor, Julie 187
Telezynska, Isabella 141
The Tempest (dir. Julie Taylor) 187
The Tempest (dir. Stanislav Sokolov) 187
The Tempest (William Shakespeare) 106, 186-187
Tennyson, Alfred Lord 182
The Testament of Dr. Mabuse (dir. Fritz Lang) 7, 55-56, 96
Thalberg, Irving 125
Theatre of Blood (dir. Douglas Hickox) 35
Theatre of Death (dir. Sam Gallu) 109
Theosophical Society 75, 129, 131
Die Theosophie und die assyrischen "Menschentiere" (Jörg Lanz von Liebenfels) 131
They Used Dark Forces (Dennis Wheatley) 80, 83
Thomas, Damien 67
Three Books of Occult Philosophy (Cornelius Agrippa) 47
Thriller (TV series) 117
Thule Society 80, 133
Till, Jenny 109
To the Devil a Daughter (Dennis Wheatley) 57, 59, 73
To the Devil a Daughter (dir. Peter Sykes) 57, 73-74, 76, 118, 141
The Tomb of Ligeia (dir. Roger Corman) 97
Torn Curtain (dir. Alfred Hitchcock) 24
Torture Garden (Octave Mirbeau) 17

Totem and Taboo (Freud) 1
Tourneur, Jacques 8, 75, 122, 140
Trilby (George du Maurier) 89, 91
Triumph des Willens (dir. Lena Riefenstahl) 3, 7, 84, 92-94, 95
Trotz, Adolf 86
Troughton, Patrick 117,119, *119*, 127
Trump, Donald 152
Tubular Bells (Mike Oldfield) 122, 124
Turner, Robert 47
Tuttle, Frank 57
Twins of Evil (dir. John Hough) 67, 115
"Two Augurs" (Villiers de l'Isle Adam) 34
The Two Faces of Dr. Jekyll (dir. Terence Fisher) 7, 21-22
2001: A Space Odyssey (dir. Stanley Kubrick) 8, 155, 156

Ulmer, Edgar G. 7, 15, *16*
The Uncanny (dir. Denis Héroux) 78

Vadim, Roger 37
Vampyr (dir. Carl Dreyer) 7, 52
Der Vampyr (Heinrich Marschner) 67
van Rijn, Rembrandt 172
Vaughan-Hughes, Gerald 74
Vault of Horror (dir. Roy Ward Baker) 34, 35
Veidt, Conrad 7, 57, 82, 84, 86, 92
The Vengeance of She (dir. Cliff Owen) 77-78
"Véra" (Villiers de l'Isle Adam) 33
Véra, Augusto 33
Verdi, Giuseppe 64
"The Very Image" (Villiers de l'Isle Adam) 35
Vickers, Mike 154
Village of the Damned (dir. Wolf Riller) 8, 95, 96, 97, 136-137
Villiers de l'Isle Adam, Auguste 19-20, 21, 28-38, *29*
Visconti, Luchino 110
Voltaire 158
Von Braun, Wernher 133, 179
Von Heute auf Morgen (Arnold Schoenberg) 124
Vonnegut, Kurt 157
von Sydow, Max 121, *121*, 122, 124, 174
Voodoo Man (dir. William Beaudine) 79
Vril Society 133

Wachsfigurenabinett (dir. Paul Leni) 84
Wagner, Richard 4, 7, 12, 29, 32, 41-45, *43*, 47, 82, 84-85, 102, 108, 114, 130, 133, 135, 136, 139, 155, 160, 180, 182, 183
Waite, A.E. 66, 105-106, 112
Walbrook, Anton 57
Walker, Stuart 7, *13*
Walpole, Horace 75
Walsh, Edward 23
Walsh, Kay 72, 98,164
War in Heaven (Charles Williams) 43
Warlords of Atlantis (dir. Kevin Connor) 8, 137-140, 159

Warner, David 77
Warning Shadows (dir. Arthur Robinson) 7, 52
Warren, Barry 34, 61
Watson, Bobby 159
Weber, Carl Maria von 67, 177
Webern, Anton 120
Wegener, Paul 44, 56–57, 63, 182
Welles, Orson 111
Wells, H.G. 104, 143, 144
Wendkos, Paul 98, 152, 153
Werewolf of London (dir. Stuart Walker) 7, *13*, 14
Whale, James 36, 61, 181
What's Opera, Doc? (dir. Chuck Jones) 182
Wheatley, Dennis 5, 7, 40, 42, 44, 46, *46*, 49, 57, 59, 65, 68–71, 73, 77, 79, 80, 81, 83, 91, 133
Whistler, James McNeill 9
White, Fred M. 14
The White Dominican (Gustav Meyrinck) 52
White Zombie (dir. Victor Halperin) 78
Whitelaw, Billie 118
The Wicker Man (dir. Robin Hardy) 153
Wicking, Christopher 100, 115
Widmark, Richard 74
Wiederhorn, Ken 134
Wiene, Robert 7
Wilcox, Fred M. *181*, 185

Wild Strawberries (dir. Ingmar Bergman) 6
Wilde, Oscar 11, 12, 13, 14, 17, 18, 20, 22, 28, 52, 58, 60
"William Wilson" (Edgar Allan Poe) 57
Williams, Charles 43
Williams, John 126
Willis, Edwin B. 17
Willman, Noel *19*, 20, 65
Wilson, Colin 66
Wilson, Edmund 29, 30
Wincer, Simon 8, 88
The Witches (dir. Cyril Frankel) 72, 98, 164
Woolf, Virginia 45
Wordsworth, William 144, 151
The World as Will and Representation (Schopenhauer) 3
Wright of Derby, Joseph 172
Wyndham, John 136

Yeats, W.B. 129
Yellow Submarine (dir. George Dunning) *147*, 148–149, 155
Youssoupoff, Prince 26, 86, 88

"Der Zauberlehrling" (Johann Wolfgang von Goethe) 177, 183, 184
Zeffirelli, Franco 89
Zola, Emile 11
Zucco, George 79

www.ingramcontent.com/pod-product-compliance
Lightning Source LLC
Chambersburg PA
CBHW032057300426
44116CB00007B/777